THE IMPERFECT CITY: ON ARCHITE

Para Maria Luisa

The Imperfect City:
On Architectural Judgment

Samir Younés
University of Notre Dame, USA

LONDON AND NEW YORK

First published 2008 by Ashgate Publishing

2 Park Square, Milton Park, Abingdon, Oxon OX14 4RN
711 Third Avenue, New York, NY 10017, USA

Routledge is an imprint of the Taylor & Francis Group, an informa business

First issued in paperback 2016

Copyright © 2012 Samir Younés

Samir Younés has asserted his right under the Copyright, Designs and Patents Act, 1988, to be identified as the author of this work.

All rights reserved. No part of this book may be reprinted or reproduced or utilised in any form or by any electronic, mechanical, or other means, now known or hereafter invented, including photocopying and recording, or in any information storage or retrieval system, without permission in writing from the publishers.

Notice:
Product or corporate names may be trademarks or registered trademarks, and are used only for identification and explanation without intent to infringe.

British Library Cataloguing in Publication Data
Younés, Samir.
  The imperfect city : on architectural judgment.
  1. Architectural criticism. 2. Architectural design--
  Evaluation.
  I. Title
  720.1-dc23

Library of Congress Cataloging-in-Publication Data
Younés, Samir.
 The imperfect city : on architectural judgment / by Samir Younés.
    pages cm
  Includes bibliographical references and index.
  ISBN 978-1-4094-4667-5 (hbk) -- ISBN 978-1-4094-4668-2 (ebk)
 1. Architectural criticism. 2. Architecture--Philosophy. I.
Title.
  NA2599.5.Y68 2012
  720.1--dc23
                                                                    2012004146

ISBN 978-1-4094-4667-5 (hbk)
ISBN 978-1-138-20497-3 (pbk)

Contents

List of Figures vii
Acknowledgements ix

Introduction 1

PART ONE   EXTERNAL CRITERIA FOR ARCHITECTURAL JUDGMENT

1   Architectural Judgment Based on History, Part 1   21

2   Architectural Judgment Based on History, Part 2   31

3   Architectural Judgment Based on History, Part 3   51

4   On the Nature of Modernity   67

5   Political Content and Architectural Form   83

6   Desire, Imitation, and Conflict   109

PART TWO   INTERNAL CRITERIA FOR ARCHITECTURAL JUDGMENT
THE FACES OF CHARACTER

7   Architectural Expression: Form, Quality, and Purpose   143

| 8 | Character, Imitation, and Invention: A Discussion of Three Historic Moments | 159 |
| 9 | The Limits of Architectural Expression | 199 |

Conclusion: The Usefulness of Conflict for Judgment   223

Bibliography   *241*
Index   *251*

List of Figures

I.1	Temple of deified Hadrian and Borsa, Detail, Rome.	2
I.2	Palazzo Montecitorio, G-L. Bernini, Detail, Rome.	3
1.1	Historia, Iconologia, Cesare Ripa, *Historiae et Allegoriae*.	22
1.2	Portrait d'architecte revenant de voyage, 19th Cent.,V. Dahlerup.	23
2.1	Seagram Building, Mies van der Rohe, New York, 1958.	32
2.2	Rome's layers, from the Forum of Trajan to the Church of Domenico and Sisto.	33
3.1	Types according to J.N.L. Durand.	52
3.2	Types according to C.W. Westfall and S. Younés.	53
3.3	Tholos: San Giovanni degli Eremiti, Palermo.	54
3.4	Tholos: Santa Maria in Montesanto and Santa Maria dei Miracoli, Rome.	54
3.5	Temple, San Francesco, Noto.	56
3.6	Temple, San Pietro, Modica.	57
3.7	Regia, Palazzo dei Consoli, Gubbio.	58
3.8	Regia, Palazzo Nobili Tarugi, Montepulciano.	58
3.9	Theatre and domus, Piazza del Campo, Siena.	60
3.10	Theatre, Piazza de Toros, Sevilla.	60
3.11	Taberna and domus, Piazza Grande, Arezzo.	61
3.12	Taberna and domus, Piazza dell'Erbe, Verona.	62
3.13	Hypostyle, Mezquita, Cordoba.	63
3.14	Hypostyle, Market, Siena.	64
4.1	Social Housing, Piazza Bartolomeo Romano, Garbatella, Rome, Plinio Marconi, 1926.	68
4.2	Bauhaus, Dessau, Germany, Walter Gropius, 1926.	68
5.1	Piazza Pius II. Pienza.	84
5.2	Loggia del Capitano, Palladio, Vicenza.	92
5.3	Palazzo Cenci-Bolognetti, Arnaldo Foschini, built in the 1930s, becoming later the seat of the Communist Party.	98
5.4	Reichstag, Berlin.	100

5.5	Casa del Fascio, Giuseppe Terragni, Como.	101
6.1	Palazzo Ducale, Cortile, Venice, Antonio Rizzo.	110
6.2	Palazzo Pamphilj, Girolamo Rainaldi, Rome.	115
6.3	Palazzo di Giustizia, Guglielmo Calderini, Rome.	116
6.4	The Albaicin quarter, Granada.	120
6.5	Theatre of Macellus, Léon Vaudoyer's inscription, Rome.	122
6.6	New Pavilion for the Ara Pacis, Architect's signature, Rome.	123
6.7	Mimesis: The Boy and the Castle.	127
6.8	Cain and Abel, Gustave Doré.	130
6.9	Decapitated bust of Vitruvius, Viale di Villa Medici, Rome.	132
7.1	Rome from the Gianocolo.	144
7.2	Tempietto at San Pietro in Montorio, Donato Bramante, Rome, 1502.	145
7.3	Stockholm Public Library, Gunnar Asplund, 1928.	146
7.4	Piazza del Duomo, Ortigia, Sicily.	150
7.5	Comic scene, Sebastiano Serlio, *The Five Books of Architecture*.	152
7.6	Richmond Capitol building, Thomas Jefferson, Virginia.	155
8.1	Face and entablature, Francesco di Giorgio, *Trattati di architettura, ingegneria e arte militare*.	160
8.2	Superposition of human figure and building, Francesco di Giorgio, Trattati di architettura, ingegneria e arte militare.	160
9.1	Pumping station, Friedrich Ludwig Persius, Potsdam.	201
9.2	Temple of Concord, Rome. After Constant Moyaux.	203
9.3	Temple of Mars Ultor, Rome. After Louis Noguet.	204
9.4	Santa Maria della Salute, Baldassare Longhena, Venice.	205
9.5	The Zecca, Jacobo Sansovino, Venice.	207
9.6	The French Panthéon/Ste. Geneviève, Jacques-Germain Soufflot, Paris.	208
9.7	Munich Glyptothek, Leo von Klenze.	209
9.8	Academy of Athens, Theophil Edvard Hansen.	210
9.9	The Italian Pavilion, Exposition Universelle 1900, Paris.	211
9.10	The United States Pavilion, Exposition Universelle, 1900.	212
9.11	The World's Columbian Exhibition, 1893, Chicago, Illinois, Machinery Hall.	213
9.12	Sydney Opera House, Jorn Utzon.	213
9.13	Yale Centre for British Art, Louis Kahn, New Haven.	215
9.14	Magdalen College, Demetri Porphyrios, Oxford.	216
9.15	Pritzker Music Pavilion, Frank Gehry, Chicago, Illinois.	217
C.1	Looking toward the finials of Sant'Ignazio, Rome.	224

Acknowledgements

This book is the result of a long-standing interest in the ways in which architects evaluate, justify, or reject architectural form. Since the eighteenth century, architectural judgment has combined evaluative criteria that derive from architecture itself with an increased influence from criteria outside of it such as history, *technique*, politics, or psychology. Consequently, architectural judgment today resides in the ways in which architecture is taught and learned, the ways in which its history is written, the ways in which it is called to serve the City politically and physically, the ways in which it enters into the aesthetic psychology of the architect, and the ways in which it expresses the public and the private realms. Whether they do so willfully or not, architects are engaged in building the criteria for judgment on a daily basis for the simple reason that they justify, or condemn, form on a daily basis. However, all too frequently do architects proffer definitive judgments of architectural form based on inconsistent and fragmentary knowledge of the very criteria they are supposed to know very well. Architects also use their rivalries and their subjective formal preferences in order to override these criteria. As a result adverse critical stances come to impair the possibility of reasoned judgment. If architectural judgment were a city, a city of ideas, then it is a very imperfect city.

Over the years, I have discussed these concerns with a number of esteemed colleagues – architects, historians, and philosophers. I am thankful to the useful exchange of ideas with architects Léon Krier, Demetri Porphyrios, Norman Crowe, Lucien Steil, José Cornélio da Silva, Ettore Mazzola, Thomas Rajkovitch, and Kent Bloomer; with architectural historians Carroll William Westfall, Robert Jan Van Pelt, Branko Mitrovic, and Brian Hanson; with philosophers Roger Scruton, Anthony O'Hear, David Lovekin, and Nick Zangwill; and with psychologist James Hillman. With them, I have enjoyed a most valuable exchange of ideas, and for that I am grateful, but the responsibility for the opinions expressed in this book is all mine.

Introduction

THREE KINDS OF ARCHITECTURAL JUDGMENT

We find peace near our idols.[1]

René Girard

Architects walk in the city carrying their aesthetic responses and their compositional skills. They mentally draw compositional adjustments to the buildings they observe, adding or subtracting parts, elaborating or simplifying other parts. They also mentally erase the buildings of which they disapprove, and mentally replace them by others that they consider more appropriate. Architects judge buildings, as well as the minds that produced them. They judge the qualities of form and the qualities of the thought behind the form. They judge architectural composition, its appropriateness to an end, and the reasons for which an architect decided to adopt one form versus another. Their training and their practice make them acutely aware of the differences between the many possibilities of making architectural forms and the various trials and tribulations encountered when realizing these forms. It is precisely from evaluating the difference between levels of formal potentiality on the one hand, and the conditions of material realization on the other, that much of architectural judgment arises. Architectural judgment generally involves the judicious and evaluative assessment according to which buildings are justified and acclaimed, or repudiated and condemned. Ideally, this evaluation operates on the basis of declared criteria regarding the nature, the ends, and the means of architecture within the context of realization, that context being the city or the countryside. Architectural judgment also concerns more than the spectrum of evaluations and criticisms used by architects as they undertake their assessments. Judgment is part of how architecture is taught, learned, and then practiced; how architectural history and theory influence the teaching and the learning; how forms are selected for the purpose of architectural composition; how composition serves architectural character; how social meanings are associated with or projected onto architectural character; how personal taste relates to architectural norms;

I.1 Temple of deified Hadrian and Borsa, Detail, Rome.
Source: Photo by Author.

I.2 Palazzo Montecitorio, G-L. Bernini, Detail, Rome.
Source: Photo by Author.

or how multiple architectural images animate the architect's psychology. As all of these factors enter into architectural judgment, it is useful to discuss the kinds of judgment architects employ.

Because judgment is part of understanding, architects are constantly making judgments. The bases for these are essential determinants for well-reasoned conclusions. If asked about the grounds for judgment in their art, architects will most certainly answer with a self-evident declaration: they judge following a complex questioning concerning the coherence, compatibility, or divergence of a building in relation to a set of evaluative criteria. When architects judge buildings, we find that they proffer judgment based on two explicit sets of criteria. The first is *intrinsic* to architecture and depends on a theory of architecture and urbanism. Such a theory includes character, composition, proportions, tectonics, materials, propriety, and the reciprocal influence between buildings in their urban context. These may be said to be determining concepts exercising an essential influence on the making of architectural form. Employed by practical reason, they justify a certain course of action in view of achieving certain ends by employing determined means, and serving not just those who make buildings but also those who observe them and live in them. Intrinsic criteria serve to order or align architectural convictions for the purpose of judgment. The second set is *external* and depends on larger factors that inform the intellectual *milieu* in which architectural debates unfold. Such, for example, is the kind of judgment of architecture placed at the intersection and overlap between philosophies of history, theories of modernity, or political ideology. These may be said to be conditioning factors in that they exert peripheral, though significant, influences on architecture. We can then distinguish between intrinsic and determining criteria, and external yet conditioning ones.

Together, intrinsic and external criteria constitute the framework that allows for the evaluation and judgment of architectural qualities. Naturally, these two sets of criteria are not the only ones to influence architectural judgment. Because the relationship between architecture and judgment is deeply psychological, there is another group of intensely subjective measures that weaves its way around and penetrates within the first two sets. These measures concern the general psychology of architects marked as it is by intense desire for architectural form and personal identification with this form. Whereas desire for form is necessary for learning and practicing form, associating the persona with the form plays a significant role in turning critical practices into an acute rivalry – the kind of rivalry that philosopher René Girard termed *mimetic rivalry*, as we shall see. Architects rarely admit that these subjective measures strongly influence their judgments. Their generalized intention to show that reason reigns supreme in architectural judgment makes them seldom acknowledge publicly that a considerable part of their judgment is tied to their desire nature, their wish-life for preferred forms, and conversely, their rejection of forms they find objectionable. Writings on architectural evaluation and judgment have consequently neglected this important trait in the architect's psychology. Whereas desire, rivalry, and critical practices seem on the surface to have little to do with intrinsic and external criteria, their role in architectural judgment is quite considerable. They have also greatly contributed to today's world of architecture which is brimming over with conflicts and antagonisms.

Taken together, intrinsic criteria, external criteria, as well as the psychology of mimetic rivalry constitute a three-part framework for the evaluation and judgment of architectural qualities. It is in this sense that architectural judgment is understood in this book.

The intrinsic criteria for judgment has generally been elaborated upon by architects, while the external criteria has been elaborated mostly by historians, by philosophers of history, by social philosophers, and by architectural theorists whose work seeks to situate architecture inside larger cultural currents.[2] With respect to architectural judgment, this has led to opposition between the notion of architecture as an autonomous discipline with its own traditions of image-making, and that of architecture as a plain resultant or even a mere symptom of external forces that condition or determine architectural form. The proponents of autonomy argued that to understand architecture as a symptom also means to see a new work of architecture as entering history already as a symptom. The proponents of external criteria countered that to claim a complete autonomy to architecture makes it difficult or impossible for architecture to justify, on its own terms, the place it occupies as a social force; for it is inextricably tied to historical trends, to other arts, and to technology. Autonomy does not mean self-sufficiency.

It is not the purpose of this book to argue for the exclusive justification of one set of criteria versus another. This has been so extensively debated over the past three to five decades that one doubts if many opinions will be changed. But what one can confidently assert is that much in architectural evaluation (such as periodization, stylistic classification), indeed the very discourse for evaluation today firmly takes place on grounds already provided by historians. Indeed, many of the theories and many a crisis that accompanied architecture since the late eighteenth century concerned architecture's relation to history. Two opposing views saw architectural practice either in relation to a past ideal(s), or in relation to a massive historic rupture followed by a possible future ideal(s) that will eventually emerge from the experience of daily contingency. It is this sometimes conscious and sometimes unconscious relation to history that forms the ground against which many architects measure their positions. Architects need to prove that the forms that they produce are sanctioned by history, by the authority of history. They cherish the conviction that a historical explanation constitutes an incontrovertible justification for their forms. This sanctioning by history – sometimes neglecting to note that an explanation is not necessarily a justification – is equally claimed by those who see their work in the lineage of a tradition, as well as by those who see their work as a definitive rupture from any tradition whatsoever. Both groups are modern, and both claim the authority of the historical explanation in order to justify their modern position. For the first group, to be modern entails rationally receiving, improving, and transmitting architectural historical experience, considering tradition as the receptacle of reason in history. For the second group, to be modern is not just to claim presentness, it is also the frenetic pursuit to occupy the leading edge of presentness, confidently breaking with history based on the confident backing of a historical justification.

The architect's mind is essentially poetic, or *poietic* (in the sense of the Greek verb *poein*, to make, to fabricate, to produce something), and his or her modes of conceptualizing occur primarily as an imaging and imagining activity.[3] It is worthwhile to recall the distinction between seeing and imagining, because an image is more than what one sees but the ways in which one sees, especially from the standpoint of a maker of images: the architect. Architects look at the world aesthetically, finding meanings in the images that they receive and in the images that they make for the world they inhabit.[4] Seeing, for architects, involves two additional features: *seeing as*, and *seeing in* (in Ludwig Wittgenstein's words), and both pertain explicitly to the most expressive part of architecture, namely, architectural character.[5] Above all else, it is to architectural character and to the maker of this character that architectural judgment is keenly directed.

Since architecture makes us see the image-maker in ourselves, she returns the gaze of her maker and her observer and invites the naming of her component parts. She also invites evaluation, or judgment. This is so not only for the architect, but for all who encounter architecture. As such, architecture concerns anyone who is interested in assessing the success or propriety of the building endeavor. It is architects and historians, however, who are mainly responsible for elaborating the forms and the discourse of architectural culture. In this sense one can generalize broadly by saying that architectural judgment is mostly made by those who build and those who provide a narrative of the development of buildings. In other words, architects can be said to judge from the "inside" and historians from the "outside", although both groups know architecture inside and out. This book, written by an architect and not a historian, seeks to address selected aspects of external and internal judgment. It does not cover these judgments in their entirety. Instead, the following chapters seek to treat the five most prevalent and most divisive external and internal criteria on the basis of which architecture is judged. We briefly enumerate them and then lay out their partitioning into chapters.

External Criteria

The first set concerns the historical criterion we already mentioned. The second set concerns the nature and ends of modernity and modernism. As with the concept of pluralism, modernity and modernism remain in use by architects and historians as justifiers of architectural form as if by definition. Architectural form comes to be accepted or dismissed on this basis, even if pluralism acknowledges, in theory, that different views of modernity may find embodiment in different forms. The third set examines why architecture and politics serve the city, the public realm, and the spurious association between architectural form and political content. It considers the difference and similarity between artistic freedom of expression and political freedom of expression. Today's democratic political *milieu* aims to foster individual expression based on the working proposition that the indefinite acceptance of multiple expressions enriches society and lessens, in the long term, the possibilities for conflict. Consequently, individual expression comes to be justified based on the vast rights of expression offered by pluralistic space. This political right is frequently invoked by the citizens of the pluralistic city, especially when their individual expression encounters obstacles for its own realization. Pluralistic claims serve to justify the aims and the expressions of individuals and groups, and architects and historians are no exception to this significant social phenomenon. They justify their forms on the basis of their artistic freedom in a pluralistic space, while concurrently seeing these forms as adequate representations of this space. They also project this justificatory method onto present and past architectures, associating their preferred forms with tolerant political ideologies, and disliked forms with varieties of political intolerance. This phenomenon becomes at once justification and judgment – understood here in a negative sense. It frequently overrides the criteria for architectural judgment.

The fourth set pertains to the phenomenon of judgment based on desire for form, for the architectural image, including the engaging desire to make form, to appreciate it aesthetically from a distance, or to possess it and personally identify with this possession. Since desire for form is at the source of its imitation, architects imitate preferred forms and preferred makers of forms. But when imitation, personal identification with form, and the desire to exclusively own the form all converge, the result is intense rivalry. Here, the architect's subjectivity (discriminatory preferences, biases) enters in full force, often prevailing over internal or external criteria for judgment.

Internal Criteria

The previous four sets of criteria all converge on a fifth set which is concerned with architectural expression, namely: architectural character. Character is the ultimate result of layers of architectural making in relation to layers of social meaning. It bears the influence of typological thought, from the most abstract forms to the most concrete models and direct precedents. It is the product of that fateful couple: imitation and invention, requiring all the skills of composition including proportion, distribution and disposition. It is also the outcome of tectonic culture, of how forms are joined, of how forms project or recede, of how forms bear loads and are themselves borne by other forms. Considered additively, Nature and building culture (the sum of all the individual architectural characters within a given area) shape a regional or a national character.

To put it in different terms, this book examines judgment of the architectural image in its historical, cultural, political, psychological, and expressive dimensions. This is not to suggest that these five sets of criteria are the only ones worth considering, or that they should dominate judgment as they presently do. There are certainly no necessary and sufficient reasons to assume that these criteria form one coherent and complete whole. Yet although they do not completely explain architectural judgment, they still account for a considerable part of this judgment. A more comprehensive explanation of architectural judgment would need to include many other important external and internal criteria such as a philosophy of becoming, in relation to historical development in general and to architecture in particular; or the relationship between architecture, science and ecology; or cognitive theories, tectonic theory, theory of proportions, etc. Rather, these five sets of criteria were selected because they play, as we have said, a fairly divisive role in architectural judgment, for good or for bad, whether internal or external. They dominate because they divide. A close look at architectural debates and criticism reveals that architects selectively deploy, divert, or re-position parts of these criteria, or purposely merge them together in order to justify their personal or group judgment, or in order to achieve the desired aim of winning an argument. One example is the so-called "definist fallacy" in which architects tend to define concepts in ways that are sympathetic to their own positions and antagonistic to those of others, while leaving little room for alternative definitions. This phenomenon has been particularly *en vogue* since hyper criticism led to wars of definition and wars of exceptions to these definitions. In this case, problems of definition become problems of judgment – especially given the muddled use of terminology on the part of many architects. Such practices are by now widely established and broadly used; however, widespread use in itself in no way signifies validation or justification. Collectively, the five sets of criteria have the remarkable capacity to attract and to provokingly incite many other evaluations. When architects, for example, justify certain buildings because they are "modern" and reject others for being "un-modern", they immediately call forth questions about how and why does a building become an expression of modernity, about different kinds of modernity, about multiple images of modernity, about why steel is deemed more modern than stone, and why should modernity be the criterion that outweighs most other evaluative criteria?

Why, the reader might ask, does this book concern itself more with the external criteria for architectural judgment, and why does it begin with these external criteria? The explanation is twofold. First, internal architectural judgment consists of nothing short of the foundational principles of architectural theory in their entirety. The professional and academic discourses amongst architects and historians have generously dealt with the internal criteria for judgment resulting in their being better known than the external ones. Yet, for many architects today, the external criteria pass almost for granted, as if they are fixed and unassailable givens of architectural judgment, and sometimes this judgment is explained-away in this fashion. Clearly, however, architectural theory by itself is insufficient to explain architectural judgment in its entirety. It still needs to account for evaluations coming from the philosophy of history, from art theory, or from psychology. Second, a significant number of criteria for judgment lead to, and converge on, architectural expressiveness. That is, on architectural character in its fullness as an object in the world. For these reasons, the internal criteria have been placed within Part Two.

We now turn to a general description of the chapters. Part One consists of six chapters. The first three are dedicated to architectural judgment based on history in comparison to the modern architect's acute consciousness of time and the historian's role in privileging certain narratives over others. Any discussion of architecture at present, especially concerning judgment, cannot ignore the weight of classicism and historicism and their retreat as grand narratives that justified architectural production, and against which architectural production measured its success and failure during the past two centuries. Historicism itself arose, in the early nineteenth century, because of a crisis in depth in historical consciousness. The discovery and direct comparison of several architectural paradigms from different cultures and continents (the Egyptian, the Chinese, the Greek) complicated the idea of measuring architectural practice against one single paradigm. Yet, useful though the plurality of paradigms may be, it also engendered the relativism of judgment, and many philosophers and historians employed themselves at precisely avoiding the pitfalls of relativism. Notwithstanding these efforts the recent retreat of historicism caused yet another crisis, one in which pluralism collapsed into relativism. This collapse deeply affected the ways in which architects hold paradigms because both pluralism and relativism bear directly on the practical, as well as the theoretical, uses of reason. Both concepts strongly affect the possibilities of choice, the possibilities of judgment. The result has been a disorientation in architectural judgment because many previously unshaken paradigms and their very social anchoring have been shaken, suspended, or removed. Some contend that paradigms of a collective scope have disappeared, and that all we are left with are morsels of choices that can only be considered paradigmatic on an individual level. Others see cultural paradigms multiplying and shifting fairly frequently, while some still affirm that many great paradigms are alive and well notwithstanding their being eclipsed by the deafening contingency of contemporary life.

The relationship between architects and the study of history is, to say the least, in a state of crisis at present. On the one hand, as many architects and historians have correctly noted, the instrumental use of historical knowledge in architectural schools and the profession is decreasing in a most disquieting way. On the other, history enters in full force when there is a need to make an architectural justification that requires an assumption about the architect's position within a historical sequence. For good or for ill, architectural judgment based on history still obtains, although in a state of disorientation. Historians and philosophers of history have for centuries provided ample material for the architect's judgment. Their thinking has strongly impacted the architect's thinking about history and its instrumentality. Is another history possible, however, one that is built less on the premises of the historian and more on those of the architect? Chapter 3 concludes by proposing an outline for a history based more on the ways in which architects conceive and compose architecture while incorporating the scholarly concerns of the historian.

Chapter 4 discusses two elusive and yet highly influential concepts in the architect's intellectual life: modernity and modernism. Few artistic concepts have received as much polemical content as the one embodied in these two words. They have been used to validate, condemn and judge works of art and architecture. Yet, while many architects claim to directly justify their work and judge the work of others based on notions of modernity, they find considerable difficulty in defining, locating, and demonstrating the nature of this modernity. This chapter expounds on the nature of modernity, its successes and failures, moving back and forth from the early *cultural differentiations* that occurred during the Enlightenment to the immense *cultural dissociations* of the recent past. This chapter will show that the elusiveness of the concept of modernity derives in part from the fact that the concept has been given the task of absorbing numerous cultural currents – too numerous for the concept to maintain any stability. Hence the constant need for the advocates of modernity – and in particular, modernism – to relocate the concept, temporarily housing it in different cultural addresses – a phenomenon that quickly deteriorates into vacuous demands about the ever-renewed need for change. Some of these cultural currents bear directly on architecture and the arts, being at once intrinsic and external. Consider for example, the intimate, complicated, and problematic relationship between architectural modernism and *technique*.[6] Other currents are external and involve philosophies of history such as the Great Chain of Being, or modernist views of architectural history and its compartmentalized stylistic underpinnings. This chapter concludes by speculating on a possible cultural synthesis that rises beyond the ever-increasing dissociations within contemporary cultural spheres. And if some intend to work toward such a synthesis, then what, one might ask, might be its main lines both culturally and architecturally?

Architectural judgment takes place inside the contemporary democratic *milieu* – rife as it is with the polarizing effects of pluralism, monism, liberalism, eclecticism, subjectivism and relativism. Contemporary parlance has reduced these different concepts to one large Manichaean duality: monism and pluralism. The first is considered limiting and limited because it regards cultural matters from one single point of view; and in politics as well as in academia, monistic beliefs invariably become forms of tyranny. The second is frequently confused with relativism where commonly shared beliefs – e.g. the idea of universals, the sense in common, traditions at large – are excluded in an *a-priori* way in favor of local or subjective preferences. This duality weighs heavily on architectural judgment, and Chapter 5 shows how both monism and pluralism have been, and continue to be, abused and even taken to extremes. Although pluralism encourages prolonged tolerance, there is a marked difference between a flexible and benevolent tolerance and indiscriminate neutrality in artistic and political endeavors. More specifically, there are similarities but also many differences between political and artistic freedoms. Political freedom and artistic freedom are not the same. To be more precise, different kinds of artistic freedom are directly related to the kind of art that one practices within the political context that contains this practice. These freedoms are related to the limits or boundaries between the arts; and judgment, whether intrinsic or external, cannot ignore this important question. In addition, Chapter 5 also addresses two other criteria that strongly influence architectural judgment. The first is the association between political content and architectural character; the second is the teaching and practice of one architectural ideology as if it were the sole legitimate ideology. Contentions about architectural form and political content have ranged from some architects arguing for no relationship whatsoever, to others seeing architecture, and art, as direct representations of political aims. And whereas the clash between these positions seems to have subsided recently, it is not because the antagonists have necessarily adopted a set of clear resolutions. Rather they seem to have temporarily put aside the argument, having found no way to arbitrate their differences.

Chapter 6 examines that set of powerfully subjective measures mentioned above, one that weaves its way around and within intrinsic and external criteria for judgment. It discusses desire as a force that moves the mind to action, and as such becomes a basis for judgment. One may say, without too much exaggeration, that architects live on forms. They avidly desire forms they find pleasing. They also vehemently reject forms that displease them. Their aesthetic mode of being predisposes them to judge all artistic forms, be they visual, auditory or literary. Architects are self-sculpting aesthetes who refine their craft with discipline, introspective patience, and fortitude. This is a decisive aspect of their psychologies. In addition to this self-sculpting, they intensely project their sense of selfhood into their buildings and the ideologies that support these buildings. Desire for form and identification with form thus become predisposing features for judgment. They explain, in part, the architects' separative stances, deep divisions, and rivalries. Furthermore, since much in human learning is imitative, from children's early imitation of their parents' actions to adults adopting the work of valued teachers as models, desire for form (buildings, painting, sculpture, rhetoric) becomes mimetic desire for the realization of preferred forms. But many obstacles combine to frustrate the realization of these forms, including rivalry. The paradoxical side of imitation (*mimesis*) is that it is at once a basis for learning as well as a source for conflict. The frustration of mimetic desire caused by rivalry evolves into mimetic rivalry.[7] This rivalry provokes architectural judgment at its most emotional and aggressive levels. Many are the weapons deployed and the urge to reach and use them is immediate, including above all the trenchant blade of criticism. Erudite arguments are sometimes used with the intention to intimidate, barely concealing what in reality are harsh sectarian antagonisms. Judgment based on desire for form and on mimetic rivalry is important because evaluation concerns architects too, and not just their buildings. The psychology of those who build the world is inseparable from their judgment in the choice of form, its refinement, distortion, destruction, and rebuilding.

Part Two, in three chapters, is titled "The Faces of Character". It is concerned primarily with architectural character, an issue that is tacitly assumed in many discussions about what architecture expresses even if, at present, many architects do not distinguish character from style. Architectural character has the remarkable capacity to converge and reflect many of the external as well as the intrinsic criteria for judgment because it calls forth architecture's relation to historical antecedents, societal meanings, the architect's theory of modernity, or the idea of expressing a civic purpose. Character is strongly related to the ways in which all the elements of architectural composition, from the general massing to ornament, express a building's purpose with propriety, with suitability. This purpose ranges between the civic realm (the *res publica*) or the private realm (the *res privata*), and the difficult role faced by architects frequently resides in giving proper expression to three purposes: the civic, the private purpose of a patron, and both in relation to the architect's ever-pressing need for self-expression. To say that architectural forms express or represent the civic or the private realms implies that architecture possesses a symbolic quality, and Part Two returns to the concept of imitation, or rather to the dual concept of imitation and invention in relation to character. What is architecture imitative of (the larger cultural context) and what is imitative in architectural character (the elements of architectural composition); what are the modes of imitation that distinguish architecture from the modes of imitation that distinguish the other visual arts; and what are the limits or bounds of architectural imitation? These are the central questions addressed in Part Two, which will also focus on a selection of significant texts that dealt with architectural character. The selections are culled from three moments of great historic importance: the Italian Renaissance, the French Enlightenment, and the period of Modernism and after Modernism. This is followed by a discussion of some significant buildings in order to discuss the range and the limits, or bounds, of architectural character.

We appreciate character because it articulates a range of expressions that might be termed civic (the courthouse, the church, the theatre), or vernacular and private (the house, the villa, the office building). We also value character because it emerges from a place and it constructs the sense of place. In its travels, it merges with other architectural characters and thereby participates in shaping another sense of place. We esteem character when it migrates between places and keeps the memory of its origins side by side with the transformations it invariably absorbs. We also revel in the rich differences in composition that can be obtained by modifying only a handful of architectural elements. Therefore, because the types, the characters, and the styles of buildings are valued in their origins as well as in their transformations, various conservation laws are adopted with the intentions of protecting the sense of place on the scale of streets, squares, quarters, cities, and regions. And yet, paradoxically, charters such as the Charter of Venice, while aiming to conserve traditional buildings, also disallow the construction of new traditional buildings that continue the very architectural character that was valued in the first place.

In the long history of the architectural treatise, the body and building analogy has been an enduring theme. Because of our proclivity to see the human measure in all objects of our making, we are as attentive to the different expressions of architectural character as we are attentive to the changes in our facial countenance. The slightest change evokes our concern because the face and the façade are two of the elements through which we express our modes of being. Just as we prepare our facial countenance in anticipation of our encountering other facial countenances, so do buildings present a countenance and are affected by that of other buildings. In order to understand the different faces of character, we seek historical, cultural, political, psychological, and above all, expressive criteria, because character is that superlative quality without which architecture becomes mute. And given its indelible effects on the mind, the emotions, and the senses, character has been the subject of intense polemics, its criteria justified or doubted, its suitability praised or criticized, and its complexity explained as a result of social and artistic crises. For these reasons, the concept of character forms part of several chapters throughout this book.

So rapid have the changes in architectural character been over the past two to three centuries, and so varied and contentious have been their explanations, that words such as: polemic, criterion, criticism, and crisis have become an inseparable part of the daily architectural parlance. Therefore, before closing the introduction it might be of use to recall the etymology of these four familiar words because their meanings are significant for judgment, and such meanings are sometimes overlooked in the heat of debate. The word polemic derives from the Greek word *polemos* (war); and when *logos* (discourse) is associated with it, it designates arguments susceptible of causing conflicts and antagonisms. The words criterion, criticism, and crisis share a common linguistic origin. All are related to the Greek verb *krinein*, to separate. Criterion is a standard upon which to base a judgment. It derives from the Greek *kriterion*, a means for judging from *krites* to judge, again: from *krinein*, to separate. And that is what critics do when they separate or isolate the qualities of a certain building that they analyze and subsequently find that it failed to meet some previously announced criteria. Critics – from the Greek *kriticos*: discerner, from *kritos*: separated, chosen; and the Latin *criticus* – proffer judgment on the merits or faults of a building, and then proclaim that they personally differ from the building and its maker. Whereas they might not necessarily offer better solutions, critics profess to "know better". Critics never marvel. They have seen it all, and classified it all. So excessively valued has criticism become amongst architects that to be critical is considered by many as synonymous with being rational. Instructors in architecture are referred to as critics. Architects are reproached for not being critical enough when evaluating a building or reading a book, and they are admonished by the culture of difference and methodological skepticism to keep a critical distance from an argument with which they might have otherwise found agreement. It is important to note, however, that *whereas valid criticism necessitates sound architectural judgment, architectural judgment itself can operate fairly well without criticism.*

Crisis, the fourth word, implies a decisive separation from a previous condition following a turning point, either toward improvement or deterioration. The word crisis and phrases incorporating this word such as crisis in history, the age of crises, the crisis of values, have been unavoidable parts of contemporary intellectual discourse since the Enlightenment consecrated criticism as a methodology. Some observers frequently qualify any cultural or political conflict as a crisis, while others have come to use the word crisis, indiscriminately, as a synonym to the word change. Surely, any change does not necessarily lead to a crisis, and different crises have different depth-effects inside society. As Jakob Burckhardt outlined in his justly famed study on freedom and history, there are surface crises which dissipate rather quickly, and crises in depth whose effects are enduringly felt in society or a smaller group within society.[8] A crisis in the arts might be felt quite intensely among architects and artists, but it may be of a passing interest for society at large. An economic crisis though, produces a lasting effect on all. Burkhardt, however, saw our deep-rooted desire for change as an aspect that invariably leads to crises, and when several crises intersect their additive effects lead to an upheaval. Eventually, as Karl Marx underscored, the multiplicity of quantitative changes leads to a decisive shift in quality; and given its scale this shift is in the nature of a crisis. Notwithstanding the many uses of the word, its persistent deployment points to a widely shared historical consciousness regarding the pervasive cultural transformations that we have been witnessing since the late eighteenth century. It is in this sense that we speak of the French, Bolshevik, industrial, or communications revolutions.

Given the persistent discussions about crises, the contemporary democratic cultural *milieu* is highly attentive to the individual's subjectivity *vis-à-vis* collectively held beliefs. Because of its keen attunement to humanism and criticism – the two invariably travel together – it is sensitive to any opinion that passes for judgment. The pluralist democratic *milieu* encourages intellectual freedom and dissenting criticism as a form of acceptable resistance. It expends much effort in order to uphold differing cultural expressions and sustain the resulting enrichment to society. Such a phenomenon may be an unavoidable adaptation to competing forces for the sake of maintaining stability, in other words: peace in the cultural and political spheres. The pluralist milieu, however, preserves peace while uncomfortably setting aside some larger and difficult questions in the hope of returning to them at some indefinite point in the future. Desirable though the multiplication of opinions is, it also means division between the protagonists, both politically and artistically. A sensible observer might ask, what happens to a state when the dissenting internal forces loom so large so as to threaten the very existence of the state? Does partition become preferable to disintegration? Analogically, what happens to the stability of a cultural sphere (for example, art and architecture) if rivalries and divisions proliferate to the extent that they presently do? What happens to architecture when adverse critical stances come to saturate its field and its boundaries as they presently do?

Profoundly unsettled is the contemporary architectural world, and this book is born out of disenchantment in the ways in which architects judge each other's work. Fortunately, many architects share the belief that architectural form is justified on the basis of a framework of ideas, and yet many of them also proffer definitive judgments based on unsteady intellectual foundations. This book does not seek to indiscriminately criticize architectural judgment and then proceed to overconfidently prescribe what that judgment should be. Architectural judgment is an inevitable accompaniment of the intellectual and emotional lives of architects as they painstakingly mold their aesthetic gaze. But habits of judgment that are taken for granted are in special need of periodic examination, revision, and hopefully improvement. This is why architects judge the very criteria they have established in order to evaluate architecture in the first place. Because broad intellectual debate is presently lacking amongst architects, this book intends to unveil, clarify, and partially reform the familiar, easy, and at times, facile judging habits with which architects justify some buildings and the sleight of hand with which they condemn others. This book intends to disturb the waters that reflect the architect's gaze, without however causing too large a splash. The book intends to engage, not offend.

Finally, judgment is also an expression of dedication to architecture. It reflects the architect as citizen-aesthete, one who is called to build the City in whose bouleterion the judging mind ritualizes its performances. Judgment holds considerable influence on the steadiness or instability of the discipline. Judgment, in the final analysis, is not only confined to determined opinions about buildings. Whether positive or negative, its layered accumulations affect the whole architectural endeavor: the City and the relations between those who imagine it and build it. Is it possible to cure, or at least attenuate, the architect's addiction to conflict and antagonism? And finally, are certain kinds of conflicts not useful for human advancement in general and architectural advancement in particular? These are the questions discussed in the book's Conclusion.

NOTES

1 *Des choses cachées depuis la fondation du monde*, (Grasset, 1978), p. 279.

2 Architectural theory has worn many faces, and those who influenced it have not always been architects or practicing architects. Claude Perrault was a medical doctor; François Blondel was a diplomat, mathematician and military engineer; Marc-Antoine Laugier was a priest and a diplomat; Francesco Algarotti was a writer and collector; Johann Joachin Winckelmann was an art historian; Antoine Chrysostôme Quatremère de Quincy was an art theorist and historian; and John Ruskin was an art critic and political thinker.

3 On imaging, see E.S. Casey "Towards a Phenomenology of Imagination", *Journal of the British Society of Phenomenology*, 5, (1975); R.A. Finke, *Principles of Mental Imagery*, (MIT Press, 1989); A.R. Luria, *The Mind of a Mnemonist*, L. Solotaroff (Tr.) (Basic Books, (1968), 2002); N.J.T. Thomas, "Are Theories of Imagery Theories of Imagination? An Active Perception Approach to Conscious Mental Content", *Cognitive Science*, 23, (1999), pp. 207–45; J.J. Prinz, *Furnishing the Mind: Concepts and their Perceptual Basis*, (MIT Press, 2002).

4 "In all matters, but particularly in architecture, there are these two points: the thing signified (*quod significatur*) and that which gives it its significance (*quod significat*)". Vitruvius, *De architectura*, I, 1, 3.

5 On *seeing as*, including, but not necessarily limited only to the Gestalt reversing of images, see David Seligman's "Wittgenstein, on Seeing Aspects and Experiencing Meanings", *Philosophy and Phenomenological Research*, 37(2), (1976), pp. 205–17. On the intentionality of *seeing in*, see Richard Wollheim, *On the Emotions*, (Yale University Press, 1999).

6 In this book, the word *technique* is used in the sense given to it by French philosopher Jacques Ellul.

7 This chapter develops René Girard's notion of mimetic rivalry, applying it to relations between architects.

8 Jakob Burckhardt, *Force and Freedom, Reflections on History* (1929), J. Hastings Nichols (Tr.), (Boston, 1964).

PART ONE
EXTERNAL CRITERIA FOR ARCHITECTURAL JUDGMENT

PREAMBLE TO CHAPTERS 1, 2, AND 3

Architectural history provides narratives that connect a long sequence of buildings in relation to other cultural productions including artistic movements and products, ethical and political ideas. Describing buildings as embodiments of these social forces, historians are not content with simply narrating the conditions that surrounded their emergence, they also speculate on the meanings and directions that historical events and buildings might be taking. Historians and philosophers of history also extend their conjectures in order to assert that past and future events happened or will happen as if by necessity. One example of such scholarship is the teleological thinking that animates some broad surveys of architectural history. But historians also resist philosophizing about the direction of history, even if their thorough reflection on historical material makes it quite difficult to avoid such philosophizing. Therefore, architectural judgment based on history requires the architect's familiarity not just with the results of historical scholarship, but also its underlying philosophical aims as well as the historians' own evaluation of their discipline.

Permeating all aspects of cultural life nowadays is an acute awareness of history. Science and religion, art and architecture, and ethics and politics, explain their present qualities in comparison to a selected sequence of historical events alternately emphasizing continuities or ruptures where one or the other are needed. Within this broad intellectual ecology architectural judgment based on history presents a particular dilemma. On the one hand architecture receives its justification from cultural history broadly considered. On the other, architecture has its own specificity as the art form that gives form and contains the very milieu where most human activity takes place: the City. Architecture and architectural meaning, justification, and evaluation at once mold the City and emerge from it. Consequently, architects are torn between how much in architectural justification and evaluation is to be based on cultural history, or on a philosophy of history, and how much is to be based on architectural principles such as urbanism, composition, or tectonics which themselves have their own histories. The dilemma resides in favoring one over the other, as both choices entail different consequences. Therefore, architects turn at once to the historians of architecture, to philosophers of history, as well as to their own experience as makers of form. Many architects will at one point or another attempt a rapprochement, or even conciliation between history and philosophy in relation to their practice. This thinking is usually found behind justificatory statements such as: "mine is an architecture of our time", or "at this point in history my architecture is the result of a decisive rupture from the historically given". Here is where architectural judgment based on history encounters complications.

Historical narratives, as we mentioned, usually reveal an underlying philosophy of history which is brought to bear on the material history of architecture. To the extent that architects accept the historical explanation (as we shall see) they tacitly accept the linkage between the history of ideas, philosophical conjectures regarding the direction of history, and their convergence on architectural form. Whereas many of them agree on the general relevance of such a linkage, many will disagree on its specific relevance because of the difficulty in proving how historical or philosophical beliefs help to produce architectural form. Here, we are in the presence of an old problem: to what extent do ideas play a causal role in the production of forms? This problem is related to ideas of causality, becoming, finality, determinism, indeterminism, irreversibility, teleology, and the philosophy of time. Nonetheless, many architects *do* judge buildings based on the history of ideas and the material history of forms, and in so doing their explanations follow those of historians and philosophers in suggesting that architectural forms had to appear the way they did, as if by necessity.

The difficulty concerning architectural judgment based on history, resides in reconciling what is asserted to be a general historical necessity with the nature of the architectural object that is presented as if it were a symptom of such necessity.

The next three chapters will engage this intricate problem on three levels. Chapter 1 will consider the triangular relationship between the architect, the historian, and the philosopher. If history and philosophy mutually condition one another, then in what ways is such conditioning useful for architectural judgment especially in relation to competing historical narratives?

Chapter 2 will examine how historians think about history, exemplified by how grand historical narratives, Classicism and Historicism, shaped architectural culture. It also examines how the retreat of grand narratives gave way to a multitude of smaller histories where the individual historian's theoretical inclinations (whether it is post-structuralism, critical theory, or new historicism) are brought to bear on architectural judgment based on history. The increase in theoretical presuppositions on the part of historians is invariably accompanied by an increase in the relativism of values and evaluations, thus complicating judgment even further. Architects benefit from the demands they make on history as well as knowing the demands that historians themselves make on history. Yet although historians, philosophers, and architects make different uses of architectural history, it is important to note that for many architects judgment based on history is based mostly on the historian's model, that is, the methodologies and conclusions embodied by the history of ideas broadly considered, and architectural history in particular. But architects also need to acknowledge that the aims of the historian and the philosopher do not necessarily coincide with the aims of the architect. Might there be another model for architectural judgment based on history than the one provided by the historian? Might there be a way to consider an architectural history that is written from the standpoint of the architect?

This leads us to Chapter 3, whose aim is to provide a new outline for a history, one that is made from a combination of the scholarly methods of the historian and the operative design methods of the architect. Chapter 3 offers another way to study history that goes beyond periodization and classificatory schemes and beyond theories that purport to explain the aims of history. Instead, it adopts an approach to architectural history that is built less on the premises of the historian and more on the ways in which architects might conceive of their art. It proposes an approach based on the nature, ends, and means of architecture without negating all that is useful in the scholarship of the historian or the speculations of the philosopher.

1
Architectural Judgment Based on History, Part 1

> ... all the characters of history or historiography are reducible to the definition and identification of history with individual judgment. And, as individual judgment, history is a synthesis of subject and predicate, or representation and concept. The intuitive as well as the logical elements are inseparable in history.[1]
> Benedetto Croce

THREE GROUPS OF JUDGING ARCHITECTS

Architectural judgment is significantly shaped by versions of architectural history and by their underlying theoretical or philosophical content. Architects deploy conclusions derived from such contents in order to justify preferred forms and trends, or by contrast, in order to repudiate disapproved forms and trends. When architects justify their work based on traditions and their conventions (precedents), they use the kind of historical justification in which architectural history is considered as a receptacle of exemplars, an accumulation of lessons from which they learn how others approached similar problems. Exemplars are chosen paradigmatically[2] depending on their previous success, and new buildings are made by combining judicially selected parts of previous buildings. Judgment based on history, in this case, depends primarily on the success of architectural composition in the sense of *imitatio* and *inventio*, of combining and re-combining pre-existing forms. Judgment pertains to measuring the individual architect's work in relation to the established rational use of conventions from which architects learn and to which they contribute.

    Other architects justify their work based on a theory or philosophy of history that validates the architectural forms they produce by virtue of their present position inside a historical sequence. This sequence is linked to hypotheses concerning a general order inherent in history, a grand narrative (e.g. historicism) containing philosophical pre-suppositions (e.g. progress) about the becoming of architectural form, inexorably moving this form toward an aim, a finality.[3] New buildings are

1.1 Historia, Iconologia, Cesare Ripa, *Historiae et Allegoriae*.

composed with a critical awareness of the architect's position within this sequence while presenting a dense opacity toward the historically given, its larger traditions and its regional conventions.[4] Judgment, in this case, rejects imitative theory and considers invention as *inventio ex nihilo*, an invention out of nothing, following the commanding impetus of a technologically determined society. Judgment based on history, depends on the extent to which deliberate distancing or rupture from the historically given justifies the acceleration to reach a desired historical finality – a finality that may materialize in the imminent present or in some distant future.

Even if their uses of history differ widely, both of these groups share an ever-heightened consciousness of the individual's choice and agency in history. For the first group, historical continuity is directly instrumental in everyday practice. This group is made up of traditional architects. For the second, a radical opposition to continuity instrumentalizes history in order to justify an architectural practice which, once established, can then proceed to sever its connections to history. This second group is made of modernist architects. Both groups maintain a state of tension between two qualities: to integrate architecture into a historical continuity or to differ from such continuity in order to fulfill another historical purpose. To integrate or to distinguish became two parts of the mystique that provided an élan vital, a vital impetus, for the architect's *disegno*, the will-to-make, and gave impetus to judging the work of others. In other words, history for these two groups remains the scenographic backdrop that empowers their explanations as well as their justifications.

A third group, however, rejects this historical scenographic backdrop altogether. It denounces grand historical narratives as well as claims to know history in its objective totality, and it denies consensus and unity as bases for the legitimization of architecture. Among its beliefs are the avoidance of assertions about the universal validity of ideas, the encouragement of difference, and the promotion of multiple historical methodologies because no single methodology can make an exclusive claim to reveal the truth about history. Only local and fragmentary histories are now possible; and given the relativity of opinions about history, where historians write their individual narratives based on their own value judgments, judgment based on history is an impossibility. It is also irrelevant to the cultural justification or legitimization of architecture since buildings are primarily the individual or rather the differentiated expressions of their authors.

Architectural judgment based on history is here understood as the validation or repudiation of a movement, a period, a building, under one or another of the three aforementioned categories. As forms of dialectical reasoning, each of these three approaches involves a kind of synthetic judgment because architectural history does not only offer buildings on the one hand, and architects as inscrutable subjects on the other, but rather individuals or groups who thoroughly engage the contingencies of their specific historical situations. Architects seek to be influential cultural agents; they do not remain passively influenced by histories of architecture. They take part in debating, or questioning the nature and ends of the historical endeavor, the historian's methodologies and the philosopher's conjectures. They take sides and alternatively become protagonists or antagonists of various positions on history. They enjoy historical speculation, but would like to know their proper stand in history with a high degree of certainty. They recognize empirical facts, but they wonder about the meaning of that diffused infinity of atomized forms at their disposition. They entertain the idea of a meta-historical construction of a prior unity of reason within history, but they worry that this philosophy will crush the individual historical phenomenon. They revolt against the notion of being determined by historical forces, but they delight in the idea of being carried by history to the culminating point which they presently wish to occupy. Most of all, they cherish the historical explanation that justifies their preferred forms.

1.2 Portrait d'architecte revenant de voyage, 19th Cent., V. Dahlerup.

To explain a historical event or architectural form is not only to describe why it happened, how it came about, what are its antecedents, or how it relates to other homologous phenomena; it also includes the knowledge claims, inferential methodologies and classificatory schemes of history as a discipline (the knowledge of it). Historians pursue this evidence-dependent knowledge with the tacit belief that the reality of the past is accessible through their rigorous methodologies.

Philosophers, or theoretically inclined architects and historians, add yet another layer of inquiry regarding a historical event or architectural form. They inquire about the sort of object architecture is by reflecting on its nature – for example the ideas of type, of character – and the justification of its existence in a time and place in comparison to how the mind apprehends, categorizes, judges, or constructs historical reality (the ontology of it). Naturally, there are numerous exceptions to these generalizing statements. There are many historians who inquire into the *a priori* suppositions of the mind, and many philosophers who prefer empirical epistemological pursuits over ontological reflections. But the writing of architectural history is rarely a purely epistemological or purely ontological pursuit. It is difficult to draw a definite demarcating line between history and philosophy since philosophical concerns are frequently woven into the fabric of the most adopted form of history-telling: the historical narrative.[5] Thus, given that architects draw a considerable part of their judgment based on history from the discourses of historians, they tend to combine fragments of epistemological and ontological approaches while striving to fashion them into a coherent argument.

This occurs whether architects consider themselves versed in architectural history and theory, or matter-of-act pragmatists who prefer to deal with practical matters of construction or patronage, or temperate artists who attempt to blend the two. They speak of a historical consciousness precisely when a certain dynamic from the past determines their understanding of the present, or justifies their will-to-make in the present. Many architects today assume that all objects of human production are ruled by temporal relations. In this assumption, they oppose the notion of time having an absolute value and existing by itself to that of time as an awareness that emerges empirically from numerous relations between multiple phenomena. Considering history to mean: the embodiment of the consciousness of time in architecture, they project "pastness" or "presentness" onto their buildings as if these conceptions were artistic values that can be inserted into or withheld from architectural composition. This phenomenon is not unrelated to the contemporary architect's aesthetic formation, shaped as it is by sanitized images of buildings shortly after they were completed, before weathering, settling and humans leave their imprint.

This acute consciousness of the place architects occupy in their epoch is closely related to their sense of being responsible for history by participating in the historical becoming of form. Since the Enlightenment consecrated the individual's full rational autonomy, this consciousness greatly emboldened architectural production and its justification. Prior to the Enlightenment, many considered Reason and History to be two separate things. After the Enlightenment, many consider them to be one. Consequently, it is difficult nowadays to dissociate architectural justification from a theory of history. In parallel, it is significant that the ideological polemics amongst architectural historians begin to acquire intensity in regards to the history that dates from the Renaissance onward. These polemics gain much vehemence with respect to the Enlightenment, and reach an epidemic fierceness when it comes to the architecture of the past one hundred years.

ARCHITECTS, HISTORIANS AND PHILOSOPHERS

In order to judge architecture based on history, architects necessarily ponder on what ordinary parlance calls the "march of things", combining many considerations deriving from two sources: the history of architecture and the philosophy of history. These considerations are uncomfortably shared by two groups of scholars: the kind of historian who opposes philosophizing about history and for whom history is always a search for "how things really were" with truth and objectivity, and the kind of philosopher, or philosophically inclined historian, who projects overarching patterns onto historical events. Wilhelm von Humboldt and Leopold von Ranke, and their admonishments to penetrate the spirit of a culture, a period if you will, are examples of the first kind of scholar. Georg W.F. Hegel and Karl Marx, and their comprehensive philosophical systems, are examples of the second kind of scholar. Although their motives may vary, architects, historians, and philosophers of history, commonly reflect on the interpretive theories of the past based on the concerns of the immediate present. They combine classificatory reasoning, causal judgment based on the archaeological materiality of buildings, the contextualization of historical evidence on urban and sociological levels, deterministic forces, whether history has a direction or whether time has an arrow, or if development necessarily leads to progress. All of this leads one to question whether architects and historians today are able to recall or recover a way of looking at architecture *prior* to their being exposed to an interpretive theory of architecture.[6] Quite often today, theory precedes history.

But what do architects want from historians and philosophers with respect to architectural judgment based on historical knowledge? Just as scientific history is expected to speculate on the mysteries of human origins and of human destiny, so does the architect expect from architectural history to unveil the origins of forms, explain their evolution, their regional characters, the complex cause and effect relations between form, content, and context, as well as speculate on the direction in which they may be moving (becoming). Put differently, architects wish to use the historian's material, critical, and speculative modes of inquiry for the purposes of judging architectural forms. Architects also wish to understand the methods through which historians explain stability or change in architectural forms. For what reasons, for example, are changes in architectural form explained-away as reflections of socio-economic changes by historians whose scholarly aim is to accumulate facts precisely for that purpose?[7] Conversely, what revisions to architectural judgment must be made after historians took upon themselves the task of detaching socio-economic changes from chronologies of stylistic changes, especially when closer examination revealed that these two sets of changes are not always synchronous? What revisions to architectural judgment based on periodic classification must be accommodated when architects, on the one hand, study history from the angle of conflicts for stylistic dominance, while on the other, historians regard styles as scholarly inventions that facilitate the study of architectural forms based on patterns of commonalty?[8] How is judgment affected if concepts such as Renaissance or Modernism pertained more to a state of mind unbound by temporality rather than the enclosures of specific periodizations? Why is it that when a style is classified-away, it is deemed no longer conducive of certain societal signifiers by some architects and historians? Architects wish to understand from historians why is it that when certain building characters are exported, they retain a strong imprint of their birthplace, e.g. the Florentine palazzo, the Ottoman mosque. What were the historical justifications that led to the validation of Gothic architecture in such diverse contexts as the thirteenth and nineteenth centuries in France, Germany, England, and nineteenth and twentieth century America? Or by what justification did the Gothic and the Classical achieve equal exemplary value with the rise of historicism in German national consciousness?

Above all, to understand their place as free agents within history, and as judges of historical forms, architects ask historians for certitudes. But their very empirical observations show that historians are part of the very becoming they wish to trace. After all, historians themselves are historically situated.[9] Far from being neutral recorders of events, historians are at once observers of and agents in history. Their writing of history is consequently inseparable from their chosen philosophical beliefs or their preferential aesthetic choices despite intense efforts to attain historical "objectivity" and "truth". Architects are apt to forget that history also tells the story of its own past, and that various histories are linked by cause and effect relationships. Rightly or wrongly, many architects believe that architectural history is a faithful mapping of architectural reality and they frequently overlook the advice of many thinkers, namely that the map is not the territory.

From philosophers, or philosophically inclined historians, architects learn that if history were a book, then they would like to know the driving principles that connect its chapters, and whether these chapters constitute partial conclusions that will eventually combine in an encompassing finale that might explain a movement, a period, an age. A philosophy of history can only succeed if it considers the alignment of historical events according to a certain schema, either looking at history as a unity – what David Hume called the "overall shape of history" – or at the unity of certain historical strands taken en bloc, while uncovering the connecting links. Taken together, the lessons of history and philosophy serve to provide the thematic grounds for architectural judgment based on history. But the question we have posed regarding what architects want from historians and philosophers addresses the scope of judgment based on history only partially. To be more inclusive, the scope of the question should consider that architects, historians and philosophers alike judge form based on history, and that each of these groups makes different demands on history. We shall return at a later stage to the question of what historians themselves want from the writing of history.

With the wisdom derived from comparison, architects, historians and philosophers observed how the subjectivity of historians conditioned the writing of their histories, their selection of facts, the role of their imagination in weaving the historical narrative, and the philosophical content of their explanations. Thus they distinguish between the past and its histories; between the way in which historical events may have unfolded and the many possible narratives in which these events might be told. Such, for example, is the narrative form of the architectural history survey which points to two directions at once: first, it purports to disclose the coherence of architectural history as a structure or a process; and second, it seeks to convince the reader of its correctness, producing what Roland Barthes called the "effect of reality". Nowhere is this form of narrative survey more literally evident than in the narrative form of the museum (a historical survey based on images rather than text) as it purports to physically match periodicity with stylistic classificatory schemes. But philosophers of history and historians are not simply content to narrate, describe or predict a certain course of events that happened in the past from the standpoint of their effects on the present. They also prophesy or make proclamations based on assumptions regarding the meaning and direction of history. As Manfredo Tafuri suggested, certain "operative historiographies" were undertaken as veritable architectural projects aimed at molding public opinion.[10]

It is commonplace to grant that prolonged reflection on the possible connections between historical phenomena makes it difficult to avoid philosophizing about them, even if the connections are not established with certainty. Such may have been Raymond Aron's meaning regarding one of the crises of historicist thought when he remarked on the "impossibility of philosophical truth, and the impossibility not to philosophize".[11] History, in this case, uses philosophy as a support. More insistently, Benedetto Croce emphasized that there is an identity of purpose between the philosophical logic that links disparate events, and the historical logic that classifies and categorizes those same events.[12] History and philosophy mutually condition each other within the context that saw their emergence and without which they might not have occurred in the forms in which they have been cast. Historical concepts and systems, paraphrasing Croce, are the results of that form of explanation we call philosophy, while individual judgments and narratives are the results of that form of explanation we call history.[13]

This leads us to some important specificities regarding the judgment of architectural form based on history. *In the act of justifying their own work or judging the work of others, architects bring into their arguments a deliberately aligned historical sequence that tows behind it a critical selection of architectural forms. They select their own significant historical ensembles, their own subjective history, which are then brought to bear on the current moment of judgment. When they justify their own work and judge the work of others, architects expect a full transparency between the forms they practice, on the one hand, and historico-philosophical beliefs on the other.* It is no hyperbole to say that there is a historian inside every architect. Georg Simmel's characterization of Ernst Troeltsch as barely a philosopher, but one who knew enough philosophy so as to be a true historian, seems quite apposite for architects.[14] In order to intelligently engage in judgment based on history, architects need to master enough history and enough philosophy.[15]

Ever since the late eighteenth century, when the architectures of Egypt, Greece or China came to be gradually known – in addition to a widening interest in Gothic architecture – the notion of one dominant paradigm against which to measure one's work was seriously challenged. Whereas this situation made available a massive fund of formal compositions, or manifold architectural characters and styles, it significantly complicated judgment on account of the very multiplicity of choices. On the one hand, judgment had to be carried out in comparison to a plurality of paradigms, while on the other hand, the tenets of historicism advocated that every architecture was to be evaluated based on its own unique terms in a given place and time. Escaping this relativism, which opposed the idea of universals across cultures and regions, became a preoccupation of historians and philosophers. Our contemporary conditions, however, are considerably more complicated. What are architects, historians, and philosophers to do with respect to architectural judgment based on history now that all of the world's formal traditions are effortlessly available in any location on the globe? Furthermore, what are they to do now that the grand historical narratives have retreated from their previous positions as landmarks of cultural evaluation and judgment?

[Margin notes: What is the role of the architect? What is the role of the philosopher? What is the role of the historian?]

NOTES

1. B. Croce, *Logica come scienza del concetto puro*, Laterza, (Bari, 1947), my translation, p. 180.

2. Greek: *paradeigma*, to show side by side.

3. In this chapter, the influence of philosophy on architecture is understood under the heading of the philosophy of history and its impact on the writing of history as well as architectural judgment. Architectural theory, or philosophical and aesthetic reflections about architecture, arose primarily out of the reflections of architects and historians of architecture. Philosophers, however, have rarely developed sustained considerations about architecture. Plato's *Timaeus, Parmenides, Cratylus, Republic*, and *Laws* contain many profound remarks about artistic making in general: causes, essences, Forms, imitation, beauty and proportions; but no direct treatment of architecture. Aristotle's *Poetics* laid important foundations for mimetic thought. Fragments of his *Metaphysics, Parts of Animals, Physics, Rhetoric, Nicomachean Ethics, Eudemian Ethics*, and *Politics*, develop several paradigms of general artistic applicability such as his four causes, unity and universals, actuality and potentiality, propriety and experience. In the *Didascalion*, Hugh of St. Victor made the parallel between architecture and the study of scripture. In the *Philebus Commentary*, Marsilio Ficino discussed Platonic Forms, time and change; and proportion, beauty and suitability. His *Commentarium in convivium* compares the differences between the abstract level of Ideas and the realization of architecture. Thomas More's *Utopia* and Tomasso Campanella's *City of the Sun*, shed light on their vision of the city's form in relation to the general Good. Denis Diderot made some brief remarks on architecture in the context of his *Theory of Aesthetic Relations*. In his *Philosophical Inquiry into the Origin of the Sublime and Beautiful*, Edmund Burke expanded somewhat on the relation between the dimension of buildings and the resulting pleasure of the observer, on light in buildings, and on dissociating proportions and propriety from beauty. Immanuel Kant's only fleeting remarks about architecture in his *Critique of Judgment*, pertained to a building's adequacy for a needed purpose. By far, however, Georg W.F. Hegel's *Aesthetics* presented the most extensive philosophical treatment of architecture, its general character and particular determinants, its symbolism, its relation to the other arts, as well as its evolution. Prominent twentieth century philosophers, with the exception of Martin Heidegger and Jacques Derrida, made only passing comments related to architecture.

4. On transparency and opacity in modernism, especially in the work of Konrad Fiedler, see Philippe Junod's *Transparence et opacité*, (1976), (J. Chambon, 2004).

5   As expressed concisely by Hayden White "... the principal difference between history and philosophy of history is that the latter brings the conceptual apparatus by which the facts are ordered in the discourse to the surface of the text, while history proper (as it is called) buries it in the interior of the narrative, where it serves as a hidden or implicit shaping device". Hayden White, *Tropics of Discourse*, (Johns Hopkins University Press, 1978), pp. 126–7.

6   A point pithily made by Edmund Husserl in his attempt to develop the concept of "life-world" enabling the observer to recover such an untainted position. *Phenomenological Psychology*, J. Scanlon (Tr.), (Martinus Nijhoff (1925), 1977), p. 59.

7   Richard Goldthwaite's *The Building of Renaissance Florence, An Economic and Social History*, (Johns Hopkins University Press, 1980), examines market forces as shapers of art and architecture form.

8   See Joan Ockman, Deborah Berke, and Mary McLeod (eds), *Architecture, Criticism, Ideology*, (Princeton Architectural Press, 1985); Marvin Trachtenberg "Some Observations on Recent Architectural History", *Art Bulletin*, 70(2), (1988), pp. 208–41; Stanford Anderson, "Architectural History in Schools of Architecture", *The Journal of the Society of Architectural Historians*, 58(3), Architectural History 1999/2000 (1999), pp. 282–90; Dana Arnold, Elvan Altan Ergut, and Belin Turan Ozkaya, (eds), *Rethinking Architectural Historiography*, (Routledge, 2006).

9   It is important to note that many architectural historians were also architects, or received training in architecture, for example: Eugène-Emanuel Viollet-le-Duc, Banister Fletcher, Henry Russell Hitchcock, Bruno Zevi, Manfredo Tafuri, Kenneth Frampton, Charles Jencks, Joseph Rykwert, Paolo Portoghesi.

10 Tafuri directed these comments at the work of Siegfried Giedion and Bruno Zevi. See *Teorie e storia dell' architettura*, (Laterza, 1986), p. 176. On the historiographical methods of modernism see Panayotis Tournikiotis, *The Historiography of Modern Architecture*, (MIT Press, 1999).

11 Raymond Aron, *Introduction à la philosophie de l'histoire*, (1938) (Gallimard, 1986), my translation, p. 376.

12 Croce's pronouncements, of course, affirm that history *is* philosophy, and even that history and philosophy are one and the same thing. *Logica come scienza del concetto puro*, Laterza, (Bari, 1947), pp. 208–11. This parallels Robin G. Collingwood's admonition that "all history is the history of thought", *Idea of History*, (Oxford, 1946), pp. 214–15. The position that history is philosophy has been previously adumbrated by some historians of the Renaissance. See David Quint, et al., (ed.), *Creative Imitation: New Essays on Renaissance Literature in Honor of Thomas Greene*, (Mediaeval and Renaissance Texts & Studies, 1992).

13 *Ibid*, p. 209.

14 Quoted by Hartmut Ruddies in "La vérité au courant de l'histoire. Réfléxions sur la philosophie de E. Troeltsch", Pierre Gisel (ed.) *Histoire et théologie chez E. Troeltsch*, Labor et (Fides, 1990), p. 34.

15 An old and valuable piece of advice voiced by Vitruvius regarding the proper education of the architect, history and philosophy being two of nine recommended disciplines. *The Ten Books on Architecture*, I, 1, 12.

2
Architectural Judgment Based on History, Part 2

The selection for emphasis among the many specimens of architecture, the arrangement and interpretation of facts known about them, the personal judgment of each historian, the vantage point of the time within which he or she operates – all these variables help create as many histories as there are historians. In that sense history is manufactured by historians, and any building or person or event in this process can acquire as much weight as is consonant with each historian's purpose.[1]

Spiro Kostof

TWO GRAND NARRATIVES: CLASSICISM AND HISTORICISM

The views developed by those who look for the reasons of constancy and the reasons for change in architectural history, have oscillated between two grand narratives: classicism and historicism, corresponding to the first two groups of architects we mentioned in the last chapter. Much of the history and theory of the past two centuries has been written under the shadow of these two narratives. The classical narrative, operating well into the nineteenth century, and beyond, took nature as the superlative source for cultural paradigms. It saw a causal relation between the laws of Nature (*natura naturans*) and the products of nature (*natura naturata*). Architectural principles evolved from a dual origin: from the observation of Nature and nature, on the one hand, and on the other, from the artistic conventions that imitated natural laws such as proportions and hierarchy. Architecture, as opposed to painting and sculpture, did not have a direct example in nature; but by imitating the laws of Nature, architecture produced forms that could have been authored by nature had nature been the architect. Architectural history, and history in general, was written in order to demonstrate how cultural values derived from Nature, from natural law. For classicism, nature-made objects, and by imitation, human-made objects, have an essence that endures beyond everyday modifications. There are forms that undergo little change in history; and when change occurs, these

2.1 Seagram Building, Mies van der Rohe, New York, 1958. *Source*: Photo by Noroton.

forms still retain identifiable and enduring qualities. A palazzo retains its enduring character notwithstanding the many additions and alterations it received over the centuries. Classicism developed a history of enduring ideas such as the authority of reason embodied in tradition.[2] In this view, individual buildings, as particular historical phenomena, are contingent manifestations informed by enduring and formative ideas that gave meaning and provided the measure to empirical daily experience. Such, for example, are the two Vitruvian triads of solidity, utility and beauty, along with symmetry, eurythmy, and propriety. To achieve their contemporary work, architects looked to the enduring aspects of tradition from two standpoints. The first advocated the maintaining of tradition based on the authority of great historical exemplars. The second operated on the assumption that the continuation of a tradition is justified only by collectively reasoned agreement about what has proven successful in that tradition, otherwise this practice would be discontinued. This rationalist approach particularly characterizes the contemporary practice of classical architecture.[3]

The second grand narrative, historicism, assailed the first considering it as a fixed and absolutist outlook that uniformly applied the same theory to the study and the evolution of the nature-made and the human-made.[4] Historicism separated the natural and the human realms, seeing no common principles that animated both. It rejected the belief in universal ideas which are abstracted from development and from temporality. It also opposed certain concepts of Enlightenment rationalism, such as the unchanging laws of nature and unchanging human nature, and replaced them with a view of nature and society in constant change. The radical aspect of the historicist interpretation of reality was its affirmation of the primacy of historicity, of temporality, its emphasis of the particular over the universal, and its assertion that all phenomena and their cognition are always in a state of becoming – forms arise, change, transform into newer shapes, or dissolve. As all human productions, architecture can only be studied and understood according to the social context in which it emerged, and the historian's task was to understand that social context from within (as in J.G. Herder's einfühling, feeling into) while refraining from projecting into it an external content that may alter

2.2 Rome's layers, from the Forum of Trajan to the Church of Domenico and Sisto.
Source: Photo by Author.

the understanding of its past reality. Architecture was a unique expression of its culture and time, and was progressing according to laws of growth and change deriving from the unique historical experience of that social context. Society and architectural style were linked causally, while style was considered the bearer of societal meanings. Historical change followed some determining patterns which the historicist explanation sought to prove through an extensive accumulation of facts arranged in a chronological order. But these determining patterns did not reside in the paradigm of transcendent Nature as embodied within the traditions of classicism; rather, they were located within the immanent cultural values of a continuously changing culture. Ideals no longer resided in the glory of an unsurpassable past as an *a-priori* given. Rather, ideals were to emerge from the clashing events of daily empirical experience.

Central to understanding historical reality itself was the notion that cultural forms were ever in a state of becoming or in gradual change – a notion pivotal to the very essence of modernity. To historicist change Hegelian and Marxian thought added a progressive character in which becoming meant a transition from "lower" to "higher" forms. Thus was the notion of a universally valid and past ideal replaced by that of a future ideal. When historicism assailed the certainties of classicism, it did not erase the notion of certainty itself. It simply replaced one set of certainties with another. More precisely, historicism accepted a variety of certainties, some weaker, others more forceful.

Historicism's emphasis on the uniqueness of a culture or a movement, its proclamation of the relativism of values, of historical knowledge, and therefore judgment, served to diminish the influence of paradigms that applied across cultures. One of the new historicist certainties made it unfeasible or ineffectual to judge one culture or one architecture by the standards of another. By focusing on the increasing independence or differentiation of historical periods, as well as on cultural specificity, historicism did not initially account for forms and conventions that naturally travelled between cultures and regions and richly influenced them. Though forms and conventions arise in one place, they are either willfully imported by another culture and made to combine with local forms, or imposed on it by force. Nonetheless, it is noteworthy that not all forms and conventions imposed by an external power (e.g. colonialism) are subsequently rejected; as many of them eventually become part of a culture or region.

A more forceful historicist certainty was historical determinism. With the considerable authority exerted by Hegelian teleology, determinism reached an overarching historical scope where cultural productions were inescapably led by a spirit of the age (zeitgeist) influencing nations and individuals.[5] This spirit was evolutionary in the sense that it was considered as the moving force behind the formal changes, e.g. governing the passage from the Romanesque to the Gothic, Gothic to Renaissance, Renaissance to Baroque, and so forth. An era's cultural products were not only expressions or conformations of the assumed zeitgeist, but the products themselves were justified based on this very assumption.[6] For this overarching reason Hegelian historians tried to associate the compositional laws of architectural style with the determinations of the zeitgeist. Some philosophers and historians, but especially artists and architects, seemed particularly adept at identifying the spirit of eras in general, and especially the spirit of the modern era, at the same time as it was manifesting; whereas others, more cautious, preferred to speak of a spirit only in retrospect. Nevertheless modernist architects and artists, the true historicists, believed they knew with certainty what this impending spirit was and how to imminently embody it in their daily work. As promethean artists, they knew how to sculpt the real and render it pliable to their will which was the will of their age. Many architects also believed that they were called upon to fulfill a historic mission to manifest the zeitgeist and be its most faithful and enthusiastic apologists.

That the modernist architect and artist considered themselves the embodiment of autonomy and freedom from any conformism, did not prevent them, however, from holding this position simultaneously with the providentialist belief that the architectural and artistic forms of the modern age obediently reflected the unquestionably dominant zeitgeist. To achieve their work in faithfulness to this spirit, architects had to sever their connections with previous traditions by the continual search for new forms, and these forms/images were expressed by the latest technology which, in turn, represented the new society – the technological society. The world was apprehended within a new kind of image: a technicist image, which modernist architects heralded as the one image valid for their preferred cultural resonances. It is worthy of note that in contrast to the German romantics' use of the term weltanschauung, in the sense of a view of the world, recent post-modernist uses of the term have tended to employ it in the plural sense of "images of the world". Hence M. Heidegger's observation that the peculiarity of the modern era was to see the world as bild, as an image.

Zeitgeist and weltanschauung are used today in the plural, showing the contemporary capacity to artistically adapt almost any set of values. But the fact that a decreasing number of architects today use these two concepts as overt justificatory criteria, does not necessarily mean that architects and historians agree that they are no longer applicable. Rather, the meanings associated with these concepts still strongly underline ordinary judgment as a given, as if they have automatically fallen below the threshold of architects' critical self-consciousness. These meanings presently commingle as loose fragments along with other historical beliefs deriving from post-modernism. The latter showed little faith in the grand narrative of historicism, its deterministic qualities, or in the remote abstractions of modernist forms. But post-modernism did not offer a full counter-narrative, or an inclusive counter-theory of history. Rather, it offered multiple fragmentary oppositions to selected fragments of the historicist narrative, stating that rupture from history cannot be sustained, that disallowing the use of multiple architectural styles leads to an impoverishment of architecture's symbolic function, and that the propensity to elaborate conventions is an inseparable trait from the human character that cannot be held in abeyance for too long.

THE RETREAT OF GRAND NARRATIVES

Among the reasons that significantly affected the writing of history, and thus judgment based on history, are three interrelated clusters of considerations whose conjugated effects caused an intense questioning of the validity claims made by sweeping narratives. The first, concerns the dispute about the nature and utility of the historical explanation itself. The second, regards the criticism of historicism in its relation to the complex network of concepts that came to attach themselves to it such as: progress, teleology, development, and world-view. The third, pertains to the critical examination by historians of the claims and methodologies of their discipline, seen especially in the confrontation between the modernist and post-modernist approaches to historical knowledge.

I

Because the decisive problem in history is comprehension, the assessments of historical events have been strongly marked by the scientific and the historical explanations; and it is significant for architects judging from history to be aware of the long-standing assumptions underlying both forms of explanation. In what came to be known as the covering-law theory, the scientific explanation posited one paradigm applicable to all forms of explanation.[7] Historical events are explainable to the extent that they are instantiations of general laws and widely confirmed empirical observations, just like a scientific law receives justification if it is not contradicted by experiments.[8] Explanations are to show that events in history are predictable because they depend on some causal law. One such explanation, for example, justified the rise of modernism by asserting that the ends of architecture had to change because the technological means of producing it had changed. The change of means occupied a causal position regarding the ends of architectural form, while knowledge of this change of means made the change of forms predictable. To claim, however, that the change of means can be linked causally to the change of forms is one thing, and to claim that this was a general historical law is another.

Chief among the objections to covering law theory was that it was too deterministic; it assumed that events had to happen the way they did. Other objections clarified that an event preceding another is insufficient a reason to establish causality between the two. Similarly, to outline the contextual forces that surrounded a historical event or a building, does not mean that these forces necessarily played a causal role in the formation of this event, this building. Given these objections, historians such as William Dray proposed the rational explanation as a remedy to covering-law. Rational agents in history act with intended aims, and the historian must satisfactorily explain historical events by reconstructing the reasons that ostensibly justified them in the very eyes of these agents rather than presenting historical events as instances of some general law.[9]

Humanist culture also objected to covering-law theory on the basis that it did not do justice to the history of art and architecture which assesses individual artistic expressions and psychological patterns of behavior. Artists and architects can explain their forms based on the principles and rules of their practice which they elaborate into conventions. These conventions are artistic laws, not historical laws. In doing so, the humanist critique reminded that the ways in which art and architecture operate should not be conflated with the ways in which their history is studied. Philosophers since Wilhelm Dilthey, Robin G. Collingwood, Benedetto Croce, Raymond Aron and others, had been hard at work underlining the significant differences between scientific and historical explanations and warned against reducing one to the other. They also emphasized the individual uniqueness of cultural forms as historical events within a specific context to which they belonged. Unlike the laws of nature which are universal, history does not possess homogeneity; and the fact that different historical periods are specific and heterogeneous makes the establishment of general historical laws impossible. However, the fact that history does not follow universal and certain laws does not mean that it does not follow causes. If both laws and causes are suspended, then history becomes unexplainable. History is not the result of chance events. Causality in history derives from the mind of the agent, and it was the historian's task to reconstruct the thinking behind the causal linkage of forms even if thought is not accessible to external investigation as are buildings. Contrary to physics, where causes can be subsumed under general principles (e.g. the fall of objects in space and Newton's law of universal attraction), in history, every event has a specific cause which is impossible to arrange under a universal formula. It is therefore significant to distinguish between law and causality.

II

Built into the contemporary architect's grasp of the historicity of buildings are several intertwined notions. Cause, origin and beginning are usually understood within the concept of genealogy; whereas time, progress, development and teleology, are grouped under the concept of historical directionality and irreversibility. Yet each of these notions elucidates different understandings or aspects of historicity, unveiling what is implicit in an historical narrative: the linkage of historical facts based on external or intrinsic causes. Cause, origin and beginning remain under the general concept of genealogy until historians or architects actually attempt to justify architectural form genealogically. At a certain point two questions confront each other: where does a form originate from, and, from what beginning does a form descend?

1. A beginning assigns a date, a determined point within a chronological sequence.
2. A beginning can be archaeologically determined and genealogically demonstrated.
3. Thus, its existence can be explained; and
4. its characteristics understood.
5. A beginning also validates – or denies – some of the formal qualities of a building.

All five parts are needed to use beginning as a justification; but they do not explain the more subtle and abstract notion of origin.

Both origin and beginning occupy causal roles *vis-à-vis* form, but the first is causal on the level of paradigm[10] (a type, a foundational myth such as Laugier's hut), while the second is causal on the level of a historical sequence (the particular model, the archaeological precedent). Origin denotes a principle from which, whereas a beginning denotes a point from which, a chain of historical events might proceed. An origin, or type, cannot be excavated and dated, yet it can justify an architectural form on the level of essence. Its value resides in the extent to which history is considered as the mutual support between an "originating" meaning, and the sedimentation of subsequent meanings. The distinction between origin and beginning corresponds to the distinction between the context of justification and the context of discovery.[11]

One example of origin, or type, is the circle which explains what is in common between the Pantheon, the Buddhist stupa at Sanchi, the rotunda of the Dome of the Rock in Jerusalem, the US Capitol in Washington, the Stockholm public library, the ballerina's pirouette, the circular dance of the Turkish whirling dervishes, or the grouping of people around a camp fire. One example of a beginning is the introduction, ostensibly for the first time, of the pycnostyle intercolumniation (1:1.5 the column diameter or less) in the Temple of Venus Genetrix in the Forum of Caesar in Rome.[12] Both origin and beginning, however, are sometimes conflated as when historians dismiss the possible existence of a primitive wooden hut as a precedent to the stone temple because their excavations did not reveal one.[13]

Inherent to the historical explanation is an assumed correspondence between the slicing of time (epochs, periods, movements, generations) and the evolution of things. As a theoretical activity of the historian, periodization assumes a certain homogeneity of events grouped under the same period, and the possibility, based on intrinsic characteristics, to determine beginnings and ends to periods. With the idea of progress appeared the idea of a specifically human time that transcended natural time while taking the century as a measuring unit. But this necessary condition to the arbitrary habit of thinking in centuries puts architectural historians in the difficult position of having to make architectural developments correspond to a precise chronology. The architecture of the eighteenth century does not entirely correspond to the years 1700 to 1799. What really marked our understanding of the century was the convergence of the end of a century with the end of a world. When we mention 1789, we denote time in the sense of calendar. When we mention the French Revolution, we denote time in the sense of history, or historic event. As Condorcet expressed it: "One instant put a century's distance between the man of today and that of tomorrow".

Portraying the architecture of that period as revolutionary or visionary, some historians[14] saw it as the material representative of this shift or rupture in historical consciousness, whereas in reality it was the same architecture practiced under the ancien régime. This shift in historical consciousness became one of the justifications used by historians to trace a progressive change in architectural form in order to demonstrate an irrevocable movement toward modernism.

Proceeding retroactively from modernism in a backward direction in time, their narratives alternately emphasized or minimized selected stylistic processes using either rupture or continuity in order to provide modernism with an evolutionary genealogy connected to beginnings in the eighteenth or even the sixteenth centuries.[15] Just like some architects theorize about what architecture ought to be, some historians write a historical narrative about what architecture ought to have been in order to justify an architecture that, according to their preferences, ought to presently be. Irrespective of the different beginnings or adumbrations assigned to modernism, these historians cast the pursuits of volumetric and stylistic abstractions on the part of a selection of preferred architects within a progressive genealogy. This progressive, or rather teleological, narrative was meant to shape the course of contemporary architectural practice and its historical assessment or judgment.

Progress is a particular way to represent historical time that differs from the simple notion of development in that progress advances toward a finality. Progress implies that history moves according to a unified direction, and that historical periods constitute the various steps of that progress in which a principle gradually realizes itself and justifies all the changes. For Jacques-Bénigne Bossuet, this principle is God governing history; for Voltaire and Nicolas de Condorcet it is Reason accompanying history; whereas for Hegel, Reason systematically justifies the progressive movement of historical periods on their way the realization of the Concept. Historical events or periods gain their significance depending on the place they occupy within a unified and progressive chronological development. Consequently, progress implies the merging of meaning with direction.

One example of writing progress into history is the way in which the cross-vaulted and pointed arcuation inside a Gothic church is deemed to be an advancement over the round arch vaulting in Roman and Romanesque buildings. In a Roman building with square structural bays, the four round arches are all equal, and so are the two longest span arches on the diagonals; but in a rectangular bay, the arches on the shorter side must be stilted in order to rise the same height as those on the wider side. In a Gothic church, the pointed arch solves the "problem" of stilting by allowing a steeper pointing on the short side of the bay and a less steep pointing on the long side, while the diagonal arches are obtusely pointed. The progressive linearity of this argument assumes that the Roman structural bay inherently had an unresolved problem which received a more satisfactory solution in the later one. Another example of writing progress into history, is the claim that modernist architects invented the free plan in contradistinction to their predecessors who failed to do so notwithstanding centuries of trial and error. The free plan allowed for a maximal flexibility in the disposition of multifaceted, regular, and irregular forms inside a regular structural grid.[16] Yet, the hypostyle halls of the Temple of Amon in Egypt, of the Palace of one hundred columns in Persepolis, of the Porticus Margaritaria in the Roman Forum, of the Mosque of Cordoba, the Mercato Nuovo in Florence, had offered precisely that flexibility in disposition.

Progress differs from teleology in the sense that teleology does not necessarily imply improvement. A *telos* (Greek: goal, end) might lead historical events toward undesirable conclusions. Such, for instance, is the difference between promise and progress. In their good aspirations early architectural modernists sought to wed their preferred architectural forms to their progressive social ideals and their beliefs in the redemptive role for technology with the full expectation that historical events will gradually unfold in the direction of their goals. Yet, the decades that followed showed that modernist architecture became a tool of daily market forces having little to do with earlier stated ideals, while the unrestrained belief in technology led to disastrous environmental consequences and a long-standing unwillingness to admit these consequences.

Teleology and progress, however, have in common the thinking about history with respect to a goal, an internal or an external finality. Teleology assumes a principle that guides evolution, whether it is a principle that directs history while being independent from it (Bossuet), or a principle that directs history from within (Hegel). The criticism of the teleological conception tended to question the belief in a direction to history that may be too abstracted and removed from daily contingency, thus obscuring the specificity of a historical event or form. In fact, the teleological conception of history tended to re-use the same methodological schemes as the theologies of history, provoking adverse reactions against the transcendent as well as immanent historical explanations, and giving rise to historical studies that attempted to avoid the imposition of external norms.

Progress for architects has been deeply entangled in means, and when the technological means developed to an infinity, the ends for which the means were developed disappeared from sight. But the post-modernist self-conscious reaction against the Enlightenment's justification of progress, most importantly modernism, was not embraced in all cultural spheres. In fact, progress has now become such a routine belief that it passes unreflectively for a historical given. Yet, when some thinkers saw the weakening of the Enlightenment certainty regarding the progressive direction of history, they concluded that this was the dissolution of history itself.[17] Others went further, arguing that the acceleration of events has proceeded so exponentially that it is now beyond our capacity to see them as history. Others still, went as far as to propose that the immense network of self-referential signs within consumer society makes it such that we can no longer distinguish historical reality from the myriad consumer images that occupy the reality of experience.[18] The multitude of images that now inhabit the technological consumer society have the power to condition contemporary understanding to such a point that they already frame intellectual assessment within this society becoming a kind of lens through which historians look both at the past and the present. Accordingly, architectural judgment is strongly affected if its grasp of the present-as-history is enclosed within this context.

III

We now return to the question we posed earlier regarding what historians themselves want from the writing of history in light of their critique of their own discipline, taking account of the differences between the modern and the post-modern approaches to historical knowledge. Historians elaborate their explanations based on a correspondence between their conceptions of history and their description of facts, or between their subjective inferences and their goal to attain objectivity. To this effect, their methodologies vary widely, from their intention to introduce a deterministic philosophy that privileges one dominant narrative, as we have noted, to opposing the injection of theory into history based on a certain dispassionate and practical realism, or based on a supposed ideological neutrality. The latter methodology (realism and neutrality) considers that theoretical approaches such as phenomenology, semiotics, structuralism, post-structuralism, critical theory, deconstruction, new historicism, gender studies, and others, have more to do with the concerns of these particular theories and less with architectural history itself, and ultimately leads to distortions of history.[19] The question, in regards to these approaches, is not whether theory influences history, but rather which theory is used in the writing of history.[20] Hence the five points we made earlier in the chapter, contending that:

1. because history is inseparable from the subjectivities of historians, and their cultural beliefs and theoretical biases;
2. it is to a considerable degree a narrative about the past based on the concerns of the present;
3. that implicit in the historical explanation, as a reconstruction of events, is a linkage between external and intrinsic causes;
4. and that since different histories aim to mould opinion; and
5. it is useful to distinguish between the past and its histories.

Without too much exaggeration, one can state that many historians wish their task to be an objective, although not necessarily impartial, inquiry and understanding of what "truly" happened in the past, as well as a faithful and accurate narration thereof.[21] Herein lies a set of important differences between the modern and post-modern approaches to history. The truth validity of the modern, or Enlightenment paradigm, is that it is representational, and depends on the accuracy in which the subject, the historian, maps the empirical and pre-given world. History is supposed to represent reality just like a map is supposed to represent a territory. The more accurate the map, the closer the truth correspondence between the historical narrative and the reality whose story it purports to tell. Post-modernism, however, opposed the belief that there was one empirical world, one history, and it showed that there is more than one map. It attacked, as fiction, the realist notion according to which the construction of knowledge consisted in a faithful mapping of the world, as if the historian was a neutral filter through which all empirical data passed unchanged from "history" to the writing of history. The historian was not effaced behind the narrative and the facts. But the most important post-modern contention was that neither history, nor the historian are pre-given. Both exist in contexts that have their own histories. Historians are not only historically situated, they are also situated in a context of their own authorship. They are not left untouched by the very histories they write as well as those to which they belong.

Their mapping of history is influenced by the very picture they bring to history, as in Gaston Bachelard's contention that "nothing is given, all is constructed". From this perspective, architectural history itself appears as a performance of the architecture it seeks to map.

As many historians (not only post-modernists) acknowledge, history is received or perceived already as a story, as if the world unfolds like a chronicle.[22] Contrary to the deep seated belief that facts exist independently of historians whose task – to use the expression of Leopold von Ranke – is to "resuscitate" the past using an inductivist method, the writing of history is a literary form, a narrative about a segment of the past. This narrative has a deep psychological dimension. It is unavoidably colored by the subjectivity of historians, their necessarily selective choice of significant facts and the theoretical content of their explanations – what Raymond Aron termed: perspectivism, and what Hayden White termed: emplotment, or imposed narrative.[23] As aesthetes (desirers of form) who empathize with the objects of their study, historians espouse and project themselves into existing narratives or polemics, or vehemently oppose others. As passionate intellectuals they exhibit partiality toward their preferred subject or ideology; and in their attempts at giving coherence to their arguments, they construct relationships or wholes that may or may not have existed as such, emphasizing certain trends while remaining silent about others.[24] Such occurrences cast doubt on the possible ideological neutrality of historians. For example, how could a relativist historian be neutral when writing a history of universals without contradicting his or her beliefs and methods?

In criticizing their own discipline, historians clarified that the emphasis on a dominant narrative and its representative landmarks and protagonists, made historians overlook or ignore the existence of other significant developments operating at exactly the same time. For instance, the profound influence exerted by the Renaissance narrative on architectural history since Giorgio Vasari posited that in its centrifugal expansion from Italy, older traditions had to fold back in the face of the new architecture. Assuming a universal validity, this narrative tended to overlook simultaneous architectural developments that sought to combine a variety of Byzantine, Romanesque, or Gothic elements depending on countries and regions. It also treated departures from the Renaissance superlative model as strange anachronistic deviations. The anachronism may be correct from the standpoint of the narrating historian, but not necessarily from the standpoint of contemporary architects who may have only partially espoused the idiom that Vasari called rinascita, and that Jules Michelet more explicitly and systematically called la renaissance.[25] Similarly, the modernist narrative honors such protagonists and landmarks as Le Corbusier's Villa Savoye (Poissy, 1929–31) or Giuseppe Terragni's Casa del Fascio (Como, 1932–36), while ignoring the work of traditional architects who were their exact contemporaries such as Cesare Bazzani's completion of the façade of Santa Maria degli Angeli (Assisi, 1924–30) and Federico Frigerio's Banca commerciale (Como, 1926).

It is this general mentality of privileging certain dominant narratives that led Michel Foucault, Richard Rorty and others, to stress that history is always ideological, that it is written from the standpoint of, and for the purpose of legitimizing power structures between individuals and groups, or to affirm a group's identity. But in their furious intent to escape the tyranny of the dominant narrative, some post-modernists proposed an extreme form of constructivism, stating that since not everything in cultural narratives is pre-given, determined, or ordained, then, there are no universal truths, no factual certainties, only relative beliefs.[26] With epistemological origins in the work of Friedrich Nietzsche and Ludwig Wittgenstein, post-modern relativism assailed long-enduring dualities such as subject and object, form and content, fact and fiction as illegitimate ways to ground historical truths.[27] A more moderate form of constructivism emphasized that world-views are constructed slowly, each image progressively giving way to the other, while transcending the limitations of the other. Another strain in post-modernism, manifested especially by Jean Baudrillard and Guy Debord, with sharp Nietzschean nihilism, undermined the distinction between reality and its image. Reality itself is seen as a construction made of various images or representations built under the pernicious effect of the mass-media in consumer society, establishing a milieu that disrupts the sense of reality and referentiality because the relation between signifier and signified has been severely weakened. Thus artistic productions become objects of a "real without origin or reality".[28] If classical thought and forms operated based on the imitation of a truth, a reality, and if modernist thought and forms operated based on a deliberate opacity toward imitation, post-modernist thought and forms undermined the relationship between origin and reality while losing sight of finality.

The crisis that emerged from the retreating certainties of grand narratives, which post-modern history and philosophy helped bring to the fore, showed the extent to which meaning depended upon self-referentiality. Hence the apparent triumph of relativism over objectivity. Hence the interest in the architectural fragment, itself to be studied with fragmentary historical approaches rather than grand narrative history. But the fact that there is a wide relativity of opinions does not mean that historians ought to abandon even approaching objectivity. It only means that historians know not only the limits and hazards of methodology (objective comprehension), but also the limits and hazards of understanding intentionality (psychological comprehension). Even if, in the best of circumstances, historians have extensive access to the knowable historical conditions, e.g. the building, the architect's measured drawings, the architect's text that explains the building, as well as extant contracts and comments from contemporaries, the architect's own intentionality remains unavailable for investigation.

For reasons such as these, prudent architects judging from history know that they read history, not the history. They are not troubled by the deep subjectivity of historical narratives, especially given their professed respect for the historian's intellectual autonomy. As many thinkers about history since J. Burckhardt have explained, histories written in times of war, or of socio-economic and epistemological crises, strongly bear the imprint of these events. Thus the legitimate efforts of historians[29] to "correct the map", whether it is confirming the historicist-modernist paradigm while rectifying its shortcomings, or criticizing post-modernists for their ability to disparage dominant narratives and their inability to offer a holistically better solution to the problems that affect history, are useful steps toward avoiding some of the problems that beleaguered the writing of history.

Taken together the three interrelated clusters that we discussed, and other influences such as the dissociation of boundaries between disciplines to which we shall return in Chapter 4, show the destabilization of the concepts of historical objectivity and certainty upon which architectural judgment implicitly depends. Some observers are not troubled by this apparent destabilization because they consider the very notion of historical objectivity, or ideological neutrality, to have always been an illusion. There are those who hold that the discipline of the history of art has lost much of its vitality and validity, and that it is consequently looking for a purpose. Others exhibit serious doubts regarding the very conceptual model of a history of art or architecture, indeed the whole heritage from Vasari to Hegel, seeing history only as a mediation to a constructed understanding of the past which is known only through its traces.[30] Others still, revisit the previous speculation about the end of the history of art, preferring to speak of a post-history. All these positions are heterogeneously shared by architects and historians. However, although the three clusters that we discussed show that the retreat of grand narratives seriously weakens the certainties upon which architectural judgment depends, they do not serve to altogether eliminate certainty and judgment. To evaluate the extent and duration of this weakening we need the benefit of a retroactive historical perspective.

Might there be, even on a modest scale, an alternative understanding of history, one that includes the more successful approaches of past histories while learning to avoid some of their problems? Might it be possible to avoid the impasse according to which history is either written according to a relativism of disparate opinions, or according to an abstract totalization that blurs the distinction between genuinely individual historical facts? For too long have historians and architects focused on contingency, on difference, and on the inexorable rupture from the historically given. These are, of course, legitimate intellectual choices; but might a view of history be developed where careful attention is also given to enduringness, commonality and continuity? For they do exist, and it would be unreasonable to exclude them. The reasoned legitimization of architectural practice and its history-telling is considerably improved if architects and historians judicially approve a continuity that has proven successful, and cautiously endorse a departure from a practice that has failed.

NOTES

1   *A History of Architecture*, (Oxford University Press, 1985), p. 8.

2   A full bibliographical volume is required to give justice to the vast literature covering the classical tradition. Some important texts since the late seventeenth century include: Roland Fréart de Chambray, *Parallèle de l'architecture ancienne avec la moderne*, (Paris, 1650); Blondel, F., *Cours d'architecture*, 5 vols, (Paris, 1675–83); Perrault, Cl. *Les dix livres d'architecture de Vitruve avec notes de Perrault*, (Paris, 1673); and *Ordonnance des cinq espèces de colonnes, selon la méthode des anciens*, (Paris,

1683); Robert Morris, *An Essay In Defence of Ancient Architecture*, (1728); Guarino Guarini, *Architettura civile*, (Turin, 1737); Charles Batteux, *Les beaux-arts réduits à un même principe*, (Paris, 1747); Briseux, C.E., *Traité complet d'architecture*, (Paris, 1750); Francesco Algarotti, *Saggio sopra l'architettura*, (Bologna, 1756); Laugier, M-A., *Essai sur l'architecture*, (Paris, 1753); and *Observations sur l'architecture*, (Paris, 1765); William Chambers, *A treatise on Civil*, (1768); and *A Dissertation on Oriental Gardening*, (1772); Francesco Milizia, *Principi di architettura civile*, (1781); Jean-Nicholas-Louis Durand, *Précis des leçons d'architecture données à l'école royale polytechnique*, (Paris, 1823); James Stuart, *The Antiquities of Athens*, (1762–1818); A.C. Quatremère de Quincy, *Essai sur la nature, le but et les moyens de l'imitation dans les beaux-arts*, (1823); and *The True, the Fictive, and the Real: the Historical Dictionary of Architecture of Quatremère de Quincy*, (1832), Samir Younés (Tr.), (London, 1999); L. Hautecoeur, *Rome et la renaissance de l'antiquité*, (Paris, 1912); and *Histoire de l'architecture classique en France*, (Paris, Picard, 1943–57); G. Scott, *Architecture of Humanism*, (1912); Rudolf Wittkower, *Architectural Principles in the Age of Humanism*, (London, 1949); H. Honour, *The Age of Neo-Classicism*, (1972); Robin Middleton and David Watkin, *Neoclassical and 19th Century Architecture*, (1980); Middleton, R. (ed.), *The Beaux-Arts and Nineteenth Century French Architecture*, (Thames and Hudson, 19820; David Watkin, *German Architecture and the Classical Ideal*, (MIT Press, 1987); George Hersey, *The Lost Meaning of Classical Architecture*, (MIT Press, 1988); John Onians, *Bearers of meaning*, (Princeton University Press, 1988); James Ackerman, *Distance points*, (MIT Press, 1991); Demetri Porphyrios, *Classical architecture: the living tradition*, (McGraw-Hill, 1992); *Building Classical*, R. Economakis (ed.), (Academy Editions, 1993); Richard Etlin, *Symbolic Space: French Enlightenment Architecture and its Legacy*, (University of Chicago Press, 1994); Roger Scruton, *The Classical Vernacular*, (St. Martin's Press, 1995); Joseph Rykwert, *The Dancing Column*, (MIT Press, 1996); Léon Krier, *Architecture, Choice or Fate*, (Papadakis, 1998); G. Tagliaventi, (ed.), *L'altra modernità 1900–2000*, (Dogma, 2000); Riccardo Florio, *Origini e permanenze della classicità in architettura*, (Officina, 2004).

3   See Léon Krier, *Houses, Palaces and Cities*, (Architectural Design, 1984); *The Architecture of Community*, (Island Press, 2009); José Ignacio Linazasoro, *Le Projet Classique en Architecture*, Archives d'architecture moderne, (Bruxelles, 1984); Demetri Porphyrios, (ed.), *Classicism is Not a Style*, (Architectural Design, 1982); *Classical Architecture: the living tradition*, (McGraw-Hill, 1992); Rob Krier, *Architectural Composition*, (Rizzoli, 1988); C.W. Westfall and R. Van-Pelt, *Architectural Principles in the Age of Historicism*, (Yale, 1991); Andreas Papadakis, (ed.), *Paternoster Square and the New Classical Tradition*, (Academy Editions, 1992); Richard Economakis, (ed.), *Interventions in Historic Centres*, (Academy Editions, 1993); Gabriele Tagliaventi, (ed.), *Urban Renaissance*, (Grafis Edizioni, Bologna, 1996); Norman Crowe, Richard Economakis and Michael Lykoudis, (eds), *Building Cities: Towards a Civil Society and Sustainable Environment*, (Artmedia Press, 1999).

4   Many meanings have been assigned to historicism rendering the concept very ambiguous, and forcing every discussion to provide a warning regarding which definition of historicism is being used. F. Troeltsch greatly valued historicism as the thought that values change as one of the primary characteristics of the nineteenth and twentieth centuries reflections on history. F. Meinecke saw historicism as the highest level of understanding of human phenomena in their individualized specificities, one that provided a substitute to the generalizing tendencies of natural sciences. Later in life B. Croce used *storicismo*, historism, to designate his vision that history is at once the principle and the source of creativity. Positive though these opinions may be, the concept of historicism has often been used as a negative value judgment. L. Feuerbach (and Croce) denounced the historical relativism inherent in historicism because it led to the uncritical acceptance of all events, all phenomena, as given. K. Popper gave historicism a specific meaning linked to the demarcation between the

scientific and non-scientific discourses. He criticized historicism or any theory that pretended to predict future developments based on its claims to have discovered the laws, patterns, rhythms, or "general tendencies" underlying historical change. He also criticized the analysis of history based on hypothetical-deductive models, as well as those who hold that the methods of the human sciences diverge fundamentally from those of the natural sciences. Some important studies on historicism include: Ludwig Feurbach, *Manifestes philosophiques, 1839–1845*, (Gallimard, 2001); Benedetto Croce, *Estetica*, (1902), (Adelphi, 2005); and *Storia come pensiero e come azione*, (1938); Raymond Aron, *Introduction à la philosophie de l'histoire*, (1938), (Gallimard, 1986); Friedrich Meinecke, *Historism*, J.E. Anderson, (Tr.), (London, 1972); Karl Popper, *The Poverty of Historicism*, (1944), (Routledge, 2002); Louis Althusser and E. Balibar, *Lire le capital*, (2 vols., Maspero, 1968); Nikolaus Pevsner, *Studies in Art, Architecture and Design*, (Vol. II, Walker & Co, NY, 1968); Peter Reill, *German Enlightenment and the Rise of Historicism*, (University of California Press, 1975); David Watkin, *Architecture and Morality*, (Oxford, 1977); Michael Podro, *The Critical Historians of Art*, (Yale, 1982); Leopold von Ranke, *The Theory and Practice of History*, Georg Iggers and K. von Moltke (eds), (Irvington Publishers, NY, 1983); P. Paret, *Art as History: Episodes in the Culture and Politics of Nineteenth-century Germany*, (Princeton, 1988); Alan Colquhoun, *Modernity and the Classical Tradition*, (MIT Press, 1989); H. Aram Veeser, (ed.), *The New Historicism*, (Routledge, 1989); Robert J. van Pelt and Carroll W. Westfall, *Architectural Principles in the Age of Historicism*, (Yale, 1991). See also P. Rossi, "The Ideological Valences of Twentieth Century Historicism", *History and Theory*, 14(4), (1975), pp. 15–29; E. Garin, "Lo storicismo del novecento", *Giornale critico della filosofia italiana*, 72, (1983), pp. 1–57; C. Guignon, "The Twofold Task: Heidegger's Foundational Historicism in Being and Time", *Tulane Studies in Philosophy*, 32, (1984), pp. 37–44; A. Flew, "Popper and Historicist Necessities", *Philosophy*, 65(251), (1990), pp. 53–64; J. Rhée, "The Vanity of Historicism", *New Literary Theory*, 22(4), (1991), pp. 961–83; A. O'Hear, "Historicism and Architectural Knowledge", *Philosophy*, 68(264), (1993), pp. 127–44; F.R. Ankersmit, "Historicism: An attempt at synthesis", *History and Theory*, 34(3), (1995), pp. 143–61; G. Iggers, "Historicism: The history and meaning of the term", *Journal of the History of Ideas*, 56(1), (1995), pp. 129–52.

5   Arguably, one of the most determined propagandists of modernism and the zeitgeist was Swiss engineer and art historian Sigfried Giedion (1888–1968) whose *Space, Time and Architecture* (1941) developed a linear teleological history of architecture, a "fundamental axis", in his words, that connected the Renaissance with modernist architecture.

6   Alois Riegl's notion of *kuntswollen*, for example, asserted that behind the smaller wills of individual artists stood the greater will of art itself as the source for the manifestation of individual works of art. "The Modern Cult of Monuments: Its Character and Its Origin", (1903), in *Oppositions* 25 (Fall 1982), pp. 21–51.

7   The position that history should offer explanations like those in the natural sciences had two main proponents: Karl Popper and Carl Hempel. See Karl Popper, *Objective Knowledge: An Evolutionary Approach*, (Oxford, Clarendon Press, 1972); Carl Hempel "Reasons and covering laws" in *The Philosophy of History*, P. Gardiner (ed.) (Oxford, 1974); *The Philosophy of Karl Popper*, Paul Arthur Schilpp, (ed.), (Open Court, 1974); *In Pursuit of Truth: Essays on the Philosophy of Karl Popper on the Occasion of his 80th Birthday*, Paul Levinson, (ed.), (Harvester Press, 1982).

8   Popper's falsifiability argument.

9   See William Dray, *Perspectives on history*, (Routledge and Kegan Paul, 1980); and his "La philosophie critique de l'histoire", in *L'Univers Philosophique*, André Jacob, (ed.), (Presses universitaires de France, 1989), pp. 319–26.

10   Theories of origin – since Vitruvius – have emphasized empirical experiments leading to a beginning or beginnings, to the *archi* in architecture. This shows that the hut is a beginning and not an origin, for a certain distance had to be traversed to arrive to it. The locus of the origin was somewhere between a natural shelter and the first interpretations of constructive elements devoid of purely natural connotations. Thus the "first" construction was not the hut, for this building converges many experiences, and its details imply a sophisticated way of addressing the built work from the exterior.

11   See M. Flonta, "The Context of Discovery and the Context of Justification", in *Revue roumaine des sciences sociales, Philosophie et Logique*, (25, N° 3–4, 1981), pp. 175–80.

12   Pierre Gros, *L'architecture romaine*, (Vol.I, Picard, 1996), pp. 140–43.

13   See John James Coulton, *Ancient Greek Architects at Work*, (Cornell University Press, 1977).

14   Emil Kaufmann, *Three Revolutionary Architects: Boullée, Ledoux, and Lequeu*, (American Philosophical Society, 1952); Jean-Claude Lemagny, *Visionary Architects: Boullée, Ledoux, Lequeu*, (Gulf Print. Co., 1968); or Jean-Marie Pérouse de Montclos, *Étienne-Louis Boullée, theoretician of revolutionary architecture*, (Brazilier, 1974).

15   For example the work of historians: Emil Kaufmann, *Von Ledoux bis Le Corbusier*, (1934), (French translation, 1994). Sigfried Giedion, *Mechanization Takes Command*, (Oxford University Press, 1948); *The Eternal Present: A Contribution on Constancy and Change*, (1962), (Princeton University Press, 1981); Nikolaus Pevsner, *An Outline of European Architecture*, (1948), (Penguin Books, 1968); *Pioneers of Modern Design: From William Morris to Walter Gropius*, (1949), (Yale University Press, 2005); *The Sources of Modern Architecture and Design*, (Oxford University Press, 1968); Henry-Russell Hitchcock *Architecture: Nineteenth and Twentieth Centuries*, (Penguin, 1958); Leonardo Benevolo, *The Origins of Modern Town Planning*, (Routledge and Kegan Paul, 1967); *History of Modern Architecture*, (Routledge and Kegan Paul, 1971); *The History of the City*, (MIT Press, 1980); Manfredo Tafuri and Francesco Dal Co, *Modern Architecture*, (1976), (Harry Abrams, NY, 1979); Kenneth Frampton, *Modern Architecture: A Critical History*, (1980), (Thames & Hudson, 2007).

16   The free plan, le plan libre, had been presented by Le Corbusier as one of his Five Points for a New Architecture in *Vers une architecture*, (Crès, 1923). See Kenneth Frampton, *Modern Architecture: A Critical History*, (Thames & Hudson, 1980), pp. 157; Freredic Jameson, "Is Space Political" in *Re-thinking Architecture: A Reader in Cultural Theory*, Neil Leach, (ed.), (Routledge, 1997), pp. 255–70; Alan Colquhoun, *Modern Architecture*, (Oxford, 2002), p. 148.

17   See Gianni Vattimo, *La fine della modernità*, (Garzanti, Milano, 1985).

18   See Jean Baudrillard, *Simulacres et simulations*, (Galilée, 1981).

19   See Irving Lavin, "The Crisis of Art History", *Art Bulletin*, (LXXVIII:1, March 1996), pp. 13–15.

20   On a priori theories and history, see Mark Bevir, "Objectivity in History", *History and Theory*, 33, (1994), pp. 328–44.

21   See D. Carr, "Narrative and the real world: An argument for continuity", *History and Theory*, 25, (1986), pp. 117–31.

22   The narrativist school was already opposed in the 1930s by L'École des annales, proposing to examine historical questions based on an exhaustive accumulation of facts from a broad spectrum of disciplines without "arbitrary" ruptures, be they chronological or epistemological. The *annales*, also criticized heavily the presentation

of the historical "fact" contending that the fact only exists in relation to a hypothesis made by the historian. For example, the Marxian reading of history that arranges facts hierarchically in order to emphasize the influence of the economic infrastructure will not be the same reading made by an empiricist historian. Writing history then cannot be limited to classification or chronology, nor can it be limited to their criticism, or even a system of linkage, but rather the blending of all three. See Lucien Fèbvre, "Leçon inaugurale au Collège de France" (1933), in *Combats pour l'histoire*, (A. Colin, 1992), pp. 6–9. The history of the annales is documented by G. Bourdé, H. Martin, *Les Écoles historiques*, (Paris, 1983); and Philippe Poirrier, *Les enjeux de l'histoire culturelle*, (Paris, 2004).

23 White, *Ibid*, p. 85. See also Paul Ricoeur's *Histoire et vérité*, (Seuil, 1955).

24 See David Watkin's important study of the inherent moralism of the apologists of modernist history: *Morality and Architecture*, (Clarendon Press, 1977).

25 The idea of an intellectual rebirth has had several origins, from the humanist dual notion of a renewal of man and a renewal of antiquity, to G. Vasari's *rinascita*, a rebirth of artistic life which he saw as beginning in the early fourteenth century and ending with the death of Michelangelo in 1564. The systematic treatment of the historical label and the contemporary use of the term *renaissance* derive from J. Michelet's *Histoire de France* (1855), one of whose volumes was entitled "La renaissance", and Jacob Burkhart's *Civilization of the Italian Renaissance* (1860). Current general applications of the term distinguish between an early Renaissance (c.1300–c.1450), Renaissance (c.1450–c.1500), and a high Renaissance (c.1500–c.1520s).

As E. Panofsky demonstrated in *Renaissance and Renascences in Western Art* (1960), a definition of the Renaissance requires a reflection on periodization in the history of ideas, involving questions such as: How is renewal to be dated? What are the distinct characteristics of the Carolingian Renaissance in comparison with the Italian Renaissance from the beginning of the fifteenth century? Periodization also raises the problematic of the self-sufficiency of a declared historical period and its demarcating lines between the preceding and following periods. Cultural development is not entirely a matter of clear-cut boundaries of beginnings, middles, and ends. Many intellectual characteristics considered to be mediaeval continued throughout the Renaissance, while many Renaissance characteristics continued through the eighteenth, nineteenth and twentieth centuries. J.A. Symonds's study, *Renaissance in Italy: The Revival of Learning* (1882), suggests a fourfold periodization to the Renaissance:

1. a period covering the first half of the fifteenth century;
2. a paralleling period of discovery and translation of ancient texts along with the formation of library collections;
3. the foundation of academies; and
4. a period of consolidation and stabilization lasting from the end of the fifteenth to the early sixteenth centuries.

W. Tatarkiewicz's study, *History of Aesthetics* (1970–74), suggests a threefold periodization:

1. a period of discovery and renewal of antique forms covering the Quattrocento;
2. a period of the classical Renaissance lasting one generation between 1500 and 1530; and
3. a period lasting until the end of the sixteenth century.

L. Benevolo's *Storia dell'architettura del rinascimento* (1968), suggests a broad application of the label Renaissance, covering developments in Europe and the Americas from the fifteenth to the middle of the eighteenth century. For general references see: R. Wittkower, *Architectural Principles in the Age of Humanism*, (London, 1952); Ernst Gombrich, *Art and Illusion*, (London, 1960); A. Chastel and R. Klein, *L'Age de l'humanisme*, (Paris, 1963); A. Chastel, *Renaissance méridionale en Italie, 1460–1500*, (Paris, 1965); P.O. Kristeller, *Renaissance Thought*, (New York, 1965); H.A. Millon and V.M. Lampugnani (eds), *The Renaissance from Brunelleschi to Michelangelo: The Representation of Architecture*, (London, 1994).

26 Michel Foucault, *Power/knowledge: Selected Interviews and Other Writings, 1972–1977*, C. Gordon (ed.), C. Gordon (Ir.), (Pantheon Books, 1980); Richard Rorty, *Objectivity, Relativism and Truth*, (Cambridge, 1991).

27 See, Jean Baudrillard, *Simulacres et simulation*, (Galilée, 1981); Richard Rorty, *Objectivity, Relativism and Truth: Philosophical Papers*, Vol. 1, (Cambridge, 1991); Keith Jenkins, *The Postmodern History Reader*, (Routledge, 1997).

28 Jean Baudrillard, *Selected Writings*, (Cambridge, 1988), pp.144–72. See also Frederic Jameson, *Postmodernism, or, the Cultural Logic of Late Capitalism*, (Duke University Press, 1991).

29 See, Keith Jenkins, *Re-thinking History*, (Routledge, 1991); *Postmodern History Reader*, (Routledge, 1997); Alan Munslow, *The Routledge Companion for Historical Studies*, (Routledge, 2000); Beverley Southgate, *What is History For?* (Routledge, 2005); K. Jenkins, S. Morgan, and A. Munslow (eds), *Manifestos for History*, (Routledge, 2007). The founding in 1998 of the Historical Society in the United States was aimed at reforming the practice of history and its educational role. See Elizabeth Fox-Genovese and Elizabeth Lasch-Quinn (eds) *Reconstructing History*, (Routledge, 1999).

30 See Hans Belting, *L'histoire de l'art est-elle finie?*, (Folio, 1989).

3
Architectural Judgment Based on History, Part 3

> ... history is a discipline that has a great number of approaches.
>
> Ibn Khaldun

AN OUTLINE FOR A HISTORY MADE OF OLD HISTORIES: TYPE, CHARACTER, AND STYLE

In mapping architectural territory, architectural history has tended to strongly favor architectural style over other modes of classificatory reasoning or formal analysis. Architectural historians paid relatively less attention to urban and architectural types, while rarely distinguishing between character and style. These three concepts received many definitions without relating them, however, within one coherent hierarchical whole. Yet, type, character, and style serve much more than the aims of classificatory reasoning, the coherence of architectural qualities, or the descriptive identification of formal properties. More importantly, this triplicity collectively shows the gradations of the architectural image, ranging from its most essential level (*a few architectural types*), to the expressive qualities proper to several building purposes (*a larger variety of architectural characters*), to the most differentiated number of architectural compositions (*manifold styles*).[1] Put differently, type configures the ontological essence of architecture, character articulates its distinctive physiognomy, while style delineates its common compositional elements. Type and character relate more to purpose while style relates more to composition. Type can be said to reside in an imaginal location; whereas character and style are place bound, place specific. Character anchors architecture to a nation, a region, an essential building purpose. *With respect to enduringness and changeability, type can be said to change the least, while style changes the most, with character occupying a middle term.*

Rather than considering the retreat of grand narratives and the multiple theoretical approaches that followed as a pervasive differentiation that plunged history into a hopelessly fragmented state, we might adopt an integrative

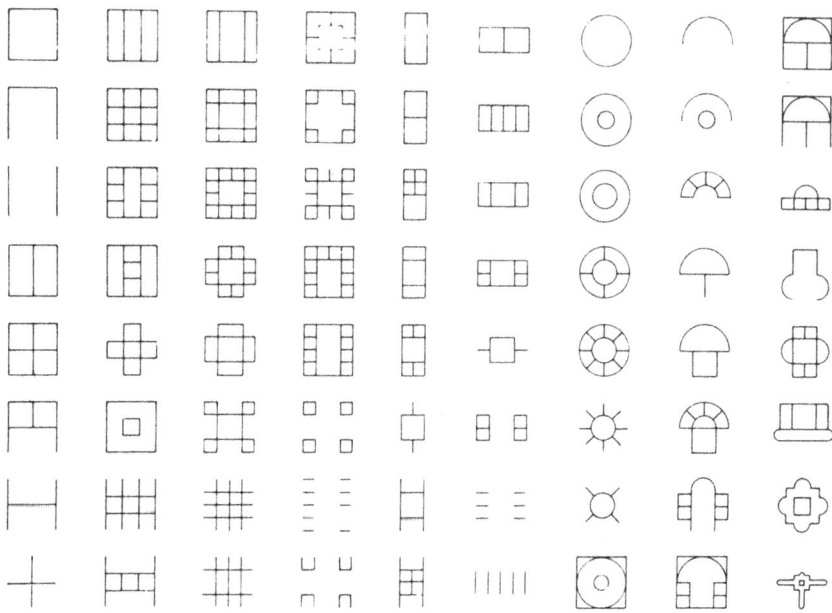

3.1 Types according to J.N.L. Durand.

approach. We might assume that out of differentiation another history can emerge, one that draws on the hard-earned lessons of the past two centuries. The historicist line of reasoning argues from the history of a building to its nature; and to the extent that it follows this path architectural judgment remains historicist. But what if historians were to adopt a reverse approach in which one proceeded from the nature of a building to writing its history, while maintaining all that is useful in historiographical methods? In broad outline, the *nature* of building can be said to include the three aforementioned categories of type, character and style; the *ends* or purpose of building pertain to shelter and the political purpose it serves in the city (civic, religious, cultural, mercantile, residential); while the *means* refer to the structural typologies (arcuation, trabeation) and materials. What concerns us presently, however, are the categories that derive from the concept of the nature of architecture. Between type on one side, and character and style on the other, the notions of causation and the evolution of form are closely entwined. Understanding this relationship, as we have seen, constitutes one of the most fundamental questions that architects pose to historians. Our present purpose is not to cover the extensive history of type, character and style; but rather to outline a program that is sufficiently detached from their competing definitions so as to allow for a history that maintains their most enduring aspects without ignoring their contingent uses.

Type

The concept of type can be traced to Vitruvius's discussion of the kinds of temples and columns (*genera*). It gained its most comprehensive definitions in the late eighteenth century following the influence of theories of origins, evolution and taxonomic classification in the life sciences, in addition to the broad epistemological reach of the *encyclopédie*. As is well known, the opposite poles regarding the concept of type in architecture, gathered their most lucid definition with the seminal work of J-N-L. Durand and A.C. Quatremère de Quincy.[2] In producing a museum of types, Durand's *parallèle* offered an efficient analytical typology which proceeds from an "infinity of variations" in the geometric combinatory possibilities of plans, volumes, and *façades*, revealing their organizational schemes. It also offered an operative typology that standardized the procedures of architectural composition, allowing architects to generate a multitude of compositions answering any number of uses with an economy in disposition and distribution. Durand's classifications range from modes of construction, to horizontal combinations (plans), vertical combinations (*façades*, roofs), to geometric assemblies (squares, parallelograms, circles), to palaces, palaces of justice, treasuries, schools, museums, libraries, markets, theatres, hospitals, prisons, houses in cities and in the countryside, stairs and courts.[3]

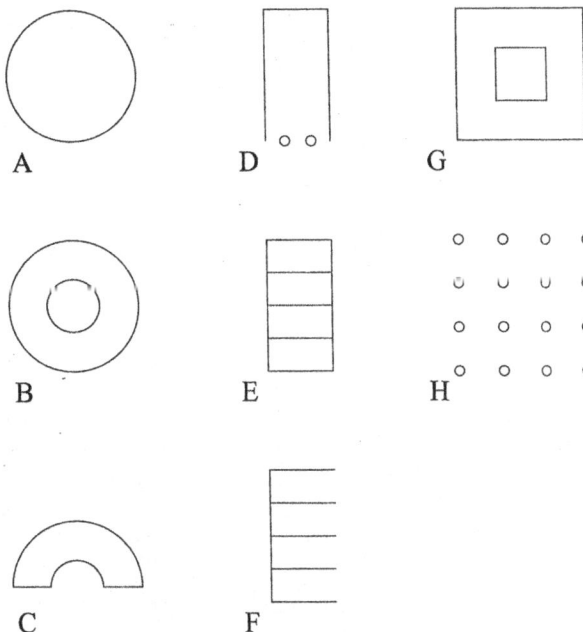

3.2 Types according to C.W. Westfall (A-F) and S. Younés (H).

Quatremère differentiated between the type and the model, emphasizing that the former is an originating reason accessible to the intellect, while the latter implies direct formal resemblance that is apprehended by the senses. Types are ideas, or conceptual forms as in the Greek: *eidos* or the Latin: *idea*. Types are irreducible images which precede empirical reality; while models are fully differentiated and composite forms, as in the Greek: *morphé* or the Latin: *forma*. Thus, in Quatremère's understanding, Durand's types are actually models. Similar to Platonic Forms, Quatremère's types are imagistic universals, generative causes that explain the essentialist commonality between buildings of varied characters and styles. Buildings descending from the same type can vary widely in their formal appearance. But although the descendents are several steps removed from the type, and vary in character and style, they always embody some indissociable qualities of the type. Type concerns more than the practice of architecture based on established typologies; it is also the view of architecture as an archetypal activity, one that restores to the daily contingencies of building the vital significance of causality. Historian C.W. Westfall extended Quatremère's reflections on type arranging in ideogrammatic fashion six, or so, building types emphasizing their

3.3 Tholos: San Giovanni degli Eremiti, Palermo.
Source: Photo by Author.

3.4 Tholos: Santa Maria in Montesanto and Santa Maria dei Miracoli, Rome.
Source: Photo by Author.

political roles in the service of the City: tholos, temple, regia, theatre, domus, taberna.[4] To these, one could add the hypostyle type, or the idea of columns directly supporting a roof. It is important to note that in this conception types are presented in their undifferentiated state, that is, before their multiple combinatory arrangements, e.g., San Francesco in Mantova combines the hypostyle in the crypt, as well as the templum and the tholos – although the dome was not realized. Durand's and Quatremère's fundamental reflections on type were considerably amplified in the late nineteenth century and throughout the twentieth, especially when the rationalist approach in urban morphology and building typology served as curative alternatives to modernist forms.[5]

Character

Whereas both type and character gain their value from shared qualities between buildings, character is primarily articulated by a criterion of identity, by a distinctive physiognomy that expresses a building's purpose.[6] J-F. Blondel, enumerated aesthetic architectural qualities based on adjectives such a grave, sublime, simple, agreeable, elegant, gracious, majestic, light, heavy, rustic, and even serious, cheerful and sad. Le Camus de Mézières associated architectural character with social hierarchy, (e.g. the house for a magistrate or the house for a soldier); Ledoux associated architectural character with national mores and laws, (e.g. the severe external aspect of a prison); and Quatremère de Quincy distinguished between three meanings to architectural character: the essential, the distinctive and the relative.[7]

Character is related to propriety (Latin: *decorum*, French: *convenance* and *bienséance*, Italian: *convenienza*) in two directions at once: in the sense of composing architectural forms, and in the sense of meanings that society comes to invest in architectural forms. This is what makes architects and ordinary citizens delight or revolt when a new building is inserted into their cities depending on whether it fits its purpose, the scale, composition, materials, and general character of the surrounding area. In expressing a building's purpose, a proper, or decorous character operates within the context of architectural and social conventions, not in the sense of their unthinking repetition, but rather in the sense of generational collective reasoning about architectural forms. An open and roofed hypostyle hall befits the purpose of a market, but not that of a theatre. The semi-circular cavea befits the purposes of a seated assembly, a theatre, but not that of a hospital. But whereas a hypostyle hall can imply a market *qua* market, and a hemicycle can imply a theatre *qua* theatre, there are limits to what architectural form can characterize. A hospital may contain several arcades, courtyards, lecture halls, laboratories, operating rooms and individual rooms for patients, all of which can be composed in a manner that expresses the hospital's role as a public building, but the architecture itself cannot express the idea of healing. The architecture of a courthouse may contain portals, colonnades, domes, and grand stairs that suit its stature as a civic building, but architecture itself, unlike painting and sculpture, cannot express ideas of justice, punishment, or clemency. Similarly, octagonal

3.5 Temple, San Francesco, Noto.
Source: Photo by Author.

3.6 Temple, San Pietro, Modica. *Source*: Photo by Author.

forms have long been associated with baptisteries, most famously that of Florence, but the octagonal form in itself, in spite of compelling symbolic associations, does not necessarily imply baptism. Custom may consecrate through association certain architectural characters, which is a perfectly justifiable use of history, but unlike painting which accept metaphor and allegory, how can architecture express healing, justice, or baptism?

Architectural character and its propriety received a significant development in the eighteenth century in the hands of architects who tried to transform the connection between signifier and signified by distending the relation between architecture and allegory. Their projects and writings tested the expressive limits of architecture as well as the transgression of these limits, (e.g. C.N.L. Ledoux's project for a house for the inspector of the Loue river's waters in the shape of a sectioned water conduit). Nonetheless, *l'architecture parlante*, or speaking architecture, including its later assimilation into experiments in "linguistic analogy" in the twentieth century, brought a useful clarification to the "limits" of formal elaborations when endowing a building with its suitable architectural character. It is when limits are transgressed that they come to the fore. A water conduit conducts water but why should the house of the river inspector be in the shape of a water conduit? A radio station transmits programs but why should the building that houses it be in the shape of a radio?

3.7 Regia, Palazzo dei Consoli, Gubbio.
Source: Photo by Author.

3.8 Regia, Palazzo Nobili Tarugi, Montepulciano.
Source: Photo by Author.

Generalizing broadly, architectural character can be understood as the ways in which:

1. a building's volumes;
2. the elements of its exterior and interior composition;
3. its proportions;
4. the assembling of its materials which transcend mere construction;
5. its colors, natural or painted; and
6. its ornament, render its distinct purpose evident.

Thus theatres, churches, libraries, markets, palaces, or houses are endowed with their own definite identities and hierarchies. Character is also national and regional (Chinese, Egyptian, French, Umbrian, Tuscan). It distinguishes cities as well as quarters within cities (the character of Rome's Campo Marzio in comparison to that of Trastevere).

Style

No other term in art and architecture has been more widely defined, disputed, praised or denigrated than style. So customary has the use of this term been since the widespread eclecticism of the nineteenth century that one is apt to forget that architecture came to be classified as a fine art only in the middle eighteenth,[8] and that the term style was rarely applied to the fine arts prior to the middle of the seventeenth. Instead, in the fifteenth and sixteenth centuries, the word maniera, manner, was used to designate some of the meanings that later came to be absorbed by style, especially in regards to the notion of personal artistic expression.

Style can be defined as the configuration of characteristic elements, the shared compositional features in a period or an individual that permits their identification for descriptive ends as well as for the purpose of recognizing normative trends. The understanding of style is linked to the notions of similarity and exemplariness on a wide cultural scale (what Richard Wollheim termed the "taxonomic"), or to the agreement or distinction of one individual's work in relationship to a group, a period.[9] Stylistic periods have been identified by, or arranged according to various subdivisions: three-part sequences (usually early, middle and late), or four-part or five-part categories (e.g. P. Frankl's spatial form, corporeal form, visible form, and purposive intention, or H. Wolfflin's linear and painterly, plane and recession, closed an open form, multiplicity and unity, clearness and unclearness). From the historian's perspective, style designates two scales: the period seen holistically (or general style), and the particular individual (or individual style and manner). Style and periodization (as opposed to mere chronology) have been linked by historians who intended to structure architectural discourse as if it were a vehicle for historical conceptions connected to the idea of the evolution of forms (beginnings, apogee, decline). Under a different conception, style can be used to designate the larger compositional themes of a period while manner can designate the personal compositional themes of an individual. From the perspective of architects, style is

3.9   Theatre and domus, Piazza del Campo, Siena.
Source: Photo by Author.

3.10   Theatre, Piazza de Toros, Sevilla.
Source: Photo by Author.

3.11 Taberna and domus, Piazza Grande, Arezzo.
Source: Photo by Author.

3.12 Taberna and domus, Piazza dell'Erbe, Verona. Source: Photo by Author.

understood from their standpoint as skillful composers of architectural elements who endow buildings with the inevitable imprint of their personal style or manner, just like a stiletto carves an image on a wax tablet.

Since the rules of style depend in essence on the rules of composition, it stands to reason that style can be synonymous to character from a certain point of view, and to manner from another. Style can be synonymous to character because both partake in the notion of a distinct qualitative identity of a building, a region, a nation, a period. Style can be synonymous to manner in the sense that manner concerns the architect's execution of buildings within the larger stylistic tendencies of a period, or a personal career.

Type, character, and style can undoubtedly be misused. Type, for example, can be understood simply as a neutral plan onto which different styles come to be indiscriminately affixed, e.g. the same plan accepting a Byzantine, Gothic, Venetan, Tuscan "styles". Type can also be reduced to a repetitive technological standard (the maison domino) which itself can accept numerous stylistic appendages. Character can be indiscriminately applied as when the temple front is affixed to a church, a bank, a museum, a school, or a house. An acute pursuit of reductionism may lead to an impoverishment of the imaginal (stylistic) qualities of architecture. Conversely, an excessive stylistic eccleticism may lead to its random proliferation.

3.13 Hypostyle, Mezquita, Cordoba.
Source: Photo by Author.

3.14 Hypostyle, Market, Siena. *Source*: Photo by Author.

Whereas most architects display knowledge of many styles, many manners, it is important to note that it is revivalist architects who practice architecture *as* a style. Irrespective of the architecture they practice, revivalists hold a special relation to the history of architecture and the history of taste, which allows them to depart from what they find objectionable in the contemporary conditions of their profession. Revivalists apprehend architecture and architectural history stylistically, and also see their role in present practice stylistically. This separates them from the rational practice of tradition based on more broadly inclusive concepts of type, character and style. Whereas both revivalists and traditionalists use traditional forms, the traditionalists do not place character and style within categories that immobilize them in a certain periodical classification; rather, they assume that contemporary practice adds to tradition by vitally composing and recomposing its forms.

Each on its own, type, character and style are well-established concepts amongst architects and historians, although as we mentioned earlier, character received less attention than the other two. What has been lacking however, is a history that links these categories; a history that serves more than the scholarly aims of historians who exhibit disinterestedness in the possible practical use of historical knowledge on the part of architects, a history that is close to the ways in which architects might construct their art. This outline for a history depends on the operative assumptions that both architects and historians are interested in the virtue of minimizing the distance between the aims of history and those of architecture; and that architects' judgment from history derives from their belief in an inextricable historical rootedness. This outline may have a salutary, and dare one say, reformatory effect on both the architectural and historical disciplines, attenuating the structuralizing importance of style as a periodic measuring motif. As an operative mode, this outline suggests a pursuit of architectural history based primarily on subjects or questions and secondarily on the theoretical commitments of individual historians, be they hermeneutics, *kulturkritik*, narrativism, post-history, or deconstruction. It can include many of these theoretical approaches but without being detracted from its essential simplicity. This outline of a history has a more modest scope than sweeping grand narratives, and at the same time, a more ambitious scope than the subjective or individual historical narratives. It takes it as a given that in the face of immense historical material, certain minds are predisposed to philosophize and project overarching systems, while other minds philosophize from the point of view of the differentiated rationality of an individual who chooses his or her own significant historical narrative. It takes it as a given that the universalizing and particularizing inclinations of the mind can be included at once. It holds multiple kinds of historical narratives to be inseparable from the intelligible assessment of form and the consciousness behind form. It holds the possibility that an integral history can be written in which long enduring themes regarding the nature, ends and means of architecture, as well as cross-cultural formal traditions and individual manner, can all find their place. Although this suggestion of a history based on type, character and style has to a certain extent an aprioristic element, by no means does it aim to supplant the empirical experience of history writing, nor is it immune from mistakes.

NOTES

1   I adumbrated this hierarchical linking between type, character, and style in *The True, the Fictive and the The Real: The Historical Dictionary of Architecture of Quatremère de Quincy*, (Papadakis, 1999), pp. 37–41. Type (Greek: *typos*), character (Greek: *Characteer*), and style (Greek: *stylos*), share a common origin in writing, in the notion of engraving, imprinting, molding, incising, or making a distinctive mark.

2   Some of the central sources that have influenced typology include: M-A. Laugier's, *Essai sur l'architecture*, (Paris, 1753); Ribart de Chamoust, *L'ordre français trouvé dans la nature*, (Paris, 1776); F. Milizia's *Principii di architettura civile*, (1781), (S. Majocchi, 1847); Ch.-F. Viel de Saint-Maux, *Lettres sur l'architecture des anciens et des modernes*, (1787); J-N-L. Durand, *Recueil et parallèle des difices de tout genre …*, (Gille, an IX, 1801), and his *Précis des leçons …* (An X, 1802); *The True the Fictive and the Real*, (1999).

3   This classificatory scheme was adopted by practitioners and educators such as J. Guadet in his *Eléments et théorie de l'architecture* (1911), and scholars such as N. Pevsner in *History of Building Types*, (Bollingen, Princeton, 1970). The latter, while purporting to be the first architectural typological survey, conflates building use with building type.

4   R-J. Van Pelt and C.W. Westfall, *Architectural Principles in the Age of Historicism*, (Yale, 1991), pp. 155–60.

5   For reflections on building typology and urban morphology since the late nineteenth century, see: C. Daly, *L'Architecture privée au XIXème siècle*, (Paris, 1864); C. Sitte, *The Birth of Modern City Planning*, (1889), (Rizzoli, 1986); W. Hegemann and E. Peets, *The American Vitruvius: An Architects' Handbook of Civic Art*, (1922), (Princeton Architectural Press, 1988); P. Lavedan, *Histoire de l'urbanisme*, (H. Laurens, 1926–52); M. Morini, *Atlante storico dell'urbanistica*, (Hoepli, 1960); S. Muratori, *Studi per una operante storia urbana di Venezia*, (Istituto Poligrafico dello Stato, 1960); G.C. Argan, *Progetto e destino*, (Il Saggiatore, 1965); C. Aymonino and A. Rossi, *La città di Padova*, (Roma, Officina, 1966); A. Rossi, *L'architettura della città*, (Marsilio, Padova, 1966); A. Vidler, "The Third Typology" in M. Culot and L. Krier, *Architecture rationnelle*, (Archives d'architecture moderne, Brussels, 1976); J. Castex, J-Ch. Depaule, Ph. Panerai, *Formes urbaines*, (Dunod, 1977); J.I. Linazasoro, *Permanencias y arquitectura urbana*, (G. Gili, 1978); R. Moneo, "On Typology", *Oppositions*, 13, (1978); R. Krier, *Urban Space*, (Rizzoli, 1979); P. Panerai et al., *Eléments d'analyse urbaine*, (Archives d'architecture moderne, Brussels, 1980); Casabella, *I terreni della tipologia*, Gennaio-Febbraio, (1985); L. Krier, *The Architectural Tuning of Settlements*, (The Prince's Foundation, 2008).

6   We shall return to character in greater detail in Part Two.

7   See J-F. Blondel's second volume of the *Cours d'architecture*, (9 Vols., Paris, 1771–1777); Le Camus de Mézières, *Le génie de l'architecture, ou l'analogie de cet art avec nos sensations*, (B. Morin, 1780); the article "Caractère" in E-L. Boullée's *Essai sur l'art*, (c.1794) H. Rosenau (ed.), (A. Tiranti, Ltd., 1953); and C.N.L. Ledoux, *L'architecture considérée sous le rapport des mœurs et de la législation*, (Paris, 1804); the essay "Caractère" in A.C. Quatremère de Quincy's *Dictionnaire d'architecture* in Panckoucke's *Encyclopédie méthodique*, (3 vols., 1788–1825), which was later recast and reduced in his *Dictionnaire historique d'architecture* (1832).

8   The first categorical division of the arts into fine and mechanical occurred in C. Batteux's *Les beaux-arts réduits à un même principe*, (1747), pp. 5–7, in which architecture and rhetoric came to be indirectly classified among the fine arts by virtue of a separate category: the useful. Diderot and D'Alembert's *Encyclopédie* also classified architecture as a fine art. For a historical survey of artistic classification, see W. Tatarkiewicz, *A History of Six Ideas*. (Martinus Nijhoff, PWN, Polish Scientific Publishers, 1980); and P.O. Kristeller, "The Modern System of the Arts: A study in the History of Aesthetics" I, and II, in *Essays on the History of Aesthetics*, P. Kivy (ed.), (Library of the History of Ideas, University of Rochester Press, 1992).

9   On style, see G. Semper, *Style in the Technical and Tectonic Arts*, (1860–1863), H. Mallgrave and M. Robinson (Tr.), (Getty, 2004); H. Muthesius, *Style-architecture and Building-art*, (1902), S. Anderson (Tr.), (Getty, 1994); H. Wollflin, *Principles of Art History: The Problem of the Development of Style in Later Art*, (Dover, 1950); P. Frankl, *Principles of Architectural History, The Four Phases of Architectural Style*, (1914), (MIT Press, 1968); M. Schapiro, "Style" in his *Theory and Philosophy of Art*, (Brazilier, 1953); J. Ackerman, "A Theory of Style", in *Journal of Aesthetics and Art Criticism*, 20, pp. 227–37; E. Gombrich's entry "Style" in the *International Encyclopaedia of the Social Sciences*, Vol. 15, (Macmillan, 1968); R. Wollheim, "Pictorial Style" in *The Concept of Style*, B. Lang (ed.), (Cornell, 1990); J. Gilmore, *The Life of a Style*, (Cornell, 2000).

4
On the Nature of Modernity

Modernity is a qualitative, not a chronological, category.

Theodor Adorno

The very mention of the word modernity provokes in architects a critical preoccupation with its history and its definition in relationship to their work. In clarifying their own positions with respect to this elusive concept, architects engage in conjectures regarding the directions modernity is taking given its changing meanings since the early decades of the twentieth century. They assess the extent of modernity's successes and failures, whether it has ended, whether it has yet to fulfill its aims, and the extent to which it is still formative of the present. In thinking of modernity architects conjure up a list of associations derived from cultural history, literary theory, or art theory, on the one hand, and from architectural history, theory, and the history of technology on the other. Architects know that the concept of modernity – as it began to exert an ever-increasing dominance on material life since the late nineteenth century – has been used to designate a broad accumulation of forces including:

1. incessant change assured by an ever-accelerating technological progress that will eventually lead to utopian well-being;
2. the universality of rationalism and efficiency in managing natural and urban resources on a global scale;
3. the vast migrations toward industrialized areas;
4. mass consumption;
5. the rebellion against church and aristocratic powers and the increase in democratic social relationships;
6. secularism, the autonomy of the individual and the autonomy of art;
7. the overt ideological confrontation with tradition;
8. the association of the spirit of the time, the spirit of modernity, with modernist art and architecture and the various avant-gardes; and

4.1 Social Housing, Piazza Bartolomeo Romano, Garbatella, Rome, Plinio Marconi, 1926.
Source: Photo by Author.

4.2 Bauhaus, Dessau, Germany, Walter Gropius, 1926. Bundesarchiv.
Source: M_H.DE, Wikimedia Commons.

9. the seeming necessity for artists and architects to be the daily embodiment of inventiveness.

Architects also recall the multiple artistic strategies and movements that sought to embody the spirit of modernity: Paris in the nineteenth century, Art Nouveau, the Secessionists, Cubism, Fauvism, Futurism, Constructivism, Dadaism, Surrealism, Art Deco, Abstract Expressionism, Pop Art, Minimalism, and other tendencies. Acknowledging these indelible influences on the architectural discourse, architects then consider how modernity is expressed in architecture passing through the Bauhaus, the Congrès internationaux d'architecture moderne, the International Style, Late Modernism, Neo-modern, Post-modernism, Deconstruction, new Traditional Architecture (also known as the Other Modern).

But, increasingly since the late 1960s, architects have also been aware that some of the most cherished principles of modernism – e.g. rationality and functionalism, object buildings, the totalizing proscriptions on the uses of tradition, abstraction and the exclusion of ornament – have had deleterious effects such as the making of alienating places, the fragmentation of the city, not to mention ecological disasters given that the building industry accounts for a considerable part of the present global pollution. Post-modernism, in part, attempted to correct modernism's constraints on freedom and its claim to universal applicability by opening the possibilities of choice from traditional architecture as well as from the recent modernist architecture. Moving from the practice of selected eclecticism, post-modernism made possible a wider plurality of forms that ranges from the new traditional architecture that takes the city's typologies and characters as its basis, to the deconstruction of modernist forms free from modernist cultural values. Mostly, however, architects apprehend modernity imagistically because they apprehend the world imagistically. For this reason, they identify modernity, above all else, with technological forms. Yet, in their reflections, many architects neglect two important distinctions: modernity and modernism; and *technique* and technology. In our explorations of these concepts, starting with the eclipse of the Great Chain of Being and ending with the possibility that modernity holds the promise of a larger cultural synthesis, we will move freely between events in the eighteenth century and the present.

THE GREAT CHAIN OF BEING

In the late eighteenth century several grand conceptions regarding natural order and human order came to be eclipsed. One of these conception, the Great Chain of Being,[1] considered the known universe as an immense hierarchical creation ranging from the most elementary form to the highest Cause of causes. The Great Chain was a view of the world that saw a unity between natural objects and objects of human-making; and this unity, at least conceptually, was exemplified by the enduring idea of art imitating Nature. The imitation of Nature operated as a poetic order (Greek: *poeisis*, to make), a paradigm that informed and justified aspects of human making such as art and architecture. The Great Chain of Being stood as the measure of the True (e.g. science, religion), the Beautiful (e.g. art, architecture) and the Good (e.g. ethics, politics). Each part of the Great Chain is qualified by two values, the one intrinsic and relates to this part's own fullness, or wholeness; the other extrinsic and governs its relationship with other parts and their place within a larger whole. What is a whole in one context is itself a part of another context as each part transcended but incorporated the previous one. This infinite series of connections, where each whole is a constitutive part of another whole, made for the fullness of a hierarchical world, and objects of human-making were not seen as separate from this view of the world. In art and architecture we see this conception exemplified in the idea of *symmetria* where each part takes its meaning from the whole while maintaining that whole by sustaining other parts. The bracket forms part of the cornice which in turn forms part of the entablature which in turn resolves the relationship between wall and roof, while wall and roof are constitutive parts of the whole building composition. In the city this conception manifests in the way individual buildings not only have fullness and value by themselves but receive a greater value and fullness in relation to the street, the block, the square, and the quarter.

SOME ACHIEVEMENTS AND FAILURES OF MODERNITY

In that same century, in the West, the major trends of what later came to be known as modernity, took a resolute outline. The arts were divided into two spheres: the fine and the mechanical, and architecture – for the first time – came to be classified among the fine arts.[2] Artistic theory gave a decided preference for aesthetics over beauty. With increasing intensity, the percipient subject was more interested in his or her own sensate aesthetics over the beauty residing within the object. This was accompanied by a break with traditional themes, mythic and symbolic thought, and with traditional compositional modes in the arts. In ethics and politics, the individual's civil rights came to be emancipated and guaranteed in equality and freedom. Liberal democracy emerged, while the state was no longer considered to be the only determinant of the Good Life. Denis Diderot's ideal philosophe submits to no authority without discussion, founding his views on that which is accessible to all: the capacity to reason and sensate experience. Diderot's claim that "metaphysics proves nothing" signaled a decided shift toward a sensate factual experience as *the* reality which science measured, weighed and classified. The *Encyclopédie* aimed at establishing rationality and efficiency as the two guides for the only reality that can be known or that is worth knowing; and this reality was the context of physical immediacy between subject and object. In other words, the sensuously evident was the locus of the *true* and the *factual*. Philosophy observed and participated in these attempts at grounding knowledge within a sense based reality and gave itself the task of justifying this reality with an acute degree of immediacy. Certainly, all of these ideas had been present within various cultural forms for a long time but what distinguished the course of events since the late eighteenth century was the forceful application of these ideas on a much wider scale than heretofore. Rationality, efficiency, autonomy, universality, and secularity pervaded all cultural spheres, becoming the determining set of measures.

This rapid generalization serves to clarify the following point. The conjugated and intense effects of these qualities caused the cultural spheres of science (as part of the realm of the True), art and architecture (as parts of the realm of the Beautiful and the useful), and ethics and politics (as parts of the realm of the Good) to differentiate from the encompassing, and limiting enclosure of long established institutions in order to form their own autonomous spheres.[3] Thus, modernity as a *project* was born.[4] This project is distinct from the idea of modernity as an inevitable awareness of time that has accompanied the human condition since time immemorial. Therefore, it is useful to distinguish between the appearance of *modernity* in the cultural spheres of science, religion, and philosophy; art and architecture; and ethics and politics, on the one hand, and the development of *modernism* in each of these spheres. *Modernity can be characterized by a high degree of differentiation (autonomy) within the values and categories of cultural spheres; while modernism can be qualified by the inveterate pursuit of this differentiation, tending toward infinity – understood here in the sense of proliferate development.* We shall return to the idea of infinity in a moment, but prior to that, we look at differentiation in its advantageous and deleterious results.

Much in modern cultural history since the Renaissance linked the increase of individual liberty to the autonomy from the oppressive influence of political and ecclesiastical institutions. These two institutions framed cultural reality their own uniform understanding of the world which they imposed on the individual's daily experience – a frame that was shattered by the revolutionary events in France in the late eighteenth century. When aristocratic political authority and ecclesiastical authority retreated from the place from which they directed society, the cultural value spheres differentiated, gradually searching within themselves for their proper legitimization. One after the other, entire components of society claimed the right to complete autonomy. In order to wrest away the knowledge of the world from the state and the church, Enlightenment thinkers separated two purposes: the purpose of promoting the Good and that of finding the True. More explicitly, Enlightenment thinkers aimed at separating those who hold power from the establishment and interpretation of truth. Rousseau's *Contrat social* underlined the human and not the divine origin of power, affirming that the common weal finds its legitimacy in what he called the general will.

For over 200 years, the increasing differentiations of modernity allowed for the deepening, the widening, and the emancipation of knowledge between previously homogenized fields as well as within those fields themselves. But the radicalization of differentiation, namely the pursuit of utmost autonomy, led to separateness, disconnection, or dissociation. Differentiation, for example, explained that chemistry was a branch of physics, and that physics, in turn, formed a branch of mathematics, while the reverse of the sequence was not true. Breaking some barriers between scientific disciplines helped in deepening knowledge, albeit in one dimension which then needed to be correlated with others disciplines. But when differentiations proliferated the results were dissociations that caused the separative barriers between disciplines, the narrowness of overspecialization and fragmentation in the academy and in practice. Soon, the mono-dimensional logic of scientific materialism came to replace the idea of a holistic unity previously associated with the Great Chain. For example, Aristotle's quartet of causes attempted to explain the principles that govern a form or an event (formal cause), the purpose for a form/event (final cause), the substance of a form/event (material cause), and the instigator of motion or change in a form/event (efficient cause).[5] This quartet formed an indissociable conceptual unity. No cause could be discounted. When this quartet dissociated formal cause fell into the domain of individual whims. Final cause was claimed as part of the domain of theologians and moralist thinkers. Material cause was taken within the exclusive realm of scientific analysis. And, with the dominance of technocratic mentality, efficient cause became the cause that outweighed all the others. The grounding of knowledge shifted because the initially useful differentiation of the value spheres of science, technology and philosophy had attained the point of dissociation.

If differentiations can dissociate, then whatever delimited and contained these differentiations must have been eroded. It is useful here to open a small parenthesis that serves to clarify two important properties of any field or form, namely: links and boundaries. A link connects at least two distinct entities, anchoring them to a place or a tradition, without commingling them, thereby assuring their identities. A boundary guarantees identity through closure and containment in time and space, separating at least two distinct entities, without excluding the possibility of their informing each other, thus guaranteeing at once: passage and distinction. Such dialectic allows various fields and arts to differentiate and inform each other, without eroding the boundaries that assure for each field or art its proper character, thereby maintaining intrinsic content (immanent meaning) and extrinsic significance (transcendent meaning). Needless to say, the sought clarity in distinguishing links from boundaries is not achieved through an exacting mathematical specificity, which is of useful value in technical applications. But the important note, here, is that links and boundaries are not barriers or limitations because they are indispensable characteristics that assure containment and identity (fullness) to any field or form; and if these characteristics are removed, dissolution follows. For example, when the teaching of architectural design assumes that the same methods of composition apply equally to painting and architecture, a painting can be transformed, in a few steps, into a building, and vice versa.

Returning to the discussion of grounding knowledge, it is clear that when a measurable and quantifiable sense-based psychology is held as the privileged key to knowledge and the only way to deduce truth in the sciences and the arts, philosophy came to see the notion of a transcendent (the knowledge of a truth beyond the senses) as contrary to reality. Knowledge had to be qualified by an immediacy, a presentational immediacy with physical reality, which was defined as the realm of empirical experience. In this view, sight was the universal guarantor that things will be perceived as they *are*, and not as they *could* or *should* be; and sight looked at the world through this image. Meaning came to be associated with a visible, quantifiable reality, and less so with an invisible and remote causal realm. Reality and the perceived image came to be synonymously identified. And in this decided shift toward factual immediacy, the sensuously evident was the enclosing condition in which the *true* and the *factual* collapsed into each other. In this mono-dimensional approach of scientific materialism, Nature, as a causal realm (*natura naturans*) that transcends and incorporates physical nature (*natura naturata*) was reduced to that which is only materially evident in nature. The world is no more than what science says it is. Nature was equal to the biosphere; and the modernist mind stood separate from Nature and considered nature to be a realm of empirical processes and exploitable forces and resources. The modernist mind saw nature according to its (the mind's) own ordering and interpretive processes, and these interpretive processes were then regarded as the aims of an existential reality that could only be known in this way. The modernist "I am and I think" meant "I am separate and I think separately". Rousseau had already warned about this new excessive zeal for autonomy, calling it "the furor to distinguish oneself".[6] By contrast, an equally rational *cogito* might be formulated as: "Although I am an autonomous thinker, I think because someone else thought before me". Every "first time" has a past.

In architecture, the constructive aspects of differentiation came to clarify the imitation from the copy; the type from the model; type from character from style; principles from rules; unity from uniformity; order from ordering and ordonnance; restitution from restoration; tectonics from mere construction; and the reasoned authority of tradition from narrow authoritarianism.[7] These concepts enriched the inward work (intellectual, artistic, ethical) of the architect, and its exterior presence (urbanity, social propriety, serving the larger Good) when they are based on a clear distinction between the *true* and the *factual*, the *nature* of architecture and her *means*, and the hierarchy of values which make some buildings *endure* beyond the *circumstantial* immediacy of their appearance. When dissociation took hold, especially in the twentieth century, an interior truth (reflection) came to be reduced into an exterior fact (a brain wave); epistemological pluralism came to be confused with mere relativism; the city became an agglomeration of fragmented mono-functional zones; proportion collapsed into dimension; beauty residing in the object was reduced to a beauty that can only be in the eye of the beholder; the type and the model collapsed into the standard; the maison domino severed the integral relation between type, character, and style; load bearing walls became impoverished veneers; tectonics changed into mere construction; the character of a building was changed into a sign; the character of cities was replaced by placeless suburbia; and finally, knowledge and significance became mono-dimensional bits of information that surf the placeless grid of a technologically determined reality.

In ethics and politics, the differentiations of power allowed for the widespread emancipation of individual rights, for the abolition of slavery, freedom of faith and speech. The rights of the individual, one of history's major forces, were passing through class struggle and evolving into what Tocqueville called "the gradual development of conditions of equality". Political pluralism's differentiation from the monistic practices of the state and the church brought many liberating results for the collective and the individual. But the dissociation, or dissolution, of pluralism led to relativism. Relativism within societies made it such that the Good would be pursued solely with respect to parameters relative to the individual. This engendered situationist ethics that militated against the larger shared ethics that form one of the solid foundations of the city.

For more than 200 years, the enlightenment project of modernity tried to integrate the following forces: belief in the infinite progress of knowledge based on the impetus of the scientific method and the redemptive grace of technology; the break with tradition with the belief that today's new form will be obsolete as it is rapidly replaced with the next form; a hyper-awareness of the consciousness of time that can be described as a addiction to the future, or in Friedrich Meinecke's terms: the "flight into the future". These forces can be characterized by the intention of precipitating modern forms into areas of empirical reality that have not yet been filled. As a consequence, we have the phenomena of the apparent acceleration of history; the aesthetics of presentness; the higher value placed on the circumstantial over the enduring; the writing of history as a history of ruptures and crises; the disruption of continuity; and the phenomenon of making different, not necessarily better or more appropriate, but different. The collision between these and other forces may explain why, for some, modernity is a state of prolonged existential crises.

This second generalization serves to clarify the following point. When modernity's desirable goal of <u>differentiation</u> is pursued with a relentless zeal, it becomes dissociation or fragmentation; but when it is pursued fanatically, it can lead to dissolution.[8] As director of the review *Les temps modernes* Jean-Paul Sartre called for the dissolution of all literary monuments, including his own, for the sake of the idea of movement, a universal movement. Unlike Ernest Renan, and certainly unlike Herodotus, Sartre saw progress not as a tranquil river, but as a tumultuous confrontation. The new does not simply succeed the old, it confronts it. Modernity does not simply succeed the Great Chain, it confronts it. Here, the pathos of modernity becomes quite specific. To be modern is a combat, and Sartre wanted to be the symbol of this militant modernism inherited from the French Revolution and amplified by Marxist philosophy. Some modernists did not foresee that their work was to cause widespread dissolution. Other modernists reveled in the relativist flux of fragments that followed, considering this state of affairs as "the way things are" in an age that can only manifest in this way. Many, still consider this state of affairs today as an a-priori given.

Post-modernists doubted that reality is entirely pre-given, because they saw reality, in large part, as constructed by the mind. But as they considered that meaning was dependent on context, and that the world that the individual mind beholds is an interpreted construction, post-modernists opposed universals while, at the same time, championing egalitarianism. Roland Barthes' ultimate egalitarianism was that we are all authors in a world without author. Every reader is a potential writer, and the author swims in inter-textuality. This opposition to universals, however, was not complete, because post-modernists – at least in art

[handwritten margin note: Uniqueness can be fleeting if designed incorrectly, or can be admired forever]

and architecture – still held the view that some form of tradition must be accepted. Paralleling this notion, post-modernists glorified interpretation in as many varieties as was being made, and came to hold all interpretations to be equally justifiable – even when out of context. When deconstruction entered the scene, it aimed at proving that an assertion made in one context was incongruous in another, and since contexts are in a constant fury of change, then meaning itself must be discounted.

INFINITY, MONISM, AND TECHNIQUE

Regarding the notion of infinity, the Enlightenment project of modernity may be described as an experience of limits between fields and within fields, as well as the transgression of these limits. Cartesianism, scientific experimentation, and free inquiry, were linked together as if they were a single ideology that applied equally to the arts and sciences regardless of their different intentionalities and values. This ideology was not only considered as an emancipation from all forms of previous determinism, but it also announced a future perfection with high certainty, even if such a contention remained to be proven. The hasty application of such conclusions to all areas of knowledge precipitated a crisis of identity in the arts as they became absorbed into a techno-scientific culture characterized by unshakable teleological aims. This ideology saw its early development in the late seventeenth century, albeit in a state where science and technology were undifferentiated. It reached a widespread development in industrialization, receiving its epistemological legitimization when the *Encyclopédie* subjected all areas of knowledge to this ideology's constant scrutiny. The *Encyclopédie* claimed to have unraveled an epistemological "système general" equally applicable to the sciences and the arts.[9] The distinction between liberal and mechanical arts, and between the *beautiful* and the *useful* was eliminated, while the *rational* and the *efficient* were considered to have an equal validity to the speculative. An inventor of the steam engine could be considered an artist, and a painter could be called an artisan.

For the next two centuries, rationality and efficiency came to be pursued with ever-increasing intensity leading eventually to the phenomenon that Jacques Ellul termed *la technique ou l'enjeu du siècle*: technique or the wager of the century. *Technique*, in Ellul's thought, may be defined as *the pursuit of utmost rationality and efficiency possible at any given moment and the consequent conquest of all areas of nature and human endeavor for this purpose.*[10] *Technique* is to be distinguished from technology, which constitutes many possible discourses on *technique*. In this sense, technology is to *technique* what physiology is to the body. *Technique*, for instance, is the mentality that conceives the city as a collection of mono-functional zones dedicated to commerce, culture, leisure, industry, and sleeping, while as a discourse on *technique*, zoning regulations and their applications are a technology. Ellul's work has been fundamental not only in demonstrating the pervasive effects of *technique* on all aspects of society and on framing the individual's mind, but also in its distinction between industrialization on the one hand, and the technological order, on the other. Whereas prior to the Second World War various industries formed a disparate set of productions, the decades following the 1950s saw the systematic and most coordinated establishment of a technological order permeating all aspects of society and global society. *Technique* became an order qualified by *autonomy, monism, universality, self-expansion*, with a *causal progression*, and an *absence of finality*.[11] These qualities explain the technological order's dual directionality. On the one hand its integrated functions make it autonomous, on the other, its external relationships act as an all-integrating function organizing natural resources as well as all areas of human endeavor – the arts, sciences, education, government – into processes, applications, products. Throughout these processes, technological growth refers to itself, replicates and resembles itself, in a causal progression and with an absence of finality. The contemporary city, for example, grows by incessant annexation of land around its periphery, transforming previous natural territory into a conglomeration of monofunctional zones. These zones attain such a size, that it becomes imperative to build more highways and more automobiles needed for the vast displacement of people, necessitating more mining, fossil fuel, metals, plastics, and the specialists to connect them all. With the increase of zones, there is an increase in highways; with the increase of highways, there is an increase of automobiles and an ever growing need for fossil fuel; with the increase of automobiles, there is an ever larger need for parking lots, and the more parking lots are needed, the more buildings and city blocks are removed to make space for them; with the decrease in the densities of cities, there is an increased need for large tracts of suburban residential and commercial developments … These phenomena recall the Hegelian "spurious infinity" in the sense of a continual circularity of events always approaching but never attaining full closure. In a formulaic way the spurious infinity can be expressed as an n+1. Closure might be attained if we had but one more technology, one more product. But closure never comes.

Technique became a monistic force because it is an empire of means that is organized in terms of itself, replicating and multiplying itself *ad infinitum*. By their very proliferation the means eclipse the very ends for which they were developed in the first place. *Technique* became its *own* ends. Because meaning in the technological order is an internal matter, it presents a dense opacity to meaning outside of its own dictates. The humanist critique, for example, has been largely unsuccessful in modifying *technique*'s pervasive influence. Thus *technique* is non-dialectical; it is the reign of immanence.[12] It eclipsed the order that operated within the Great Chain, the poetic order, and came to occupy the grounds of that cultural space. This explains why protagonists of the technological order reject the idea of artistic tradition categorically, while claiming universal validity for their rejection. No boundary remained closed to the empire of *technique*, leading initially, to blurring the distinction between the technological object and the artistic object, followed by a transgression of the boundaries that clearly defined and separated various arts and their modes of representation. As links and boundaries were transgressed, modernist artists and architects heralded rupture and transgression

– of traditions and their modes of representation – as the means to achieve their individual artistic freedom. One price for this new artistic freedom, came at the expense of the clear distinctions between artistic genres, between their limits or bounds.

The idea of making itself underwent an acute transformation that saw the rupture between imitation and invention, where in order to be called modern the practice of art and architecture must be *all* invention. Prior to industrialization, and then *technique*, the maker's inventiveness was considered to be potentially infinite, but this did not mean that the arts and their materials were infinite in potentialities to the same degree. Indeed, materials have definable limits which are indissociable from the nature, ends and means of every art. In other words, if invention (the laws governing the maker) manifests in potentially infinite combinations of form (the laws governing the made), these combinations themselves may be potentially infinite only within the art's own limits (links and boundaries) and propriety. However, when the means to realize art and architecture multiplied (tend toward an infinity) to the extent they did in the twentieth century, then the nature and ends of the arts come to be eclipsed. In participating in and in observing this process, some architects and artists assumed that a change in means must necessarily entail a change in ends, that the multiplication of means assists in expanding human invention which has slumbered for too long under the influence of limited technologies, and that was after all the glory of the present zeitgeist. Other, more revolutionary avant-gardists, delighted in the realization that *technique*'s infinite expansion was now causing iconoclastic upheavals in all cultural spheres. Invention came to be seen as opposite to the idea of limits or bounds between the arts, while the many technological means assured an unlimited artistic freedom. As a result of the unbridled enthusiasm for all things technological, the means for individuating a work of art or architecture came to outweigh the purpose for individuating. At times, the means to individuate came to be confused with the purpose for individuating.

Whereas the pursuit of the infinite (the explosion of limits) grew immensely in the twentieth century, one must not loose sight of its rise in the eighteenth. Indeed the whole of the enlightenment project, may be seen as a pursuit whose goal is differentiation, the experience of limits, and to a certain extent their rupture. One effect of the cumulative reflections of Pascal, Newton, Leibniz and D'Alembert on infinitesimal calculations, is that the infinite came to be regarded as the limit of the finite, or that toward which the finite tends continuously without ever arriving there: a spurious infinity. This is not to deny the import or usefulness of mathematical reflections on the infinite or the infinitesimal in their proper realms. Indeed, by their immense philosophical scope, these reflections intersect the idea of the boundaries of creativity. But the understanding of infinity that fits the sciences and an abstract technological order did not remain within the scopes of science and technology because the modern mind considered progress in the science and technology to be the same as progress in art and architecture. Consequently, the notion of infinite progress and development coming from technology invaded the arts and exploded the clear boundaries between them, to the point where their very identity was put in question. This precipitated a pervasive fracture in the very idea of making in art, because that which characterizes the *maker*: imitation and invention, came to be considered as the logical opposite of that which governs the *made*: rules, conventions. Imitation and invention were separated. Consequently, invention came to be classified within the exalted realm of the infinite, and by extension, unlimited artistic freedom, while imitation and rules were classified within the restricted realm of the finite, and came to be seen as confining to invention and artistic freedom.

Taking stock of what we have said so far, we have distinguished between the following word-concepts: modernity and modernism; differentiation, dissociation, and dissolution; *technique* and technology; links, boundaries and infinity. What is modern is not only the displacement of being by becoming, or rather, our losing of being inside technological becoming. It is not the displacement of the idea of perfection by that of infinite perfectibility. It is the logic that concentrates every act onto itself in order for it to manifest its singular essence. For this purpose, limits or boundaries, become obstacles to be superseded – hence the ever-increasing demand for differentiations. Following the eclipse of the Great Chain of Being, the Enlightenment project began to engender differentiations between and within all the cultural spheres. *These differentiations are of the essence of modernity. They are distinguished from modernism which is a radical pursuit of differentiation.* Once differentiation tended toward infinity, dissociation followed. *Technique's* intervention within science; art and architecture; ethics and politics, caused deep dissociations within these cultural spheres. For this reason, it is vital to distinguish between the *ends* of modernity and the *means* of *technique*.

One of the paradoxes of *technique* is that it is not a palpable or measurable object, and yet it appears limitless because it influences the production of a myriad of objects. Appearing to have no limits is analogical to saying that *technique* has no outside. This explains the difficulty of "seeing" *technique* because it is unlike finite objects that have dimensions and proportions. Such realizations led some philosophers to conclude that the question of *technique* is not just a confrontation between two cultures, the one humanistic, the other techno-scientific; but rather the confrontation is with *technique* on the one side, and all that has hitherto been known as human culture on the other.[13] The principal problem of modernity is the collapse of science, art and architecture, ethics and politics, into the mono-dimensional grid of *technique*. Whereas technology is one of the means of any modernity, *technique* has usurped of all that has hitherto been known as culture for the purposes of an abstract technological order which then comes to be seen as the only possible reality, the only possible modernity. The big irony is that modernity facilitated differentiation and the ensuing socio-cultural freedoms; but now, with *technique* we have freedom to move within what *technique* has already framed: the world of mono-dimensional technological reality, a world of whole immanence where one enjoys enormous freedom, only as a consumer within the thin surfaces of steel and glass buildings. To be free as a consumer, that is the mother of all ironies.

In the *Human Condition*, Hannah Arendt reminded that consumption implies eating, ingurgitating. Consumers become omnivorous eaters of the world. By multiplying the artifice of false needs, the consumption society removes us from nature. But this is not the core issue for Arendt. What worried her is the reduction of the world's reality to the vital processes of consumption, in the most metabolic sense of the word. No object or culture escapes this consumption. Only, the goal of mass culture is not the diffusion of culture to the masses, nor is it about liberating the masses from the dominance of classes that claimed "high" culture, nor is it about making the masses forget their condition. It is something much more trivial. It is about rendering consumable the productions of the mind, as when the consumption society literally consumes, submerges and destroys cultural objects. Art and architecture are reduced to consumable images, a particular kind of image – a technicist image. The claim to be modern is equally shared today by those who champion contemporary consumerist and technologically determined society as well as by its most vociferous opponents. And as we mentioned before, to be modern in the temporal sense is unavoidable. But to be modernist is a cultural choice among many – it is not obligatory.

ON THE WAY TO A POSSIBLE SYNTHESIS?

To judge architecture based on modernity assumes that the concept is stable, complete, and justified with precise criteria. But that is contradicted by the tumultuous cultural fragmentation vaguely known as modernity today, a disenchanted world (in Max Weber's words) of fragments and dissociations. If the nature of modernity resides in a healthy degree of differentiation that led to a useful autonomy of cultural spheres, and if this nature has been rendered unstable because of the excesses of differentiation, then architects can no longer use judgment based on modernity with the absolute certainty of their past polemics. Modernity, as Jurgen Habermas affirmed, indeed remains incomplete.[14] But this statement gains special value in the context of the other phenomena we have been discussing: infinity, the spurious infinity, and the absence of finality that characterize *technique*. Understanding modernity's incompleteness or its absence of finality – something that can only be understood retrospectively – is complicated by the fact that modernity will, for the foreseeable future, stay entwined with *technique*. Meanwhile, *technique* remains the over-determining standard for the production of goods and for the evaluation of the good; and this standard continues to have a formative and normative influence on many a modern mind. Because *technique* frames reality (Heidegger's *Gestell*) the possible is understood as that which is *technologically* possible. It is consequently difficult for the mind that is formed within the technological order to judge modernity separately from *technique*. Yet, modernity also remains incomplete for other reasons – more positive reasons. Most interestingly is the open possibility, or promise, to integrate science, art and architecture, and ethics and politics in a yet higher synthesis that embraces them all, even if much in modern thought rebels against the idea of synthesis.[15] There is no guarantee that such a higher synthesis will occur, for that will depend on the coherence of many disparate cultural forces. However, one could imagine a future cultural condition where the monistic hold of *technique* itself dissociates, which would constitute a remarkable emancipatory achievement. It is possible to imagine a future point where dissociations will have run their course, and integration or synthesis may be the logical outcome. The future modernity might thrive in a world that would truly be epistemologically pluralistic. That is if moderns will take stock of their achievements and failures, and then look at the immediate task ahead in order to reach a higher level of completion, or fullness, within which architecture will play its rightful part.

This possible synthesis is categorically different from forcing science, art and architecture, ethics and politics into the uniform technological flux, where they erode, dissolve, and loose their identity. The desired new synthesis needs to integrate things in their fullness, things with clear links and boundaries. But what needs to be synthesized goes beyond the hopelessly dissociated fields of specialization. What is required is not just an historical, but rather a historic consciousness capable, like a clear search light, of penetrating through and beyond the hopelessly dissociated fields in order to arrive at the causes behind two great historic moments. The first is that great integration of cultural forces known as the Renaissance, the second is that great differentiation of cultural forces known as the Enlightenment. This is not to say that the Renaissance was all about integration while the Enlightenment was all about differentiation, only to emphasize the principal integrative trends of the Renaissance as compared to the vast differentiating trends of the Enlightenment. And here is why tradition and modernity are important: the one preserves and builds the essential, the other engineers and practices needed change. Tradition and modernity can be considered partners in the continual construction (paradigms and their forms) and destruction of forms (paradigm shifts and their forms). With a rationally integrative frame of mind, it is possible to consider a gradated continuity between architecture within the city and the city within nature on the basis of successful past achievements. Continuity is judiciously approved where architectural production has rationally been proven successful, and change is carefully approved where and when there is a rational need to depart from a practice that has failed.

Understanding the causes of integration and differentiation might allow for the historic consciousness mentioned above to turn its gaze toward the future in order to produce such a synthesis,[16] while avoiding the pitfalls of teleological predictions. Should this synthesis (or group of syntheses) be realized, even if partially, the reconstruction of the city within nature could then proceed equipped with the essential knowledge of the Great Chain as well as the experience of differentiation. It might turn out that the Great Chain did not disappear – it was perhaps only eclipsed. With respect to architecture, this possible synthesis will need to hierarchically integrate: the essential nature of architecture (the idea of dwelling individually and collectively), the purpose to which it tends (solid shelter, the common good of cities), the forms that compose it (the various typologies on urban, architectural and tectonic scales), the means to assemble these forms (from tectonics to simple construction) and the sustainable materials out of which these forms are made. Judging the enduringness of these practices will need to be measured in relation to the idea of dwelling wisely on this planet ecologically and architecturally. Assuming the lasting presence of an effective will to realize it, this synthesis needs to transcend mere sustainability in favor of seeing nature's making and human making and dwelling as co-evolutionary projects on a planetary scale.

NOTES

1   A.O. Lovejoy, *The Great Chain of Being*, (Cambridge, 1936).

2   For a historical survey of artistic classification, see W. Tatarkiewicz, *History of Aesthetics*, (Thoemmes Press reprint, 1999).

3   Jurgen Habermas called these three increasingly autonomous spheres: 1) the cognitive-scientific; 2) the aesthetic; 3) the moral-practical.

4   This differentiation has been lucidly analyzed by Herbert Spencer, Max Weber, Arthur Lovejoy, Charles Snow, Lewis Mumford, Jacques Ellul, Michel Foucault, Charles Taylor, Jurgen Habermas, Ken Wilber, and Tzvetan Todorov. See H. Spencer, *First Principles*, (1880), (De Witt Revolving Fund, 1958); *Max Weber: Selections from his Work*, with an Introduction by S.M. Miller, (Crowell, 1963); and his *Rationality and Modernity*, (Allen & Unwin, 1987); A.O. Lovejoy, *The Great Chain of Being*, (1936), (Harper Row, 1960); C. Snow, *The Two Cultures*, (1959); L. Mumford, *The Transformations of Man*, (Collier Books, 1962), and *The Future of Technics Civilization*, (Freedom Press, 1986); M. Foucault, *L'archéologie du savoir*, (Gallimard, 1969); J. Ellul, *Le système technicien*, (Calmann-Lévy, 1977), and *L'empire du non sens*, (Presses Universitaires de France, 1980); C. Taylor, *Sources of the Self*, (Harvard University Press, 1989); J. Habermas, *Habermas: Critical Debates*, J.B. Thompson and D. Held (eds), (Cambridge, 1983), and *The Habermas Reader*, William Outhwaite (ed.), (Polity Press, 1996); K. Wilber, *Sex, Ecology and Spirituality*, (Shambhalla Publications, 1996), and *A Brief History of Everything*, (Shambhalla Publications, 1996); and T. Todorov, *L'esprit des lumières*, (Robert Laffont, 2006). Herbert Spencer in *First Principles*, and Émile Durkheim in *De la division du travail social*, treated the sociological dimension of differentiation analyzing it within their reflections on labor, seeing differentiation as the primary instigator of social transformations. Durkheim reproached Spencer for overlooking that differentiation is accompanied by complementarity and interdependence between differentiated parts.

5   *Metaphysics*, 980–1003.

6   J-J. Rousseau, *Discours sur l'origine et les fondements de l'inégalité parmi les hommes*, (1755), (Editions Sociales, 1983), p. 189.

7   Effects of differentiation and then dissociation in painting, saw impressionism, expressionism, surrealism, and abstraction as ways to deconstruct and reconstruct what was initially the simple, integral figure. Kandinsky and Malevitch sought to "liberate" art from the figure in order to produce compositions of pure lines, and non-identifiable figures with color.

8   The passage from differentiation to dissociation and then dissolution is developed in K. Wilber's *The Marriage of Sense and Soul, Integrating Science and Religion*, (Random House, 1998).

9   "Art" in *Encyclopédie, ou Dictionnaire raisonné des sciences, des arts et des métiers …* (Vol. 1, Paris, 1751–65), pp. 713–14.

10 Ellul's most seminal works in this area are: *La technique ou l'enjeu du siècle*, (A. Colin, 1954); *Propagandes*, (A. Colin, 1962); *Le système technicien*, (Calmann-Lévy, 1977), and *Le bluff technologique*, (Hachette, 1988).

11 See J. Ellul, *Le système technician*.

12 In Part Two, Chapter 8, we shall return in greater detail to the non-dialectical nature of *technique* in contrast to the fervent, if misguided, attempts to consider its products in a symbolic way.

13 See C. Snow, *The Two Cultures, and a Second Look*, (New American Library, 1969); G. Hottois, *Le signe et a technique*, (Aubier, 1984); *Evaluer la technique*, (Vrin, 1988); and P. Chabot and G. Hottois (eds), *Les philosophes et la technique*, (Vrin, 2003).

14 On the notion of incompleteness of modernity, see J. Habermas, *The Philosophical Discourse of Modernity*, (MIT Press, 1987).

15 For a recent attempt at rescuing the idea of the unity of knowledge within an Enlightenment tradition, see E. Wilson's *Consilience* (Vintage, 1998).

16 Two of the problems that presently weigh on many a historical consciousness (with respect to architecture and the arts) is the by now deep-rooted belief that a *weltanschauung* is deliberately made, manufactured, and that architecture and the arts are docile reflectors of the latest *weltanschauung*. Moreover, relativist positions have instilled a competition of contradictory *weltanschauungs*, thereby masking the necessity of tracing *weltanschauungs* to their originating causes.

5
Political Content and Architectural Form

> *... not the same is correct in politics as in poetry.*
>
> *Aristotle*[1]

Architectural character has the capacity to elicit complex thoughts and emotions on the part of the observer that go beyond the initial intentions of the architect. For this reason, those who observe and use architecture tend to project onto it or associate it with artistic, philosophical (Paul Valéry, Martin Heidegger), religious (Augustus W.N. Pugin, Quilan Terry), social (Claude-Nicolas-Louis Ledoux, Charles Fourier) or political concerns (François Mitterand, Vincent Scully). This associative and projective thinking is also common among architects and historians because they share the capacity to evaluate architectural form in comparison to its intended purposes, its many histories, its migration to different regions, and to its uses in various cultural contexts. Of these associations and projections, the political vesture has played a significant role in both the understanding as well as the misunderstanding of architectural character.

When politics provides the legislative framework for our civic association, it articulates a common *ethos*. When architecture provides the physical framework that shelters the public and private realms, endowing each of them with its own suitable character, it articulates a common *locus*. Understandably, politics and architecture have been linked. After all, both of these arts are called to serve the Good and the Beautiful. An act of justice can be appreciated ethically when it serves the common good, and aesthetically when it occurs in conformity to law. A building can be appreciated ethically when it aptly serves the purpose of a civic institution – and thus the common good – and aesthetically when its general composition serves its architectural purpose, namely character. By extension, a poem, a sonata, or a painting can also be judged beautiful and thus good. This consciousness of the good and of the beautiful operates on the basis of essential criteria such as order, proportion, or propriety with respect to a purpose. Political justice necessitates measure, order, and the equal partitioning of rights in relation to ethical norms; and law serves justice by structuring the movements and relations of daily life. This

5.1 Piazza Pius II. Pienza.
Source: Photo by Author.

form of justice, or law, is experienced aesthetically by he or she who is just. Aesthetic consciousness, by virtue of qualities such as proportion and propriety, also finds itself connected to the consciousness of the good, the just. Linking the idea of the "good" with that of the "beautiful"[2] has been an enduring aspect of the judgment of cultural production and can be traced to Plato's *Hippias Major* and *Symposium*. These considerations lead to an important twofold question. What might be the terms under which politics and architecture are justifiably linked, and by contrast, what might be the terms under which such linking is inappropriate or spurious?

In Kantian terms, aesthetic judgment can be said to have a political dimension – one that can be extended to architectural judgment because both depend on a communal sense.[3] This sense contains two important aspects that Immanuel Kant considered to be the natural vocation of humanity, namely: sociability and universal communicability.[4] Indeed, he defined humanity by the joining of two qualities in which all are called to participate: the universal feeling of sympathy on the one hand, and the power to communicate on the other.[5] Communal sense, for Kant, is not simply a notion that serves the reasoning faculty of judgment. It must truly be the "sense of community", a sense of what is worthy of esteem because it is valued and accepted publicly, a sense of what is suitable for the entire civic life and not only for the individual. It is also a sense of the *inter-esse*: the inter-subjective distance that unites and separates us at once.[6] When we judge aesthetically we affirm the universality of this action. When we aesthetically approve of a building we think for ourselves by using understanding and reason; but we also move beyond personal opinion to express a broader faculty of judgment and join the opinions held by others.[7] We experience inter-subjectivity, and at the same time a certain decentralization of our personal *cogito*. This inter-subjective experience makes possible also the modalities of communication in knowledge as well as in ethical action. It is possible then for ethical and aesthetic judgments to be inter-subjectively linked. Taken together, the communal sense, the inter-subjectivity of communications, the consciousness of the good and the aesthetic, make for a civic milieu where the political judgment of right and the aesthetic part of architectural judgment can be connected. To this we add that this connection may apply analogically as long as the terms remain quite general, as long as political form and content and architectural form and content are each justified on the basis of its own criteria.

It is one thing to state that architecture serves, shelters, and endows with suitable character the various political purposes within the city, be they governmental, mercantile, or cultural, and quite another to claim that architectural qualities represent political content. The second claim implies that one can pass from judging architectural qualities to the judging of political intentions or vice versa. More explicitly, it suggests that there is an association between architectural composition and political content. In his Entretiens sur l'architecture, for example, Eugène-Emmanuel Viollet-le-duc associated the structural efficiency of the Gothic – built by free men and not slaves as in Roman times – not only with rationality and political freedom, but also with the social secularism of the French bourgeoisie in the nineteenth century. Now architectural form and political content can certainly be used, misused, and even abused. There have been many contentions about their relationship with some architects and historians seeing no relationship whatsoever, and other architects and historians considering architecture as a direct representation of political aims. Much ink and saliva have been spilled on this issue that sharply divided architectural debates in the 1970s and 1980s, and it still does. In these decades, the debate concentrated primarily on the associations between politics and architectural character (calling it style), and on historians' use of ideological factors in order to privilege one dominant narrative, one preferred set of architectural forms. This debate, however, neglected several significant points that are germane to the link between politics and architecture. It did not justify why the citizen politician and the citizen architect are both called to build the Good City. It did not explain the difference between political freedom of expression and architectural or artistic freedom of expression; nor did it clarify that the confusion of artistic genres is related to the confusion regarding the different kinds of artistic freedom.

The clash about these questions seems to have recently receded into the background of architectural exchanges perhaps for two important reasons:

1. far from having resolved this issue the protagonists have temporarily put aside an exhausting argument fraught with intense rancor; but more significantly
2. the ever-widening democratic cultural space given impetus by post-modern thought, allowed more political choices and a multiplicity of artistic choices to find expression.

Indeed, political and artistic cultures cannot operate without the multiplicity of choices and the long-term engagement on the part of the citizenry in the selected choices. This multiplicity and its accompanying conceptual and semantic nomenclatures served to enrich knowledge, but it also caused several unintended problems. The more expressions and interpretations multiplied the more differentiation[8] increased – a phenomenon that led to dissolution when taken to an extreme. As a result, the bypassing of the conceptual boundaries between autonomous cultural spheres and the clear definition of artistic genres became commonplace. This explains, in part, the confusion regarding what is common and what is different between political freedom of expression and artistic freedom of expression, and indeed the freedom that suits every particular art. Once artistic boundaries become distorted or eliminated, spurious associations between political content and artistic form become acceptable, thereby weakening the processes through which buildings come to be endowed with their suitable character.

Cumulatively, the previous considerations suggest that any judgment that links politics and architecture needs to evaluate:

1. the cultural agreements held by society and groups within society;
2. the very plurality of evaluative criteria that fill cultural life and compete for legitimacy and primacy;

3. the sense of composure needed by the individual rational agent as he or she reflects on the multiplicity of available choices.

Judgment is deeply affected by the sheer number of available judgments. All of these carry deep implications on evaluating architecture from the outside.

I

A SENSE-IN-COMMON

Nature and the City allow us to found and find our physical place in the world – to dwell, and to choose to identify with this form of dwelling. From the house in country, to the village, to the city, we usually call the varying modes of founding and finding our dwelling: the sense of place. This sense finds itself indelibly framed and articulated by politics and by architecture. As the human creation par excellence, the City forms the ethical and physical enclosure within which Plato's fateful triad of the True (e.g. science, religion), the Beautiful (e.g. art, architecture) and the Good (e.g. ethics, politics, law) can be pursued in view of perfecting our intellectual, moral, or spiritual evolutions. Over the centuries, much socio-political thought, and especially utopian thought, was directed toward perfecting the frameworks for these ethical and physical enclosures. Utopian thought (Greek: *topos*, place) is not understood here in the pejorative sense of ill-defined dreams that are far removed from the "here and now", but in the sense of Thomas More's *U*-topia or *Eu*-topia, the well-place, the happy place; or in the larger sense: the Good City.[9] What ties Plato's *Laws*, T. Campanella's *City of the Sun*, the Renaissance architect's *città felice*, F. Bacon's *New Atlantis*, D. Diderot's *Supplément au voyage de Bougainville*, the reformatory political manifestoes that followed the French Revolution, the work of H. de Saint-Simon, C. Fourier, R. Owen, W. Morris, K. Marx, the best intentions of early modernist architects, or the revolutionary events of May 1968, is the union of socio-political thought with broad imaginal faculties regarding the city's political and physical forms. Constructing the city's political and physical forms requires much *phantasia* (creative imagination) and this world is apprehended imagistically by the architect. Architects cultivate the art of wishing, the art of desiring. They are continuously engaged in considering what the city presently *is* and imagine what it *could* be or *ought* to be. Their acute understanding of their immediate conditions makes them pose utopia at the very heart of their imagined city, with good and bad results. They imagine ways of improving even as complete a piazza as Pienza's, propose corrections to B. Rosselino's *façade* for the cattedrale dell'Assunta, and speculate on what else might Pius II have realized for his native village had he lived longer. They reflect on Beaubourg and the significant cultural loss to Paris when a perfectly vibrant neighborhood was destroyed to make space for the Centre G. Pompidou, and why did this building need to be completely rebuilt, at exorbitant expense, only thirty years after its completion. They see the grand promise of the plan for Washington, which currently stands incomplete as it contains mostly public buildings, and speculate about the exemplary effects it might have had on American cities had it been completed with private buildings.[10]

It would be difficult to categorically deny that the promise of utopia is present in the very ethical and physical constitution of the city. It would be equally difficult to deny that the highest promise of politics is to live together justly even if citizens and their elected representatives frequently deviate from such a noble goal. If politics represents the city's aims of achieving what Kant called a "just civic constitution",[11] it is because citizens are called to willfully and collectively partake in a common good that transcends the mere assemblage of their individual interests in order to reach, stabilize, maintain, and perfect the good for all. The purpose of a just civic constitution determines the form of government we wish to have, say, a democracy. The purpose of architecture in serving the just civic constitution is to endow civic, religious, educational, mercantile, industrial, agricultural, or residential buildings with a befitting architectural character – befitting in the sense of propriety, suitability, aptness, the Vitruvian *decor*, on the scale of individual buildings as well as on the urban scale. When these two purposes cohere in a relationship of reciprocal fulfillment, political and architectural forms can be said to partake in embodying the promise of the Good City. In this respect, the architect's moral imperative might be stated, in the words of Léon Krier, as building "in such a way that the maxim of your design may at the same time rate as a principle of general legislation".[12]

The extent to which architectural judgment is instrumental in this reciprocal fulfillment depends on the political and artistic choices available within a milieu that defines itself as democratic. In this milieu, individual architectural choices and decisions are considerably shaped by an aesthetic sense-in-common as well as a political sense-in-common. The expression sense-in-common, as opposed to simply inherited common-sense, is used here to designate the purposeful agreement or consensus-building effort between many minds to elaborate a shared artistic practice (a convention or a tradition), an intellectual perspective, or a political platform. It pertains to small or large groups within our civic association. Given architecture's connectedness to the arts and its role in the service of the civic association (the polity), the architect's decision to adopt one way of practicing architecture is at once artistic and political. It is artistic on account of his or her personal inclinations, talents, training, or belonging to a larger architectural tradition. It is also political because of his or her involvement in elaborating a civic responsibility aiming toward the larger good. But as we shall see, although art and architecture are encompassed within a democratic political milieu and its guaranteed freedoms, artistic freedom and political freedom are not the same. They therefore play different roles in the desired reciprocal fulfillment between politics and architecture.

Sense-in-common does not suggest that we currently enjoy a universal agreement in the arts, architecture, or in politics, for that would be an incorrect observation. Equally incorrect is the relativist statement that *explains away* differences by asserting that agreements are not possible because there are as many positions about architecture as there are architects. To be more precise, one can speak of clusters of architectural groups and political groups each of which shares an internal sense-in-common while engaging in mutual resistance with other groups. There are fewer architectural positions than a pluralist may think. However, there are many more artistic and architectural groups than there are political groups for the simple reason that there are more artistic choices available than political ones. On the one hand, we have the promise of the Good City where politics and architecture might possibly achieve a reciprocal fulfillment, but on the other, we have a small number of contrasting political stances as well as a considerably larger number of architectural stances competing not only for legitimacy, but also for primacy. The more choices increase, the more opinions are divided. Multiplication also means division. Our understanding, and therefore judgment and decision-making capacities, are critically affected by the multiplicity of available choices.

Three Words, Their Uses and Abuses: A Short Excursus.

As a response to the impressive multiplicity of cultural forms (e.g. the coexistence of a considerable number of architectural traditions) several word-concepts were developed in order to account for them and express value judgments about them. We briefly consider three of these word-concepts: monism, pluralism, and relativism, in order to underline their role in framing cultural discourse in general and their influence on architectural judgment in particular. If the world is enriched by a plurality of architectural traditions, then choice and judgment are directly affected by this very plurality. Yet, we find architects who claim the mantle of pluralism praising certain buildings for being more suitable to a pluralist milieu while condemning other buildings for being unsuitable for that same milieu. Why, one might ask, is the inherent contradiction of such a judgment not evident? Why is the word pluralism used with absolute certainty, and how would such architects explain the difference between pluralism and relativism? Might semantic vagueness adversely influence the architectural and political judgments that clarify the distinctions between the aforementioned word-concepts?

Semantic precision in the service of intellectual discrimination, and thus judgment, helps us to distinguish between the layers of meaning that separate monism and pluralism. It helps in detaching pluralist from relativist concepts (and also eclectic and subjectivist ones). Whether in architecture, the arts, or politics, epistemological monism[13] asserts the belief in a single enclosed and fixed system of thought that excludes external influences or feed-back, rejecting all views in favor of one view. This is why monism frequently provokes opposition. To the contrary, epistemological pluralism maintains that society contains multiple artistic and political traditions and forms, about which there are many agreements as well as many oppositions. Pluralism upholds the threefold notion that there are many paths to a truth, to a theory, or to the practice of architecture; that there are various ways to express, devise and make them; and that the competing views about them help to elucidate various aspects of the same reality. We encourage pluralism as an inclusive cultural aim in order to make space for a multiplicity of competing cultural positions. However, pluralism in itself does not mean that *any* position is inevitably justified simply because it has been expressed in a democratic context that guarantees intellectual freedom. In other words, whereas the encouragement of pluralism necessitates an ever-widening tolerance of artistic and political opinions, pluralism is distinguished from indiscriminate permissiveness. Pluralism does not mean *anything goes*. In pluralism there *are* opinions that are true and appropriate and others that are inappropriate or false.[14]

Pluralism, however, is not synonymous with relativism. Relativism recognizes the role of varying socio-political forces in determining diverse individual or collective values regarding cultural phenomena. As a by-product of historicism, relativism rejects cultural – or cross-cultural – universals in an a-priori manner. It maintains that a cultural phenomenon may or may not have value in itself; it is only significant for an individual or for a group within society. Relativists allow no authority to universals while claiming that relativism should be universally valid! In art and architecture, relativists link aesthetic judgment to the subjective opinion of the individual. In morals, they emphasize that the individual operates exclusively based on his or her own norms. For relativists, all truths are opinions, or interpretations. Only, relativism itself is not necessarily neutral, and it is useful to note that indiscriminate neutrality does not mean tolerance. When indiscriminate neutrality takes hold, nothing is illegitimate. This is an important and sometimes overlooked distinction between pluralism and relativism.

It is easier to arrive at a common agreement in a meeting with predominantly pluralist architects than in a meeting with predominantly relativist architects. Notwithstanding their differences, it is possible for pluralist architects to adopt a course of action based on a declaration of common principles, rare though this occurrence may be. In the best of circumstances, such an agreement might come to serve the sense-in-common if the principles it contains are animated by the will to achieve the Good City. By contrast, the justificatory motto of relativists is: my architecture is valid because it is valid for me. Narcissistic relativism becomes the culture of architectural justification as each architect judges from the standpoint of his or her own differentiated bubble. It is commonplace to declare that the contemporary cultural context is full of such justifications, such judgments, but can one build the Good City based on them? It is therefore legitimate to ask of architects which is more important: their self-expression or the civic constitution they are called to serve?[15] Put differently, do architects wish to serve a good that is larger than their own? Do they seek to serve the civic good? Underlying these questions is the assumption that architectural practice converges political freedom and artistic freedom.[16]

Keeping in mind the different meanings of monism, pluralism and relativism, may prove useful when addressing architectural judgment; because judgment is influenced at once by individual and collective views especially in today's vastly heterogeneous cultural contexts. At base, these three terms concern the rational autonomy of the individual (the culture of intellectual freedom), in relation to the collective rationality of the group (the civilization of the sense-in-common). Each cannot exist in exclusive independence from the other; especially when democratic society strives to maintain an ever-difficult equilibrium between the individual realm and the collective realm. An extremist (monistic) practice of individualism consecrates separatist stances, and leads to the tyranny of private opinions. An extremist (monistic) practice of collectivism enforces sameness, and leads to the tyranny of the state, or the academy.

As a broadly inclusive concept, pluralism can include monism and relativism, as well as eclecticism and subjectivism. When wisely used, with reason and goodwill, pluralism allows for the collective consensus to thrive side by side with individual expressions, opinions, and judgments. But pluralism comes to be abused when it is confused with relativism. Various forms and contents can then be indiscriminately associated. This is one of the reasons why many historians and architects have linked artistic form (e.g. architectural character) and political content (e.g. democracy). As we shall see, this linking is not equally valid in each of these spheres; and when it is inappropriately used as a justification or a condemnation, it engenders confusions between form and content, and divisions between architects. Quite significantly for architectural judgment, this linking continues to exert considerable influence notwithstanding valiant efforts to separate artistic and architectural form from political content. Hence the need to clearly distinguish between what links and what differentiates two important intellectual freedoms: the political and the artistic.

II

OF TWO FREEDOMS: THE POLITICAL AND THE ARTISTIC

Political and artistic freedoms of expression find themselves enhanced by the authority of collective reason. A political or artistic principle gains normative value because it has been the object of reflection and agreement between many minds enriched by the accumulated wisdom of successive generations – what are usually termed regional conventions and larger traditions. This makes for a principle's historical validity and legitimizes its continued practice. Political authority is consequently given legitimacy by virtue of its just protection of individual freedom as well as collective freedom in view of the common good. Analogically, artistic and architectural authority is legitimized when principles and rules have been proven successful. When rules become too constrictive, conventions change in order to accommodate differing individual expressions. In the best of circumstances, politics and architecture construct their sense-in-common in view of achieving the common good, in which the good citizen and the good state hold a relationship of reciprocal duty. Law regulates power and upholds the true and the good by guaranteeing political freedom, and within it, artistic freedom. In such a perspective, political freedom can be said to be more encompassing than artistic freedom and is a pre-condition to artistic freedom.[17] Now, politics may encourage, discourage or prohibit various artistic traditions, and sometimes the very same artistic tradition

5.2 Loggia del Capitano, Palladio, Vicenza.
Source: Photo by Author.

finds itself identified with political régimes separated by diverse ideologies having little to do with the ideal of a just civic constitution.

The withdrawal of the authority of reason will precipitate the collapse of any principle whether political or artistic. Collapse will also occur if an artistic principle or an art form are imposed through the unjust exercise of political authority or academic authority. However, an artistic principle remains in the domain of artistic truth even if a political entity has abused its authority by prohibiting it or by tyrannically applying it. In such situations artistic freedom may be seen as a way to resist or overcome the constraints that might arise from politically adverse conditions. Art can be used as one means to achieve a desired freedom, or a new political order, and the French Revolution's call, "*Aux armes! Aux arts!*" [To arms! To arts!], poignantly attests to this effect. Storming the academic Bastille was an act that amalgamated artistic freedom and political freedom – accompanied with much iconoclasm – in order to eliminate long-standing class privileges, to ostensibly establish fairer academic conditions, and reform educational programs and professional appointments. Political freedom and artistic freedom become ends in themselves only when they are threatened. Yet, if this statement is correct, then why do architects pursue their self-expression as an end in itself in a democratic society where both freedoms are guaranteed?

In two of our previous considerations we noted the importance of the sense-in-common as well as the value of pluralism for groups and individuals. The first stresses political or artistic agreement based on collective rationality, the second can be instrumental in encouraging reciprocal tolerance between competing political or artistic perspectives. Both have rightly been acknowledged as important constituents of a just civic constitution within which political freedom and artistic freedom are exercised. Only, as a consequence of extreme differentiation and rampant relativism, the sense-in-common, at present, does not operate as a given. Cities do not embody a unified spirit, the world is not represented as sharing, and pluralism is not necessarily used to build consensus. Instead, democratic individualism has been built around the frenetic pursuit of self-expression *as difference*. A comparison between the French Revolution's *Déclaration des droits de l'homme et du citoyen* (the Declaration of the Rights of Man and of the Citizen) and the current prevalent understanding of the rights of the individual, shows that the first attempted to establish universal rights while the second consecrates the individual's right to differ.[18] Difference and otherness have been the rallying cry of modernistic self-expression. Modernist artistic freedom is practiced as the right to differ and the forcing back of opinions to the contrary. According to this belief, the deep-seated intention to differ is sufficient justification of one's artistic and architectural forms irrespective of the existence of larger traditions. According to this belief, personal artistic expression stands in necessary opposition to, or as a rupture from larger artistic traditions, hence the pursuit of self-expression as an end in itself. But this does not necessarily mean that the adherents of the right to differ have completely renounced group agreement. They are still brought together by their refusal to build a tradition, by their celebration of pluralism as a *practice of difference*.[19] They are brought together by a prevalent inter-individualism.

modern cities [margin note bracketing first paragraph]

If the understanding of freedom is exclusively identified with individual interest and expression, then the resulting political form can only amount to an aggregation of private interests loosely held together by a larger power which itself is the most powerful private interest. This can lead to the tyranny of the private. Such a view, transforms the constitutional guarantee that secures the citizen's inalienable natural rights. It confers a higher value to individual will – interpreted as "right" – over collective will. This position has serious implications over the concept of freedom and its limits, because the individual will, if not animated by a larger concept of the common good, will necessarily interpret an affirmation of the public interest as an imposition. There is a marked difference between merely accepting other individuals' freedom and rights and between understanding the individual's free-will within a shared purpose represented by the just civic constitution: the City. Similarly, there is a marked difference between pluralism as the willful acceptance of various traditions, rules and forms, which is a consequence of the tolerant humanism of a democracy, and an indiscriminate acceptance of *any* interpretation and opinion, which is done in the name of democracy, but is ultimately a kind of random permissiveness. Is it surprising then that contemporary artists who adhere to this view of artistic freedom, produce work of a primarily private meaning – the self-referential sign – to the near exclusion of work and meaning destined for the public realm? Such a practice is of course protected in a democratic milieu, even if some artists and architects are uninterested in building the sense-in-common upon which a democracy is based. Therefore, the care that a democracy takes to protect self-expression extends even to those who give more importance to their individual expressions and meanings, to their private *doxa*, while at the same time excluding the larger symbols and meanings of their culture. Here, a democratic society pays a high price when the *doxa* becomes a tyranny of the private, turning against this very same society and assaulting it on two fronts. First, by claiming that traditions or collective symbols and meaning are irrelevant or no longer exist, while asserting that all we can really have are private *doxae*. Second, by implying that no points of view can be taken for fear of being interpreted as logo-centric, or from a spurious identification of the long-standing search for collective meaning with tyrannical régimes of the right or the left. In this mentality, anything that evades larger meanings is permissible; hence the proliferation of nominalisms. Here, the confusion between democratic tolerance and indiscriminate permissiveness contributes to the collapse of art as a symbolic mediation between what is collectively held by a culture and individual beliefs, between the enduring and the contingent, the sense-in-common and the individualistic sense.

In a cultural milieu strongly marked, for good and for ill, by the concepts we previously discussed we are faced with a difficult confluence. Our ever-renewed investment in democratic tolerance works in concert with a fervent encouragement for self-expression. We are able to define the political parameters for individual liberty with great clarity. Yet we seem uncertain about defining two other liberties:

1. the question of limits between political freedom and artistic freedom; and
2. the question of how to relate an ever-expanding artistic freedom of expression to the limits between the arts.

The notion of limits, here, is understood in the sense of clearly defined artistic boundaries. The approach to the subject is fraught with difficulty because many consider the very idea of limits as illegitimate on account of the insistent demands on expanding the right to *differ indefinitely*. To understand the limits between the democratically guaranteed political and artistic freedoms implies also an understanding of what links them together as well as what differentiates their practice. Opinions divide into several clusters. One group holds the view that the distinctions between both freedoms are so fine that they are impalpable, and that for all intents and purposes both freedoms are exercised in the same way. Another group wishes to see no constraints to self-expression, preferring to define artistic freedom only as an individual sense (*sensus individuationis*) while negating larger traditions (*sensus communis*). This group wishes to see a simultaneous increase in self-expression on the one hand, and a shrinking of the distinction between both freedoms, on the other. In this way, suspending larger artistic traditions is understood as a guaranteed political freedom. Consequently, this group justifies artistic form less on artistic grounds and more on political grounds. It is also interested in shifting the grounds for justification depending on the most advantageous situation, politically or artistically. A third group, however, clarifies that although there are similarities and overlaps between political and artistic freedoms, there are important differences. Indeed, there is a specific genre of artistic freedom that suits the expression of each art. We examine comparatively the artistic freedom suitable to poetry and the visual arts of painting, sculpture, and architecture.

Poetry states truth using a variety of allegories and helps access certain truths in ways different from the approaches of science. Poetic fictions freely allude to another order of truth: a verisimilitude, which may or may not relate to a concrete or factual experience. In this, we sometimes delight in the great departure from the factual, and sometimes we reject depicted actions that appear too improbable, even for poetry. Desiring to respect the Academy's rule that a play takes place in a fictive one-day period, Corneille, in *Le Cid*, assembled a most unlikely sequence of events.[20] Rodrigue, the hero, who was engaged to Chimène, proceeded in that one day to avenge the honor of his father who was insulted by Chimène's father by defeating the latter in a duel. Afterwards, Rodrigue proceeded to lead an army to defend the city from the attacking Moors, whom he also defeated. Later still, he returned to the royal palace to receive honors from the king and reconcile with Chimène and marry her!

H. Greenhough's sculpture of G. Washington as a Caesar and A. Canova's sculpture of N. Bonaparte as Mars, involve many fictions and parallels. J.A.D. Ingres's *Apotheosis of Homer* assembles an extraordinary gathering that includes personifications of the Iliad and the Odyssey, as well as Pindar, Virgil, Dante,

Longinus, Raphael, Racine and Molière. By contrast, a painterly depiction of a historical setting can rely on factual truth as in Canaletto's views of Venice and London, or depart drastically from factual truth while still appearing "real". Consider for example, Canaletto's *capriccio* where, three Palladian buildings: the Basilica and the Palazzo Chiericati in Vicenza, and his project for the Ponte Rialto in Venice, were brought together in a characteristically Venetian composition. In fact, his depiction appeared so true, that according to Francesco Algarotti, many Venetians asked about the location of such an area of the city which they had not seen before.[21] John Soane's plan for the Bank of England, brilliantly painted by Joseph Gandy, alludes at once to a parallel to the Roman Forum, and to a culture so admiringly conscious of the inevitable passage of time that it prefigures the future state of its own architecture in ruins. Such *capricci* allude to another order of truth and another genre of artistic freedom. By contrast, other conceptions in painting reject allegory altogether, as in the realism of the Dutch group portrait.

But what of the connection between the links and boundaries[22] which are proper to each art, in relation to the artist's intellectual freedom? For instance, how is an architect to commemorate a naval victory in a monument dedicated to it? And more precisely, how free is an architect to commemorate such an event within the limits of architecture? Comparatively, how could a painter or sculptor approach the same subject? Both the painter and the sculptor can depict the factual events, the facing of battleships, the intensity of combat. The painter and the sculptor can also use allegorical figures of war, pity, pain, ruthlessness or magnanimity. So perfectly adaptable is allegory to painting and sculpture, that both arts can be entirely allegorical should the artist so choose. Herein lies the heart of the matter for the architect. The problem is two-fold: how much allegory can architecture accept, and what happens to architectural character should architects reduce architecture entirely to allegory?

The architect may have the rare luxury of choosing the location for the monument. The architect may also combine motifs that have historically been associated with victories and armies, such as the triumphal arch. Bas-reliefs and even allusions to a ship's prow in some details may also be used. Still, to achieve this commemoration, the architect can only attenuate the boundaries of architecture to a certain extent, beyond which the limits of architecture will be misused. For example, it would be indecorous to erect a building in the shape of a ship; for buildings are not ships, and unlike ships, they are static objects. Architects are certainly free to build a musical conservatory in the shape of a trombone, a library in the shape of a book, or a restaurant in the shape of a fish; but *should* they? That is the question. Architects certainly have a right to confuse artistic genres; and the contemporary cultural milieu that includes buildings as trombones, as books, or as fish, is considered broad-minded and protective of the architect's self-expression. Yet, why does it appear intolerant when citizens of that same broad-minded milieu affirm that the clear limits between the arts also need protection and leniency? Architectural character and the architect's self-expression do not operate in a social vacuum and they depend on a reciprocal set of meanings: from the building toward society and from society back toward the building. The art of the architect, that of the musician, the bookmaker, or the cook, have their natural boundaries. The *limits* between the arts are not *limitations* to artistic freedom; and artistic genres are not a burden to self-expression.

It was this clear understanding of the relationship between artistic freedom and the links and boundaries between the arts, between what an art can and should represent, that led A.C. Quatremère de Quincy – prophetically – to caution the artist against falling in two errors. The first "consists in *stepping beyond* his own art to seek, in the resources of another, an increase of imitative resemblance".[23] The second "consists in seeking the truth *short of the limits* of every art, by a system of servile copy, which deprives the imitation of the image of that fictious part which constitutes at once its essence and its character".[24] Some architects and artists can certainly pursue their self-expression by rejecting the links and boundaries between the arts. Others pursue their self-expression not outside the links and boundaries suitable for each art, but rather within them. Both approaches are expressions of artistic freedom.

The word and the image use different modes of fiction or allegory. Thus, a universal application of the axiom: *ut pictura poesis*, should be taken *cum grano salis*. Poetry's modes of fiction or allegory differ from those of painting or sculpture, and there is considerably less allegorical potential available to architecture. This is not to say, however, that architecture does not express, for that would be equivalent to denying architectural character. In the final analysis, while there is a genre of freedom in the thematic, compositional and allegorical methods of the arts in general, there is another order of freedom still, which is proper to the nature, ends and means of each art. Artistic freedom of expression pertains significantly to the ends of architecture and each art, and these ends are served by multiple means.

But, at present, the very nature of each of the visual arts is beset by two tremendous difficulties: the confusion of genres and the multiplicity of means. Firstly, the confusion of artistic genres has become an established practice for many decades, and the conflation between political freedom and artistic freedom has only served to further complicate the situation. The result is that the confusion of artistic genres is now included among the rights of self-expression. Secondly, artists and architects possess a broad freedom of expression and a considerable variety of sophisticated means. But herein resides a dangerous element that has accompanied architecture and the arts for many decades. Until the rise of the technological order within society, the means of producing architecture and other arts conformed to their respective ends. But when the means increased exponentially, as we have noted in the previous chapter, the nature and ends came to be eclipsed and disappeared from sight.[25] The overwhelming multiplicity of means and the ever-increasing freedom to use them combine to make artists and architects disregard the nature and ends of architecture and the arts.

5.3 Palazzo Cenci-Bolognetti, Arnaldo Foschini, built in the 1930s, becoming later the seat of the Communist Party.
Source: Photo by Author.

III

THE FACE OF POLITICS AND ITS ARCHITECTURAL MASKS

Architecture has been beleaguered by two kinds of monism that have deeply influenced judgment. One kind of monism associates architecture with a preferred political system or ideology as if it were the only possible expression of this ideology. The second, declares an architectural ideology to have exclusive validity and legitimacy supported by a narrative that presents it as the inevitable outcome of a historical evolution that could only have materialized in this way. Contemporary architectural discourse still abounds with statements that explain away architecture as a result of political aims. The planning of Baroque Rome is seen as a representation of the supremacy of papal or church power. Much in seventeenth century architecture is portrayed from the angle of political absolutism. The nineteenth century plantation houses in the Southern United States are understood as representations of a dominant racist class. The architecture of the British Raj was a representation of colonialism. The architecture of Washington, DC – where fascie abound – was a representation of the federal democratic establishment, and the architecture of the 1920s and 1930s in Italy and Germany was Fascist. These architectures are consequently condemned and dismissed on account of the condemnable political circumstances that paralleled their use. Most condemned has been the architecture of the Third Reich, and in particular its most important architectural figure, Albert Speer, who clearly understood and used architecture as a representation of political ideology.[26] Yet, the Reich's abuse of one of the traditions of classical architecture – one deriving from the nineteenth century academic tradition – was clearly inscribed within a larger program that manipulated all cultural forms, all the visual and rhetorical arts and symbolism. Its aim was to convince as many unsuspecting minds as possible that the collection of images (as masks) with which the Reich surrounded itself was a direct representation of its political ideology. The deceptive syllogism was: the more attractive the mask, the more appropriate the ideology! In truth, however, all the artistic and architectural forms used by the Reich emerged within different and earlier contexts having no relationship to its sinister purposes. This cultural intervention on the part of the Reich effected a very deep schism between form and content, because if *any* form can be dissociated from its originating context and attached to *any* content, then signifier and signified have collapsed, and the symbolic nature of art or architecture has been rendered dysfunctional. Since the cities of Washington, New Delhi, Berlin, and Moscow concomitantly built similar forms of classical architecture to serve widely different political ends, how could one but conclude that the different political meanings assigned to the same architecture are a proof of her political innocence?[27]

Spurious political associations have also been extended to materials, as if masonry, wood, steel, or glass, somehow carry political meaning. For decades, going as far back as Walter Gropius' Werkbund building of 1914, many architects have insisted on an absurd association: glass, steel, and aluminum are, par excellence,

5.4 Reichstag, Berlin.
Source: Photo by Daniel Schwen.

the materials of modernity, of open government and democracy. Take for example the former Berlin Reichstag, now Bundestag, whose "renovation" was completed in 1999. The building's interior, which had survived in a damaged state following the bombardment of the Second World War, was almost completely eviscerated with the exception of the outer walls and an interior transformation made in the 1960s. The most visible part of this "renovation", from the outside, was a new steel and glass cupola containing an inverted conical structure covered with mirrors. This cupola was hailed as a symbol of the transparency of a democratic government. Yet the original cupola that was begun under the reign of Wilhelm I and completed in 1894 under Wilhelm II – suffering severe damage during the Second World War – was also made of iron and glass. In the span of one hundred years, two glass cupolas with metal armature, admittedly with different articulations, represented empire and then democracy!

Associating architectural form with a selected political content entails serious consequences for architectural judgment on at least two levels. The first is the assertion that architectural form and meaning can only be understood following the provided interpretations of modernist historians. The second is justification by opposition. Modernist architecture is justified by heaping terribly adverse political associations onto traditional and classical architecture; by comparing a selection of traditional buildings used by the most oppressive régimes of the past with a selection of modernist buildings used by the most tolerant régimes of the present. However, an intellectually honest view of history might also explain that some of the most extolled figures of modernism worked for or were prepared to work with quite condemnable political régimes. As is well known, Giuseppe Terragni built the headquarters for the Fascist party in Como, the Casa del Fascio, Mies van der Rohe had actively sought to work for the Nazis,[28] while Le Corbusier collaborated with the Vichy government in France, and produced plans (the Voisin Plan) that prefigured the evisceration of much of Paris in order to make space for his skyscrapers.[29] Similarly, while the architecture of the avant-garde in the Soviet

5.5 Casa del Fascio, Giuseppe Terragni, Como. Source: Photo by roryrory.

Union,[30] was acclaimed by linking it to an emancipatory and progressive ideology of labor, readers of architectural history would have appreciated knowing that classical architecture was also practiced in the Soviet Union well into the 1960s, and that the architects and inhabitants shared the same progressive labor ideology as those of the avant-garde.[31]

Modernist historians' embrace of futurism presents a peculiar case.[32] On the one hand modernism absorbed most of futurism's artistic beliefs such as the vehement break with tradition; the rejection of the continuity of space and time in representation in favor of immediacy and dynamism; the radical belief in the redemption of science and technology; and the cult-like apotheosis of modernity. On the other, modernist architects and historians sought to separate the architecture of futurists from their exaltation of violence and their enthusiastic associations with the rise of Fascism in Italy, by scarcely mentioning these extremes or simply remaining silent about them. These examples show that by selectively associating or dissociating political and artistic content, monistic architectural beliefs gravely compromise intellectual integrity.

This brings us to the second kind of monism, the one practiced by those who build and teach an architecture that they consider as the inevitable pinnacle of a historical development while dismissing most architectures from the past with an intolerant sleight of hand. Such was modernism's view of itself as the unquestionable ideology that is sanctioned by the metaphysical certitude of an all-pervasive zeitgeist –a kind of unalterable historical determinism. Modernism considered itself as the sole cultural presence whose technologically determined forms represented the only form of modernity possible for modern society. This judgment quickly became a kind of heroic self-assessment that considered opposing views as dangerously heretical. Consequently, when modernism became an establishment force, it banned by fiat the teaching of any other tradition in academia, and violently opposed the practice of any traditional architecture.[33] As is well known, Joseph Hudnut's influence, and to a lesser extent that of Walter Gropius, during their tenure at the Graduate School of Design at Harvard University between the 1930s and 1950s, resulted in the elimination of the teaching of architectural history, which also included the destruction of plaster casts of classical sculptural and architectural models as well as a rigid proscription on history books.[34] Monistic thought saw the application of the same architecture to all corners of the globe, dismissing the rich plurality of local architectural characters and varying climatic considerations. It is for reasons such as these that the recent renewed calls for pluralism, since the late seventies, came largely as a revolt, a will to be emancipated from modernism's totalizing control over cultural production in general and architectural production in particular. Subsequently, some schools of architecture moved to partially rectify some of the proscriptions on the teaching of architectural history by amplifying the history requirements in academic programs. This rectification notwithstanding, the effects of the proscription on the uses of history remain very deep, and teaching history to architects continues to be a restrained activity with much of the scholarship being relegated to the domain of the specialist.[35]

It is important to note that although politics and architecture are each justifiable according to its intrinsic set of criteria, the opposition between warring architectural views nowadays is fought less on architectural grounds and more on political grounds. There is a flawed and widely distributed understanding according to which the position that gained the upper hand politically and claimed an exclusive ethical imperative, must necessarily represent the most appropriate architecture. It is also significant that while detractors of modern traditional architecture falsely associate it with undemocratic régimes, they remain unable to define just exactly what is a "democratic architecture". It is one thing to ask how can politics and architecture reciprocally fulfill each other, and another to assert that one architecture (classic, gothic, or modernist) more than any other is the privileged representation of a given state, a given political ideology.[36] Given the vast associative proclivities of the mind – sometimes according to mendacious intentions – we are faced with the unfortunate prospects that political contents can be spuriously linked to an architectural form that owes its existence to completely different reasons.

Taking stock of the seven general points we made regarding politics and architecture, we noted that:

1. although both depend on a sense-in-common and serve the common good, architecture does not represent political content;

2. that judgment is affected by the considerable number of choices included in the range between monism and pluralism;
3. that although the multiplicity of opinions is quite useful, it is vital to distinguish between pluralism and relativism;
4. that it is important to note the similarities and differences between political freedom and artistic freedom, and to distinguish between the genres of artistic freedoms that suit each art;
5. that artistic freedom is closely linked to the boundaries between the arts;
6. that architectural judgment finds itself impaired when a preferred architecture is associated with tolerant political régimes while a reviled architecture is associated with condemnable ones; and
7. that architectural monism attempts to eliminate or to discourage other forms of architecture.

These problems show that as long as the judgment of architectural character remains dissociated from a clear understanding of the limits between the arts and a genuine concern about the erosion of these limits, then the current crisis regarding how buildings come to be endowed with character will only deepen.[37] The roots of this crisis extend to other crises that have profoundly marked the very idea of paradigm and how it informs artistic representation and architectural expression. These roots go back to the eighteenth century when the natural paradigm was replaced with deeply historicized societal meanings. They can be traced to the nineteenth century when the proliferation of architectural characters and styles led to the confusion of genres. They also derive from the conflation made by some architects in the twentieth century between their intent to represent the technological society and their use of the means of *technique*; and later, from the transposition of various experiments in linguistics into architectural composition. These and other reasons are usually explained as revolutionary ruptures, while changes in forms have been usually explained by linking social, technological and artistic revolutions, and by comparing architectural forms before, during, and after these revolutions with the underlying assumption that revolutions are the best context in which to study change.

The cultural circumstances surrounding the French Revolution, for example, saw the convergence of two projects with direct bearing on our topic. Following the revolutionary call, *Aux armes! Aux arts!*, the idea that cultural productions can be instrumentally used for political ends became commonplace in the writing of history. In fact the assumption was extended to assert that cultural productions have always had political ends.[38] Another project from the eighteenth century: *l'architecture parlante*, or speaking architecture, began by announcing a metaphorical association between architectural character and social significance, which quickly became an association of equivalency. Architectural character was understood as a representation of social mores. Since the confluence of these two projects in the late eighteenth century, and most acutely in the twentieth, many came to consider the notion of artistic meaning as symptomatic of, and as subservient to social and political determinants, especially in books that surveyed art and architectural history. Many scholars, consequently, assumed a causal relationship between political ideologies and their changes on the one hand, and the changes in artistic or architectural forms on the other. Artistic and architectural characters, so the argument goes, represent the world-views represented by these ideologies. This particular doctrine was pursued with relentless zeal by modernist scholars especially in their transformation of the museum institution – the institution whose given task was to tell the story of art and architecture. The museum became the means to consecrate the official views of history and to crown the artists and architects whose productions fit these official views. So deeply rooted has this doctrine been in cultural theory that modernist luminaries such as André Malraux proposed a reverse approach: to study political and historical phenomena based on the methodologies of art history and theory.

However, in considering the context of social revolutions and the architectures that accompanied them one arrives at different conclusions. Even the most cursive examination of architecture during the American Revolution (1777–83) and the French Revolution (1789–99), shows that in neither case was there a revolutionary architectural character *per se*. The same architectural traditions were practiced before, during, and after these revolutions. Pierre-Charles L'Enfant, with the valuable advice of Thomas Jefferson, probably did not consider architectural character to be a representation of political ideology, for he surely would not have selected the "royalist" and "papist" plans of Versailles, Vaux-le-Vicomte, Fontainebleau, Rome, and Karlsruhe as models for parts of his plan for Washington. With the exception of the transformation of the interior of Ste. Geneviève into the French Panthéon, the French Revolution also did not produce its *own* architecture. This, of course, does not mean that architecture was not used for political ends. A revolutionary pageant at Lyon appropriated as its symbol a garden folly – a Doric temple front forming the entrance to a cave. Yet that temple front had been built some years earlier in the garden of a banker for purposes having little to do with the aims of the Revolution.[39] Moreover, if architectural character was indeed a reflection of political ideology, then one would expect the main sources that explain architectural intentions namely the architectural treatise, to reveal this connection. Yet, the extensive tradition of architectural treatises shows that their authors did not justify architectural character based on political ideology. Rather this justification was based on the suitability of architectural compositional elements (arcades, colonnades, fenestrations, walls, roofs, and their proportional relationships) to a building's purpose (be it a public building: a church, a market, a court house; or a private building: a private palace, a town house, a villa) and that of its direct context (a street, a square, a hill, a valley).

That the mind is able to willfully emphasize, omit, use, or abuse meanings of architectural forms for political ends is true; although as we mentioned earlier, architecture remains politically innocent of her abusers' aims. That architecture is influenced by socio-political factors is undeniable. But to consider architectural character as *symptomatic* of social and political determinants, betrays a sadly common quandary: those who study architecture confuse their own analytical methods with the ways in which architecture operates, thereby denying much of her autonomy. Unfortunately, this phenomenon has by now combined with the forces of political and cultural relativism. The problem for the visual arts is that *political relativism* now masquerades as *artistic pluralism*. If architectural character is a symptom of socio-political determinants, and if these determinants are in a constant state of disagreement and change, then surely there is no possible agreement on character, and architecture is condemned to dissociation, to fragmentation. Some architects are perfectly content with such conditions, for these conditions help to justify their self-expression outside the sense-in-common. Others insist that what is essential and distinctive about architectural meaning and character transcends the architect's self-expression and the architect's sense of ownership of the buildings that he or she designed. Rather, character operates based on a reciprocal relationship between the architect's mind and the receptions and conventions of society. Although architects are the makers and custodians of architectural forms, they are only partial owners of these forms given their roles as citizens who are called to freely construct the sense-in-common.

NOTES

1. *Poetica* 1460b 13n.

2. For the purposes of the present discussion we are not differentiating between the categories of the beautiful and the aesthetic and the various uses imparted to aesthetics since A.G. Baumgarten's *aesthetica* (1758).

3. For Kant, the maxims of human understanding are: "1) to think for oneself; 2) to think from the standpoint of everyone else; 3) always to think consistently. The first is the maxim of *unprejudiced* thought, the second of *broadened* thought, the third, that of *consistent* thought". I. Kant, *Critique of Judgement*, J. Meredith (Tr.), (Oxford, (1790) 2007), §40, p. 124.

4. *Ibid*, §20–22, pp. 68–71. The concept of humanity as communicability itself has been developed by Karl Jaspers and Hannah Arendt. See her "K. Jaspers, citoyen du monde" in *Vies politiques*, (Gallimard), pp. 94–108.

5. *Ibid*, §60, pp. 182–3.

6. On Kant's inter-subjectivity in the *Critique of Judgement*, see §20–22, pp. 68–74, and §40–42, pp. 123–32. On Hannah Arendt's reading of it, see H. Arendt, *Juger: Sur la philosophie de Kant*, M. Revault d'Allonnes (Tr.), (Seuil, 1991); and Etienne Tassin, "Sens-commun et communauté: La lecture arendtienne de Kant", in *Les cahiers de philosophie*, 4, (Presses Universitaires de France, 1987), pp. 81–113.

7. The paradoxical character of Kant's third Critique is his assertion that taste, the most private and least communicable sense, is the vehicle for the faculty of judgment.

8. See our previous discussion of differentiation in Chapter 4.

9. See F. Manuel and F. Manuel, *Utopian Thought in the Western World*, (Harvard University Press, 1979).

10. See Léon Krier's Completion of Washington, in Archives d'architecture moderne, N°30, Bruxelles, 1986.

11. I. Kant, *Idea for a Universal History*, (1784), (Modern Library, New York, 1977), p. 122.

12 *Archives d'architecture moderne, Prix européen pour la reconstruction de la ville*, N°35/36, (Brussels, 1987), p. 144.

13 Epistemological monism is here distinguished from fundamentalism which designates a theological current within American Protestantism in the early twentieth century, taking its name from a 1909 brochure entitled "The Fundamentals". The followers of this current define Christianity by a certain number of essential beliefs such as biblical infallibility, hence the literal and fixed meaning attached to their view of biblical texts.

14 Above all, pluralism has been used to oppose a hierarchical view of society and the arts where cultural values and products are ranked from higher to lower, in contradistinction to the scientific explanations of natural phenomena which is decidedly hierarchical.

15 In the next chapter, we shall see why it is difficult to be optimistic about architects answering that call.

16 "What is true of human polity seems to me not less so of the distinctively political art of architecture". J. Ruskin, *The Seven Lamps of Architecture*, (1880), (Dover reprint, 1989), p. 2. As has often been rightly emphasized, architecture is the most public of the arts; yet, most citizens exert little influence on the decisions that affect the physical qualities of the public realm. Instead, these decisions are the province of architects who have the choice to practice their art as an expression of the civic good or solely as a private expression.

17 This is not to suggest that political freedom is the only condition for artistic freedom. For art, is a phenomenon that is ontologically linked to the human character.

18 Naturally, its emancipatory programs notwithstanding, the French Revolution did not exhibit the respect for cultural pluralism that characterizes contemporary democracies.

19 See, for example, the proceedings of the conference held at Columbia University in 2003, B. Tschumi and I. Cheng (eds), *The State of Architecture at the Beginning of the 21st Century*, (Monacelli Press, 2003).

20 P. Corneille, *Le Cid*, (1636) L. Lejealle and J. Dubois (eds), (Larousse, 1970).

21 A. Rossi discussed this "analogous Venice" as a locus of pure architectural values. See his *L'Architecture de la ville*, (L'Equerre, 1981), pp. 218–20.

22 See our discussion between links and boundaries in the preceding chapter.

23 Quatremère de Quincy, A.C. *Essai sur la nature, le but et les moyens de l'imitation dans les beaux-arts*, 1823. Introductions by L. Krier and D. Porphyrios. (Archives d'Architecture Moderne, Brussels, 1980), p. 68; p. 81 Engl. tr. J.C.Kent. Italics mine.

24 *Ibid*, p. 86; p. 102 Engl. tr. Italics mine.

25 Similarly, the attainment of justice is the aim of politics and the laws are the means to achieve it. When legislative means proliferate, it is possible for them to eclipse the ends which they were intended to serve in the first place.

26 See his *Memoirs, Inside the Third Reich*, (Collier Books, 1970), pp. 159–60, and his revealing assertion in his preface to *Albert Speer Architecture, 1932–1942*, L. Krier (ed.), (Archives d'architecture moderne, Bruxelles, 1982), pp. 9–10: "My buildings were not solely intended to express the essence of the National-socialist movement. They were an integral part of that very movement. That statement established the deeply political nature of my work ... Beyond the representation of political might, the

27 modern viewer can recognize a psychological intention in the buildings and projects of the Third Reich an attempt to achieve effects through architectural means".

27 This was the core subject of a much misunderstood and maligned book on Albert Speer edited by Léon Krier. This book showed that although the Reich used classical architecture as its most civilized mask, most of its buildings remained overwhelmingly industrial. It also showed while modernist historians and architects have singled out classical architecture because of its abuse by the Nazis, they remained curiously silent about the simultaneous use of classical architecture by other régimes, some of whom were considered democratic, e.g. the so-called architecture of the federal presence in Washington.

28 See E. Hochman, *Architects of Fortune, Mies van der Rohe and the Third Reich*, (Fromm International Publishing, 1990).

29 Although the relationship between Le Corbusier and the Vichy régime had been known for several decades, the content of recently released letters by the architect compelled the Swiss government to re-think naming a square in Zurich after him. See the new biography by N. Fox Weber, *Le Corbusier: A Life*, (Random House, 2008).

30 For example the work of I. Chernikov, V. Tatlin, V. Krinski, and I. Leonidov.

31 For example, the work of K. Alabian, V. Simbirtsev, A. Dushkin, A. Poliakov, and A. Shchusev.

32 See for example, F.T. Marinetti, "The Foundations and Manifesto of Futurism" (1908), and U. Boccioni, C.D. Carrà, L. Russolo, G. Balla, and G. Severini, "Futurist Painting: Technical Manifesto" (1910), Joshua Taylor, (Tr.), in Herschel B. Chipp, *Theories of Modern Art: A Source Book by Artists and Critics*, (University of California Press, 1968).

33 Today there are over 100 schools of architecture in the United States who teach various forms of modernism. Of these, only two schools teach traditional architecture and urbanism. These are the University of Notre Dame and the University of Miami.

34 For a detailed account of this story see J. Pearlman, "Joseph Hudnut's other modernism at the Harvard Bauhaus", *Journal of the Society of Architectural Historians*, 56(4), (December 1997), pp. 152–77.

35 By 2011, the National Architectural Accreditation Board in the United States will no longer evaluate the teaching of architectural history within schools of architecture.

36 A self-professed pluralist, Rome's former mayor, Walter Veltroni, declared on Raitre television that his only condition regarding new architectural interventions in the city is that they should be modernist. Aired on the 6 December 2005, *La storia siamo noi* presented by Giovanni Minoli.

37 We shall return to architectural character in greater detail in Part Two of the book.

38 See E. Kaufmann, *Three Revolutionary Architects: Boullée, Ledoux, and Lequeu*, (American Philosophical Society, 1952); J. Starobinski, *1789, Les emblèmes de la raison*, (Flammarion, 1973); A. Banham, *The Architecture of the Enlightenment: From Soufflot to Ledoux*, (London, 1980); J. Rykwert, *The First Moderns*, (MIT Press, 1980); M-L. Bivier, *Le Panthéon à l'époque révolutionnaire*, (Paris, 1982); A. Vidler, *The Writing of the Walls*, (Princeton Architectural Press, 1986); P. Bordes and R. Michel, *Aux armes & aux arts!* (Biro, 1988); J. Leith, *Space and Revolution*, (McGill-Queen, 1991).

39 See R. Rosenblum, *Transformations in Late Eighteenth Century Art*, (Princeton University Press, 1967), pp. 127–8. The French revolutionaries also appropriated the Phrygian cap with its forward-curving peak, as a symbol of their revolutionary spirit; yet it still remains that the Phrygian cap was not made for that purpose.

6
Desire, Imitation, and Conflict

Since men were of an imitative and teachable nature, they boasted of their inventions as they daily showed their various achievements in building, and thus, exercising their talents in rivalry, were rendered of better judgement daily.[1]

Vitruvius

… will is none other than desire itself.[2]

Thomas Hobbes

We now turn to the third kind of external architectural judgment, the one based on desire for form. In a brief philosophical excursus, we begin by looking at the intrinsic link between will and desire. We will then consider the subjective life of architects as self-forming aesthetes. These psychological considerations concern the artistic will to make form, the multiple desires to possess form, and the varied ways in which architects identify with form. Will, desire, and identity become foundational aspects of the psychology of architects – for good or for ill – as they shape their intellectual and aesthetic preferences. Desire is an elective affinity, it concerns preferential choice and assigns emotional values to forms and to the ways of conceptualizing them. In fact a considerable part of architectural judgment remains intimately connected to the architect's wish-life or desire-life for preferred forms, or images. Desire can then include a form of judgment, if only by virtue of the pleasure it provides for the mind, the emotions and the senses. Desire also links the possession of forms with the identity of the possessor. As we shall see, it is with possessiveness and strong association with forms as well as the ideologies that justify them that architects sculpt their identities. This phenomenon explains why, on the one hand, architects have a double mimetic relationship to each other and to their buildings; and, on the other, why they suffer deep divisions. All of these predisposing elements can lead to a kind of architectural judgment that is linked to conflict and antagonism.[3] Quite significantly, we note that whereas external architectural judgment cannot be reduced to the subjective characteristics we briefly enumerated, it also cannot be dissociated from them.

6.1 Palazzo Ducale, Cortile, Venice, Antonio Rizzo.
Source: Photo by Author.

I

DESIRE AND THE WILL-TO-MAKE

We relate to the objects of human making either from the position of an observer of forms made by others, or that of a maker of form. As observers of visual form, our aesthetic experience ranges from a spectator's passive attitude to that of an active mental and emotional engagement with form, cognitively acquiring its expressive qualities as they present themselves to our sight, or imputing, projecting onto this form some qualities that it may or may not possess.[4] Desire for form, for its aesthetic appreciation, and for its appropriation, is a feature shared by all. What distinguishes architects and artists, however, is that in addition to desiring forms, they possess the will and ability to make forms (Greek: *poein*, Latin: *facere*, French: *faire*, Italian: *fare*). For architects and artists, the will to make form and the desire for form are closely associated.[5] More specifically for architects, the will to make form, the desire for form, and the desire to dwell within form are closely associated. An architect's first mental movement, to paraphrase Paul Valéry, may appropriately be described as a will to make.[6] Making is a causal act operating in function of a will, a freedom, and a power to act over certain material, shaping it into form, and using certain means to achieve determined ends. Practical reason structurally articulates the process of making in view of the established ends as well as the available means. The architect's will-to-make can then be said to operate as a movement, a desire, a direction of the mind towards realizing a form. To will, to see, and to make, thus form an indivisible psychological reality. They become aligned within the architect's image-making faculty. Therefore, the architect's personal will-to-make, or will-to-build, can be considered a teleology on the scale of the individual in the Aristotelian sense of "final cause"; while intentionality concerns largely the thought content that animates the architect's will.

Will and desire urge action; they may be said to exhibit two directionalities at once, the one inward, the other outward. Both pertain to the subject's psychology intimately and concern natural and human made objects. This double directionality, however, is not necessarily equally divided between will and desire. As a driving force to craft forms, the will-to-make may be said to have largely an outward directionality; whereas desire, as a wish to appropriate form, may be said to have mainly an inward directionality. In turn, inward demands, or needs, come to determine the objects and the extent to which desire reaches outwardly toward these objects.[7] Artistic desire reaches out and appropriates the world as an image, or an object; and when it reaches sufficient intensity, it compellingly invokes the will to act. Desire and will, then, arise from within the innermost recesses of our subjectivity, as well as in response to something outside of us. They motivate the conjuring of mental phenomena, and furnish the reasons to justify and realize a plan of action, construct a building, compose an aria, or write a book. In tending toward a goal, a finality, desire and will are served by practical reason. They are goal-directed or object-directed whether that object is a moral act, a mental abstraction, a mental image, or a concrete physical form. To desire, will, intend, and wish, were all appositely contained in the ancient Greek concept of *boulesis*.[8] Strongly linked to the deliberations in council, or assembly – or *boule*, hence the *bouleterion* as an assembly building – boulesis marks the crossing between calculating reason (Aristotle's *logismos*) and desire in the form of an interest that moves the individual or group to action. In the case of boulesis, the will is a form of desire connected to a rational representation. And this means that every act is necessarily based on an interest and that the force of the will, an aspect of human freedom, is none else than rational representation.

Desire and will, then, have the proclivity to cause the mind and the emotions to move in a determined direction. This has led many a thinker for whom causality is vital, to reflect on whether will or desire came first. Others, of a more practical bent of mind, suggested that antecedence was a secondary notion because will and desire occur almost simultaneously in our consciousness. Of greater importance was the capacity of will and desire to influence moral, artistic, or physical activities. Others still, emphasized that although will and desire can be their own signifier, their own cause and their own aim, they are not *just* solitary decision-making sources of action. They have their associative links, their historical sequences, as well as their pathologies. They are frequently influenced by other wills, other desires, sometimes consciously, and sometimes unconsciously.

Beyond pointing to something, desire and will are also instrumental (e.g. the desire to build a house) and they operate according to a preferential choice (e.g. a house of stone is more durable than a house of wood). Preferential choice, for Aristotle, is distinguished from simple wishing in the sense that it only concerns possible actions that come after deliberation. Every action, he asserts, whether deliberate or not, is moved primarily by desire:

> *These two at all events appear to be sources of movement: appetite and mind (if one may venture to regard imagination as a kind of thinking; for many men follow their imaginations contrary to knowledge, and in all animals other than man there is no thinking or calculation but only imagination). Both of these then are capable of originating local movement, mind and appetite: 1) mind, that is, which calculates means to an end, i.e. mind practical (it differs from mind speculative in the character of its end); while 2) appetite is in every form of it relative to an end: for that which is the object of appetite is the stimulant of mind practical; and that which is last in the process of thinking is the beginning of the action. It follows that there is a justification for regarding these two as the sources of movement, i.e. appetite and practical thought; for the object of appetite starts a movement and as a result of that thought gives rise to movement, the object of appetite being it a source of stimulation. So too when imagination originates movement, it necessarily involves appetite.*
>
> *That which moves therefore is a single faculty and the faculty of appetite; for if there had been two sources of movement – mind and appetite – they would have produced movement in virtue of some common character. As it is, mind is never found producing movement without appetite (for wish is a form of appetite; and when movement is produced according to calculation it is also according to wish), but appetite can originate movement contrary to calculation, for desire is a form of appetite. Now mind is always right, but appetite and imagination may be either right or wrong. That is why, though in any case it is the*

> *object of appetite which originates movement, this object may be either the real or the apparent good. To produce movement the object must be more than this: it must be good that can be brought into being by action; and only what can be otherwise than as it is can thus be brought into being. That then such a power in the soul as has been described, i.e. that called appetite, originates movement is clear.*[9]

Thus, the practical mind, according to Aristotle, is moved to action through the mediation of desire (or appetite) that represents the ends and determines the means. The Platonic opposition between the mind and the possible excesses of desire becomes an association between two desires: mental and emotional. Desire moves the mind to deliberate in relation to a future action, and impels it to expand efforts. This endeavor, or *conatus*, according to Spinoza:

> *when referred solely to the mind, is called will, when referred to the mind and body in conjunction it is called appetite; it is, in fact, nothing else but man's essence, from the nature of which necessarily follow all those results which tend to its preservation; and which man has thus been determined to perform.*
>
> *Further, between appetite and desire there is no difference, except that the term desire is generally applied to men, in so far as they are conscious of their appetite, and may accordingly be thus defined: Desire is appetite with consciousness thereof.*[10]

Kant also held that desire exerted a pervasive influence covering the entire field of human actions, being a determining faculty in an individual's life.

> *Life is the faculty a being has of acting according to laws of the faculty of desire. The faculty of desire is the being's faculty of becoming by means of its ideas the cause of the actual existence of the objects of these ideas. Pleasure is the idea of the agreement of the object, or the action with the subjective conditions of life, i.e., with the faculty of causality of an idea in respect of the actuality of its object (or with the determination of the forces of the subject to action which produces it).*[11]

In identifying desire as the cause for the representation and the making of objects, Kant thus designated what is in common between desire and will.

Hegel characterized the very consciousness of self as a desire. Consciousness finds its own confirmation "by superseding this other that presents itself to self-consciousness as an independent life".[12] Consciousness returns onto itself following an awareness of the other. It relates to the world in order to realize itself. Therefore, when it is pursuing the pleasure of seeing its own realizations in the world of forms, consciousness is actually searching for itself, for its own realization; and desire, to the extent that it is self-consciousness, is in quest for itself. To a considerable degree, the breadth of aesthetic experience and its success derive from the reciprocal relation between the will-to-make the form, and the response of the external world to that form.[13] Architecture's great task in all of this, was its ability to join the aesthetic realm: the sensuous good, with the realm of reason: the intelligible good.[14] Combining the necessity of building with intellectual and sensuous goods Quatremère de Quincy saw architecture as a result of instrumental desire. This compelled him to define architecture as:

> *a composite art, a child of necessity and pleasure that must serve and please us by unifying the forms most befitting to the material needs of man and the harmony of relations best suited for the pleasures of the soul and the mind.*[15]

II

ARCHITECTURAL DESIRE

We find peace near our idols.[16]

René Girard

As we noted above, all of us desire visual forms, aesthetically appreciating them from a distance. The gradations of desire show that architects and artists distinguish themselves from other rational agents in that in addition to desiring form, they have a will and a capacity to make form. To this gradation we must now add a well-known feature that is specific to the art of building: the architect's mode of making is also a mode of dwelling. Moreover, architects desire to make buildings because their predilection to make and to dwell coincides with satisfying some patron's specific purpose in realizing a building.[17] But the fact that architects make indirectly, in the sense that they ideate (*disegno*, design) the forms that are subsequently built by others, does not diminish their fervent bond with forms. Indeed, architects' attachment to form frequently becomes a kind of ownership of forms, or images, because architects themselves appropriate the world as an image, as a set of images. Beyond being a mere possessive quality, this attachment often becomes a potent personal identification with their forms and images and the setting in which they have been realized. From the initial moments of conception (*having to make*), to the trials of construction (the uncertain presence of a building *having to be made*), to the satisfaction of completion (the certainty of *having made*), many architects develop a special attachment to their buildings.[18] They develop an even greater attachment to a setting after they have transformed the character of a street, the enclosure of a square, or the flank of a hill. This appropriation gains its highest intensity as soon as the building is completed, for expectation had been steadily increasing. Such a phenomenon firmly merges three personal traits that architects possess and cultivate: making, owning and identifying. And this threefold merging becomes a basic mode of dwelling for architects. It operates at a more basic and egocentric level than Heidegger's subtle etymologizing between the German verb *bauen*, to build, and the High German *buan*, to dwell.[19]

Architects also dwell in and with form by surrounding themselves with desired forms, by historicizing their forms in alluring narratives, and by identifying their selves (as personae) with these forms and narratives. A rich imagery fills the daily life of the architect – an aesthetic life that demands daily satisfaction. Architects enjoy surrounding themselves with images and objects that they find pleasing:

6.2 Palazzo Pamphilj, Girolamo Rainaldi, Rome.
Source: Photo by Author.

fragments of entablatures, sculptures, paintings of cityscapes and landscapes, vases, urns, candelabras, tapestries, mosaics, etc. In short, architects develop their own personal museums.[20] Part of this collecting derives from the accumulation of images for the direct uses of practical reason in designing, or in composing new buildings; while another part stems from the unadulterated aesthetic pleasure of observing objects for their own sake.

Visual perception insistently participates in the formation of desire, and architectural taste is a consummate aesthetic elaboration of visual perception.[21] Taste, after all, belongs to those who desire. It results from the inward cultivation of desire based on one's subjective inclinations in relation to the subjectivities of other individuals, and in relation to group inter-subjectivity. The fascinating power of the image and the insatiable "appetite of the eye" – in J. Lacan's words – induce aesthetic beings, especially architects and artists, to surpass mere participation in a perpetual exchange of desired objects toward an active construction of orders or systems of desire. In this sense, the history of architectural form, especially the kind of history with stylistic underpinnings, might rightly take its place within a larger history of desire for form. In other words, artistic and architectural history, and of course theory, can be seen as ordered constructions based on desire.[22]

Following years of self-training, from the halls of architectural education, the travels that emulate the Grand Tour, the painstaking measuring of exemplary edifices, the devoted painting of cityscapes and landscapes, the seducing

6.3 Palazzo di Giustizia, Guglielmo Calderini, Rome. *Source*: Photo by Author.

effects of architectural photography in history books, to the melting pot of forms in professional life, architects develop an aesthetic composure based in large part on the voluntary shaping of their aesthetic preferences. Architects can imitatively imagine themselves as the makers of the Pantheon, the Palazzo Farnese, or the little rustic hut in the countryside. They value the character of buildings, their tectonic clarity, the accuracy of stereotomy, and their many stylistic differentiations. All of these desirable qualities, or more precisely, all of these series of desires are fashioned by the continual formation and conformation of the mind and the emotions toward desired buildings. But preferences change. If one were to compare, for example, the architectural predilection of students at the initial and then final stages of their education, one observes the shaping of their formal preferences in different directions – especially when the preferences of teachers and those of students confront each other as they often do. Later on, architects arrange their preferences hierarchically either for reasons of their own, or because an authoritative figure from the architectural star system "said so". But accepting another architect's authority does not necessarily override one's internal discord of desires. Other architects still, may cease to desire buildings that they previously preferred. But it is unlikely that they would cease to desire buildings altogether. Their desires simply change their aims.

On the other hand, can architects desire images too much, or too little? We can engage the scope of this desire by comparing two opposing phenomena which have been taken to extremes since the late nineteenth century, namely: eclectic imagery and reductive imagery. If eclecticism can be taken to excess in the sense of disproportionate proliferation of architectural imagery, and reductivism and abstraction can be taken to excess in the sense of impoverishment or deficiency of architectural imagery, we can see how both eclecticism and reductivism can lead to weakening the notion of architectural character. Indeed the excesses of both phenomena can lead to kinds of iconoclasm. A purposeful lack of architectural imagery, is not necessarily a pursuit of purism. It leads to the eventual elimination of much architectural detail and ornament. "Less is a bore" exclaimed Robert Venturi. Conversely, the very proliferation of images, their redundancy, their superfluity, can induce the mind to reject them by withdrawing the very desire for them. Nonetheless, architects who believe that a well-furnished world includes both the agreeable and the displeasing, can tolerate certain images, even those they find objectionable. But they might reject other images, even pleasing ones, because they have been persistently assailed by them, voluntarily and involuntarily.[23] Such for example is the unintended negative effect caused by the will to propagate and popularize certain architectural preferences by their relentless repetition in architectural magazines – that is until other preferences come to replace them.[24] But architectural desire is not all concordance between mind and emotions. Architects' desire for forms and images in relation to their possible uses presents some ambiguities. The fact that architects' minds are inhabited by a plethora of forms shows the richness of possibility, while the prospects of realizing only a fraction of these forms shows the limitedness of actualization. For this reason, the frustration of the desire to build has been a frequent companion to architects.

Consider for example the notable number of architects who were successively commissioned and dismissed in order to complete the church of San Giovanni dei Fiorentini in Rome between 1509 and 1738.[25]

When architects imagine and draw a building, or draw forth the building, they realize the satisfaction of the conceptualizer, the painter. This satisfaction is in anticipation of realization. It is a partially fulfilled desire. The other part comes after the building is completed. This desire is teleological. But if the building is not completed to the intentions of the architect, there is frustration. The teleology is interrupted, the satisfaction only partial, and desire has to be modified to fit the incompleteness of desire. Qualities and forms that have not been realized in one building are now projected, or fantasized, onto the next building, as the architect's mind begins to project future formal combinations. Desire reaches past the building that temporarily held its attention because of architects' endless fascination with the seemingly infinite possibilities of formal combinations of their art. Fantasy becomes a bridge between desire, the architect's imaging faculties, as well as an anticipated experience of satisfaction. This is why architects look forward to their next building in order to realize more of the forms that inhabit their minds. They also wonder about the forms that could have been realized by other architects. They lament the incompletion of a building which could have been a masterpiece, or the destruction of buildings that resulted in a less worthy urban condition. That is what makes architects invoke the "original intention" of Raphael in his Villa Madama, had it been completed, or the entry to Piazza San Pietro in the Vatican had the Borgo not been destroyed in the early 1930s. The physical perseverance of buildings in various degrees of completion, and the mnemonic perseverance of buildings that no longer exist exert a powerful influence on the architects' imagining faculties.

They also pursue "unreachable" projects in the sense of raising ever higher their bar of achievement; and when they fail to accomplish a project, architects model themselves on other architects who are successful realizers of form. Desire then is represented in the will to pursue the realization of form notwithstanding the failure, and scorn, that results from raising the bar too high. The frustration to realize architectural form may serve to increase attachment to this form. Desire moves the mind to act, but many reasons conspire to prevent implementation. This might lead to feelings of "sterility", or to an adverse opinion of the context which is now seen as hostile to the architect's realizations. Conversely, the realization of buildings might lead to the "release" from forms in the sense of an eventual detachment on the part of the architect, especially once the building has been realized. Here, the virtuous admonitions of classical writers (e.g. Chrisippus, Epicurus, Seneca; not to mention the entire tradition of Buddhist thought) to discipline the self, to rise above satisfaction, above pleasure or displeasure, and to mold desire to fit the circumstances of the world, might prove to be useful companions.

Removed from the act of building (making), architects and their preferred architectures may be separated by such a spatial or temporal distance that they cannot immediately access them. This is why architects desire Rome when living elsewhere; and this is why the landscape painter's strongest yearning for the countryside occurs in the midst of the city. Desire gains importance because of the absence of the wanted building, and it increases with the delay in the satisfaction. The building is absent physically, but it is present within the desiring architect as anticipation for a future satisfaction or consummation. Once the desired building, or city, is found, it temporarily loses its status as an object of desire because there is temporary satiety. The thirst has been quenched; the desire satisfied. Desire grows with its repeated calling and, at the same time, the expectation of repeated satisfaction – hence the circular side of desire life.

Only, the repetition of satisfaction involves some unintended and paradoxical psychological effects. Architects' intimate relation with Rome is a case in point. Few cities have been the subject of studies so erudite, so continuous, and so voluminous as Rome. Architects, historians, painters, and archaeologists, have devoted much thought in order to understand her urban layers, topography, piazze, streets, palazzi, fountains, and all invested much desire in the aesthetic appreciation of these elements. As a consequence, living in Rome becomes a daily exercise in urbane erudition and in aesthetic appreciation and attachment. This makes them experience a sense of loss when they leave Rome, and a sense of rediscovery when they return to her. In fact, one of their first acts upon return is to walk her quarters, streets, and piazze until they sense that they have psychologically claimed the city back. But the repeated satisfaction of desire comes at a cost. The cost is the loss of surprise, that agreeable characteristic of aesthetic life that derives from discovering something new or something anew. Satisfaction contradicts the essence of desire until the building is desired again. The paradoxical side of desire is that it desires it own end, its own death as desire. Satisfaction marks the fulfillment of desire, but also its termination. But the moment of satisfaction is a temporary ceasing of desire followed by a resumption of desire. Empirically, it seems that the goal of desire was not satisfaction, but rather the continuation of desire. Here the meaning of Plato's allegory of the pierced barrel and the futile attempts at filling it, obtains in full force.

As a contrasting reaction to the circular role of desire, some architects make the peculiar claim that their preferences are disinterested. Architectural disinterestedness, even in the Kantian sense, can be conceived as a particular state where the architect is ostensibly able to suspend and overcome the habitual attraction or repulsion of empirical architectural reality while calmly undertaking judgment. Such disinterestedness might be attainable, especially if one were to consider that satisfaction has more to do with the very formation of desire inside the architect's mind (subjective aesthetic judgment) rather than in the building itself (objective properties of buildings). Be that as it may, one is at pains to reconcile disinterestedness with architects' life-long engagement in judgment based on their demanding experience as makers of buildings and as aesthetic dwellers therein. Moreover, the very fact that architects surround themselves with sundry forms is a proof of their inexhaustible, definitely *interested*, and ever-restless desire for forms of artifice and to what they regard as good and beautiful in their art; and much of this is entwined with their emotional subjectivity. It is quite difficult to achieve disinterestedness if one conflates one's identity with one's work.

III

IDENTITY, CONFLICT AND CRITICISM

> *Aesthetic intensity offers an equivalent of war by providing an obdurate enemy – the image, the material, the ideal – to attack, subdue, and convert.*[26]
>
> James Hillman

Our previous discussion established the relationship between desire and the will-to-make and some aspects of architectural desire. Looking further into architects' psychology as image-makers, we now examine their personal identification with the images and forms they produce. This form of attachment, as we shall see, is one of the causes of their conflictual relationships, and their aggressive criticism of each other's work. Identity, conflict and criticism come to play a substantial role that predisposes them to cast an external architectural judgment – a role rooted in attachment to forms. Attachment implies a sense of belonging, which in turn calls forth notions of identity and commonality and their contrary notions of difference and exclusion. Architects develop a sense of belonging to countries, regions, cities, quarters, streets and houses. This sense of belonging occurs in part because of the accident of birth, and in large part because their aesthetic choices compel them to live within or to visit their favored architectures. The sense of place, or

6.4 The Albaicin quarter, Granada. *Source*: Photo by Author.

rather, the aesthetic sense for a place, and the sense of personal belonging are closely linked. An architect born in London may experience a stronger sense of architectural belonging in Granada and consequently associate his or her sense of personal belonging with that Spanish city. Architects also harbor belongings to architectural and artistic traditions whose forms they share and develop with other architects, thus forming movements of regional or international scope. As language is identity-forming so are forms and images; and this phenomenon is strikingly evident amongst the protagonists of visual culture.

Architects exert much thought and passion in order to establish their identities as image-makers. With the help of historians, they remember the stories of their predecessors – the kind of psychological phenomenon that J. Hillman might describe as their attempts to "find themselves and found themselves" in a story that they can claim as theirs, as in the images of a mythologized narrative. Some look at their past work with nostalgia, while others classify their life work into distinct periods ("pre" and "post") in order to explain that the changes in their architectural expressions followed a gradual evolution ascending toward an eminent dénouement. This need to historicize their personal work, illustrates the architects' repeated attachment and detachment from the forms that they make available to their consciousness as makers and dwellers. As students of history, architects scrutinize carefully the historian's unveiling of architectural composition – naming it, for example, Vignolesque, Serlian, Corbusian, or Lutyenesque – and other architects' personal manners of making and their elements. Manner (or the Italian: *maniera*), as desired image, is then mimetically claimed by architects who naturally intend on developing their own architectural manners. By mimetically repeating desired images, architects work with the foundational images of their art. They are helped in this endeavor by their analysis of architectural composition which allows them to unveil and claim the images made by another, especially when that other is considered a master. Agreeable though this unveiling and claiming may be, they also entail unintended conflicts, because many architects merge their understanding of *making*, with their understanding of *being*. In this sense, every act of making, of building, includes a partial auto-transformation of its author. The architect's *cogito* might very well be rendered as: I build, therefore I am. But it can also be extended to say: what I build is part of me. When architects justify their buildings, they are justifying their personae.

The scope of this identity-attachment is immense, and ranges from associating one's name to an architectural tradition, to a style or manner, and even to the act of attaching one's name physically to a building. For example, while undertaking the archaeological work for his *envoi* from Rome, French architect Léon Vaudoyer (1785) sought to make his name endure by carving it on the Ionic arcade of the Theatre of Marcellus.[27] More recently, the autograph of American architect Richard Meier was incised on the parapet wall of his pavilion to house the Ara Pacis, the altar to Augustan peace. In the first case, narcissistic naming merged personal identity, with a tradition of forms. In the second case, authorship of form becomes a narcissistic identification with form. Michelangelo and Le Corbusier offer two opposing attitudes in this respect. The first, systematically destroyed his

6.5 Theatre of Macellus, Léon Vaudoyer's inscription, Rome.
Source: Photo by Author.

6.6 New Pavilion for the Ara Pacis, Architect's signature, Rome. *Source*: Photo by Author.

preparatory drawings,[28] while the second was an obsessive archivist of even his most minor drawing studies.

Because they amalgamate selfhood, ownership of forms, and the theories that explain and defend these forms, many architects tend to conflate their personal imaginal preferences with the essence of their art. As we noted before, architects are self-sculpting aesthetes. They simultaneously sculpt and transform their buildings as well as their personae. Many of them, and consequently many of their patrons, come to regard their buildings as vanity objects, like the books they read, the wines they drink, the cars they drive, the clothes they wear, or the paintings they own. Much time and effort are spent in maintaining this image, or the "look" as is fashionable to say. The conflation between their creations and their personalities explains, in part, their deep divisions and antagonisms; and this has a direct effect over their judgment. There also follows the will to promulgate the preference of some buildings over others, the will to prevent other buildings from being realized, or to impede opposing theoretical positions from gaining currency.

Antagonism operates as an intense level of conflict, through a mechanism where identity is confirmed through opposition, where one side must prevail. With antagonism, all becoming comes to a halt. Each position remains identical to itself. This explains, in part, the current reluctance of architects to debate each other. Conflict, on the other hand, cannot be reduced to separate and opposed identities.

It is a complex array of tensions resulting from interlaced segments of beliefs that do not necessarily or forcibly involve the identities of architects. It is possible for architects, for example, to engage in a dispute while sharing many elements of each others' beliefs and each others' personalities, as we shall see in the case of Blondel and Perrault for example.[29] What complicates the situation in the minds of architects, is that there are not always undeniable limits and distinctions within their personalities that correspond to the architectural forms that they espouse. There is always something in the building endeavor about which architects agree. There is always something in the building endeavor about which architects can say: "yes, this is me", or, "no, this is not me". This was perhaps Hegel's meaning when he said that we cannot trenchantly say when we are no longer responsible for our voluntary acts.[30] This might have also been Sartre's meaning when he said that we are still "responsible for that which we did not choose".

Floating within the current relativist flux of modern society are clusters of ideologies replete with their aesthetic predilections, hierarchical arrangements, disputes, and tribal alliances. In effect, architectural ideological antagonisms may be characterized by a kind of nationalism where architects defend their positions, wielding weapons and bearing shields on the ramparts of their ego-centric city. As in war, architectural antagonisms have their provocations, battlefields, entrenched camps, avant-gardes, arrière-gardes, strategists, demagogues, priestly castes, soldiers, deserters, and scapegoats. They also have their aggression, wounds, sacrifice, victories, defeats, and intermittent periods of lull. This is the often-noted martial aspect of architectural ideological antagonisms, exemplified especially in the confrontational form of debates.[31] The image-maker becomes the image-slayer. Because architects are attached to their buildings as their personal acts of will, and because their attachment to their preferred buildings are insistently bound up with their narcissistic projections onto the world they build, conflicts are inherently present even before they begin architectural judgment, and even if they profess to hold no pre-conceived notions.[32] To claim then, as some do, that architects judge without prejudice is the worst prejudice of all. Whether in debates, in architectural jury rooms, or in critical writings, architectural conflicts usually begin with a patriotic extolling of each side's architectural theory. Such exchanges usually confirm identities, but they do so through provocation and incitement.[33] Not surprisingly, an architectural identity might be discovered precisely because of opposition to the forms architects hold dear. Sometimes, because identity can be understood as a confirmation of one's positions in comparison to an exteriority, to being external to a certain set of beliefs, architects may define their identities too rigidly in order to oppose other identities. Conversely, other architects initiate conflicts as a practical quest for auto-affirmation.

Identity, conflict, and antagonism, begin early in the architects' careers as students. In fact, it is in architectural schools where identity and conflict are initially incited into activity by criticism and mimetic rivalry presented as educational methods. (We shall return to René Girard's notion of mimetic rivalry in a moment.) The critical culture of the Salon, of which the architectural jury room is the raucous descendent, had already paved the way for these contentious engagements. The will and ability of the architect, as a free rational agent, to make a building in one manner also implies the power, the choice to have made this building in a different manner. Criticism moves within the space available between the different possibilities of choice. It emerges from reflections about the freedom to build based on a will, and the power to realize buildings. Consequently, criticism stems from an internal struggle between what architects expect and what they actually see. The more of their desired projects and projections are realized, the less critical they become. It follows that criticism as judgment is tenaciously tied to desire.

Criticism displays two aspects. One is potentially affirmative, the other is definitely injurious. When deploying its affirmative side, criticism promotes certain positions and explicitly demands that architects and the public endorse the critic's position, or the architect's position with whom the critic agrees. Criticism sees itself as a guide for architectural formation, practice, and the formation of the public's taste. It also has a cognitive dimension in that it aims to persuade by explaining the intentionality behind buildings through structured analysis.[34] In its best applications, criticism can play a purificatory role, a catharticon, in that it concerns reflection on three levels: the work itself, the knowledge of the critic, and both in relationship to an experience of building or to a projected experiential condition of building. Criticism can be systematic, but it is not a philosophy. It is an investigative (analytical) system for buildings searching for and revealing their consistencies or inconsistencies measured against a view of their status within the architectural discipline at large. As a frequent companion of humanism, criticism can be an expression of democratic freedom, questioning both received forms as well as new forms. It can also be turned to a kind of resistance against an established orthodoxy. The presence of theory enhances the utility of criticism, because both can serve the aims of practical reason. *But criticism is not the accomplishment of architecture or architectural theory, it is one of the conditions for architectural judgment.*

When deploying its injurious side, criticism allies excessive pride with a mathematical analysis of the architectural image followed by condemnation. Injurious criticism approaches architectural analysis as means to expose, but in the sense of denuding flagrant flaws. Injurious criticism exhibits seething discordance, dissenting rants, differing stances, separative postures, antagonistic demeanor, haughty condescendence, and predatory comportments. Benefiting from the freedom available within democratic space, this kind of criticism can be turned into a generalized denigration of the beliefs of opposing groups, and a systematic derision of the other. Here, criticism becomes judgment in the sense of violent antagonism, one position rejecting or eliminating the other in its totality. Criticism, in this sense, is the artistic equivalent of societal reciprocal violence. When veiled under an academic robe criticism, though an offensive intellectual gesture, takes its place alongside the respectful dialogue that derives from classical humanism.[35]

Moreover, beyond destroying the validity of a building, one particular kind of injurious criticism also seeks to generate feelings of inadequacy, of deficiency in the criticized architect. It can also be a terrible condemnation, an excommunication of the architect's prime identity: the persona. Criticism then becomes a subversive game of mutual derision that derails reasoned judgment by erecting emotionally charged obstacles between persons and groups. "We criticize the faults of others", said François de La Rochefoucauld in his usual blend of wit and irony, "more out of pride than goodness; and we criticize them not so much to correct them as to persuade them that we are free from their faults". Regrettably, much architectural criticism is not necessarily offered with a constructive end in mind.

On the other hand, corrective advice is always an integral part of teaching, and of benevolent exchanges of ideas carried out in dialogue between architects who mutually examine each other's beliefs. Naturally, it shows the most promising results when it is given and received with intelligence and good will. This is why some architects, rare though they are, are convinced that to accept negative criticism as advice leads to ameliorating the quality of their buildings. But when injurious criticism is adopted as an educational method, the results are often quite destructive, especially considering the mimetic setting of the classroom where students learn by imitating their teachers like they imitated their parents before. The situation is not altogether different in the profession. Faced with criticism, architects exhibit three kinds of reactions. They may resort to what Sigmund Freud called "defensive rationalization" in their goal of countering the criticism by justifying the validity of their designs. They might hasten to explain that their building is a result of complex reasoning bringing together, painfully, their will to design in relation to the will of their patron, in addition to historical precedents, and a multitude of constraints ranging from site demands to budgetary limitations. Or they may well revolt with indignation and return the critic's attack, using one injurious response from the répertoire of damaging responses permissible under law.

There is a harsh circularity to this predicament that frames the architect's psychology from the early years of education to the mature years of practice. This circularity is fed by two mutually conspiring attitudes that architects themselves instituted. First, is their terrible pursuit of antagonism deriving from their expressing their identities as exclusory of other identities. Second, is the conflation between their egotistical personalities and their identification with architectural forms at their disposition.

Might this appalling situation be alleviated if they were to consider that these forms are not theirs to own, though they are theirs to use? Might the analogy help if one were to suggest that architecture is no more the property of one single architect than language is the property of one single poet? Might this state of affairs be improved if architects, with their full knowledge of their active role as transforming agents in culture, were to consider that the forms they produce, and the forms for which they are stewards, belong to culture at large?

IV

WOUNDING IDENTITIES AND MIMETIC RIVALRY

We are all brothers, but it is difficult to establish who is Cain and who is Abel.[36]
Enzo Biagi

When the notion of architecture as a strictly subjective representation came to eclipse that of architecture as an expression of a collective will to make and to dwell in nature and the city, architects multiplied their palaces of desire. Architects celebrate their desire for forms. They exalt the power of their desires, arriving at times to a kind of idolatry. In fact they engage in a double idolatry, by idolizing the work of a chosen master or model, and by idolizing this master or model as a persona. Much of this desire relates to their double imitative or mimetic relationship to each other and to their buildings, recalling our earlier note of the architect's merging between making and being. Aesthetic culture, since the commentaries of Plato and Aristotle's *Poetics* passing through the imitative theory developed from the fifteenth through the nineteenth centuries, and beyond, has treated with considerable usefulness the preeminent aspects of mimesis or imitation. To achieve excellence writers imitated the work of paradigmatic figures, painters imitated nature in her products (*natura naturata*, e.g. the human body) and in her laws (*natura naturans*, e.g. the proportional relationships between parts of the human body), while, in addition to all of these, architects also imitated natural law (e.g. proportions, tectonics) as well as the time-honored principles of a tradition. Imitation provides the intellectual discipline for artistic formation, and the theoretical foundations which enable the artist or architect to unify the best aspects of precedents with the expressions of personal invention. Imitation is the way in which the individual learns and appropriates culture, adapts to it,

6.7 Mimesis: The Boy and the Castle. *Source*: Photo by Norman Crowe.

and participates in it. Imitation allows for intersubjectivity between autonomous minds, while forming a bridge between the individual and society. This is the good side of imitation.

Due acknowledgement, however, should be given to René Girard for having drawn attention to a hitherto neglected side of mimesis or imitation – a conflictual side based on desire. According to Girard, the "very substance of human relations, whatever their nature, is made of mimetism".[37] One of the fundamental axioms of human culture, in Girard's thinking, is desire in general and mimetic desire in particular.[38] We desire an object less for what it is, and more because we imitate someone else's desire – whom we take as a model – who makes, covets or possesses that same object.[39] The model and the ideas for which the model stands become "mediators" by means of which we seek to attain our goals. Contrary to Freud's object–subject duality, this relationship is triangular, for we have:

1. two subjects, one of whom is a model to the other;
2. imitation;
3. the desired object.

In the early part of this chapter, we discussed desire from a Freudian point of view, in which a desired building, or object, exerts a strong influence on the architect who in turn wishes to imitate it, to own it, and even to identify with it. The following discussion presents an opposing point of view, one in which desire is inwardly, subjectively generated through imitation, and a mediating model.

Applying a Girardian perspective to the psychology of architects – a subject not covered in his writings – mimetic desire concerns more than the desired building and it is not limited to the desiring architect. Desire for Girard resides in the model, or the mediator of our desires.[40] In this sense, architecture itself, the architectural discourse, and the very personalities of architects are all mediating agents of architects' desires for forms. Architects not only imitate each other's works, they also mimetically desire the buildings other architects have desired. They desire each other's desires, and this precisely is the reason for which imitation is contagious. A case in point is Lord Burlington and William Kent mimetically desiring the work of Inigo Jones who in turn had mimetically desired the work of Andrea Palladio. Moreover, architects desire the "same ways" of pursuing other architects' desired buildings. One could consider from this point of view some of the landmarks that have strongly marked the education of the architect for centuries. The illustrated architectural treatise, the sketches in the architect's intimate carnet de voyage, the capriccio that assembles favored buildings in a fictive setting, and the ever-present architectural photograph, all of them fulfill admirable pedagogical purposes on account of their formative roles. All of them sustain architectural desire. More precisely, these pedagogical methods illustrate the extent to which the architect's formation is largely a mimetic appropriation of other architect's desires for forms. Moreover, architects mimetically absorb their models' non-architectural preferences. This mimetism could range from a predilection to certain kinds of music or literature, to occasionally copying the vestments or even the vocal accents of admired model-architects. Consider for example the substantial number of architects who appropriated Le Corbusier's unmistakable bow tie and thickly framed glasses. Assuming a part of the appearance in some way gives the borrower the impression of having achieved a greater fullness as an architect, acquiring the mantle and the distinguished aura of an admired figure.[41]

While desire is mimetic, it is not always in a negative sense, nor does it necessarily lead to conflict. In fact the model might serve to focus the previously vague aspirations of the imitator,[42] while intense desire spurs the effort to transform these vague aspirations into a clearer vision based on the model's exemplary work. The model itself can be collective or individual. It can comprise an entire architectural tradition or concern the work of one single architect. It also pertains to contemporary as well as past exemplars. One instance of a collective model is the *Querelle des anciens et des modernes* with its two main protagonists François Blondel and Claude Perrault. From the historical perspective of the late seventeenth century, Blondel, operating under the Renaissance definition of the classical, held the view that the ancients were unsurpassable. To the contrary, the burgeoning modern scientific outlook of Perrault, transposed into architecture, led him to believe that surpassing the ancients was indeed possible and desirable. Nonetheless, both men held strongly to the rationalist belief that the authority of the ancients cannot be accepted blindly. The authority of the antique does not prevail over the authority of reason. It is probable, however, against the insistence of many of his contemporaries regarding the unequalled excellence of the ancients, that Perrault felt a sense of rivalry toward ancient architects. This rivalry is mimetic because the object–model is the same, for notwithstanding their theoretical differences, Blondel and Perrault did not question classical architecture as a modern practice.[43]

When the model is individual it concerns a single architect whose formal preferences are imitated by admirers who shape their own architectural desires by desiring the same forms, and even the same architectural mannerisms. The imitator's motives can range from the simple wish for learning and betterment, to a profound existential dissatisfaction with personal architectural expression, or an outright envy of the model's talents. The model's reactions also vary. Girard borrows Gregory Bateson's notion of double-bind[44] in which the teacher, or the model, explicitly tells the imitator: "you can imitate me", but the teacher also tacitly says: "only you cannot surpass me". The imitated model can be flattered but he or she can also reject the imitator because the imitated model developed a sense of identity and ownership with his or her forms, which the imitator was now attempting to wrest away. It is likely that the model wishes to elicit a mixture of admiration and envy on the part of the imitator. It is even possible that the model-teacher harbors a desire to see frustration on the part of the imitator–follower who has troubled the waters into which the narcissistic model had been gazing. Tragedy is not far. In this case, the rejected follower abandons the desire to imitate *that* master, or model, while retaining the "violence" of the rejection. Subsequently, both the model and the imitator undertake to rest away from each other the object of their common desire. Mimetic desire now becomes mimetic rivalry, leading to mutual attempts to

6.8 Cain and Abel, Gustave Doré.

discredit the other, as the actions of both sides gradually increase in resemblance. Rivalry and then antagonism become unavoidable; and when mimetic rivalry turns into pure antagonism, the object of this rivalry becomes less important than personal animosity. Hostility becomes cumulative and more acute because of architects' association of their personal identity with their vocational identity. Here, criticism becomes the artistic substitute for societal violence. Criticism becomes a mimetic violence, a form of mutual psychological lapidation.

This rivalry is mimetic because it is a confluence between two sets of egotistical phenomena: the architects' personal identification with preferred forms, and their imitation of their rivals' successes in order to achieve similar success, or at least claim primacy. Mimetic rivalry often "characterizes the desire of the imitator because it already characterizes the model's desire".[45] The fact that the imitator and the model desire the same object is no guarantee that they will enjoy an untroubled relationship. Because it revolves around architecture as the mediator of their desires, mimetic rivalry, uncomfortably demonstrates to architects that their discord is only partially attributable to ideological differences, and that some of main causes for discord reside within themselves. And one main reason for discord stems from architects' aggressive "thirst for exclusive possession" – in Girard's terms. Such may have been, to cite a few examples, the reasons behind the rivalry between Hadrian and Appollodorus (if one is to believe Dio Cassius), or Michelangelo's maliciousness towards his rivals, or the plotting regarding the commission for the extension of the Louvre between the Perrault brothers against Bernini, the acute rivalry that played out in Rome between Bernini and Borromini, and the deep animosities between the leaders of modernism.[46] The crisis exacerbates the desire for appropriation of forms or fame amongst mimetic rivals, and the phenomenon becomes viciously circular, being continuously fueled by the renewed momentum of desire itself. When it migrates to the group, it can turn into what Hobbes called the "war of all against all". That is if it remains unchecked by external forces capable of neutralizing conflicts, or diffused by the presence of an expiatory scapegoat who substitutes for the actual conflict or antagonism.[47] An illustration of this phenomenon was the "scapegoating" of ornament on the way toward a collective sentencing of the classical tradition.

Next, mimetic rivals come to consider themselves as equals. They are equals who are fascinated by one another, studying each other's work carefully, and vying for the same front row position facing the collective mirror of society. This, fascination, however, is rarely admitted; for, contrary to children, adults are embarrassed to admit that they model themselves on others. It is easier for architects to admit that they imitate the work of architects from the past than to admit that they imitate the work of their living contemporaries. When contemporary architects claim that they imitate no one, it is probable that they are hiding their desire to imitate in order to claim complete independence and autonomy as inventors of form. In this way they can be faithful to the myth of the modernist genius, the romantic individualist creator who invents new objects from nothing, and who walks in no one's shadow. This shows the ambiguity between architects' natural inclination to imitate an exemplar, because humans are imitative beings, and their declared self-sufficiency and claim to make new buildings *ex nihilo*, out of nothing.

When the antagonism is between groups with different ideologies, the enemy is the other, the "stranger outside" the architectural clan. An individual's or a group's identity is confirmed by opposing the other. Exterior influences are at once excluded and seen as subordinate to the group's ideology. Evidence for this is seen in the widespread use of the language of otherness in architectural circles today, where the encounter of one ideology with another is usually employed in order to assert the pre-eminence of one over the other. Advocates of one ideology judge other ideologies by the tenets of their own while projecting the worst expectations on the other – on "them". When the antagonism is within the same group, the enemy is the "stranger inside", vying for a higher position within a pre-established hierarchy and using a commonly held ideology as a basis for dispute. Here, even the smallest difference, or what S. Freud[48] called the "narcissism of small differences", becomes the justification for ideological divisions and fratricidal antagonisms among members who share much of the same beliefs.

The winner achieves a temporary satisfaction in having prevailed over an architectural argument, or prevented another architect from obtaining a desired commission. Satisfaction might soon be succeeded by an empty feeling of victory, or eventually by a renewed search for yet another clash followed by another expected win. The winner might very well think that it was Mars who triumphed, whereas in all probability the victor was Cain. Regrettably, the love for architecture does not suffice to placate the odium between conflicting architects.

V

THE SHADOW AND THE WILL TO DIFFER

Mimetic rivals are linked by a strange kind of alliance – an alliance of silence. When psychological traits do not fit the self-image by which they prefer to be known, (e.g. envy, jealousy, rivalry, violence) individuals silently banish them into

6.9 Decapitated bust of Vitruvius, Viale di Villa Medici, Rome.
Source: Photo by Author.

a psychological space that psychologists call the shadow. And when architects bury (repress) their mimetic rivalries within the shadowy recesses of their personalities, they act in a similar way. Put differently, mimetic rivalry remains hidden for reasons that go beyond masking rivalry, because it contradicts the persona's ideal self-image in relation to the cultural values surrounding it. Sadly, repressing these qualities does not serve to eliminate them. It only conceals them from ordinary observation, and they become "subterranean" accumulations.[49] As Carl Jung, James Hillman, Ken Wilber, Robert Bly, and many others never tired to explain, the ego and the shadow are inseparable. That which is unacknowledged or admitted by the ego (e.g. the aggressiveness of certain emotions) invariably finds its exile in the shadow. The shadow, affirmed K. Wilber, "is not an affair between you and others, it is between you and you".[50] The shadow's effects are internal and external. They emerge in confrontation with the other precisely when qualities held by one individual or group are found to be in conflict with, or are incited by, qualities held by another individual or group. This is the case, for example, when personal identification with ideologies makes architects confront the qualities of their own ideology with the qualities of another. Ideological differences become personified, and the shadow side of individual psychologies then dramatically emerges and occupies the field of what was initially an ideological dispute.

When architects relentlessly and frenetically uphold difference, separateness, and their intellectual auto-centric autonomy at the expense of collectively shared aims, discord becomes inevitable. And this discord is achieved irrespective of ideological commonalities or divergence. Hyper-critical difference becomes a method[51] – a project that regards the practice of architecture as a methodological pursuit of ultra-individualism. Even inside a small group of architects who share the same ideology, the narcissism of small differences presents occasions to underline further differentiations. Small groups are then fragmented into even smaller units, leading eventually to a complete breakdown of any cohesive structure. This is one of the reasons why movements fail. In sharpening their politics of difference architects frequently overlook that opposition to other architectural identities is insufficient to form an identity of their own, although as mentioned earlier, opposition and judgment provoke or incite identity. Most importantly, the insistence on personifying difference with respect to judgment, sometimes makes architects overlook a fundamental constituent of judgment, namely, the ground upon which judgment is based. And clearly, that ground is informed by a theory of architecture concerning intrinsic and external criteria for judgment. Theoretical differences as valid bases for controversy become subordinate to the vanity of personal differences. All of this bears heavily on architectural judgment.

Nowhere is the architect's narcissistic determination to differ more evident than in public, in the midst of an audience. There, the architect must be understood as the illumined actor on stage, a constructed dramatic figure being at once subject and object, mediator of desire and the object of desire, exhibitionist and voyeur, judge and partisan, executioner and victim.[52] With the charisma of theatrical postures, with the art of clichégenic statements, architects deliver their sweeping judgments, exhibiting discriminating knowledge of the most arcane subjects, displaying a wide aesthetic culture and an appreciation of different aesthetic cultures. They demonstrate sensitivity to forms, proportions, materials, colors, and expand on visions of wide ecological breadth. They know the reasons for inclining columns and curving stylobates for the purpose of eurythmic adjustments. They can expertly contrast the proportions of the Doryphoros with those of Bernini's Apollo and Daphne, while describing the different aesthetic pleasures that derive from preferring one over the other. They are sensitive to the tenebrism of Caravagio and Juan de Ribera, and the contrapuntal inventions in Johann Sebastian Bach's fugues. With gastronomical delectation they worry about the temperature of a Saint-Emilion and the necessary breathing time for a Sassicaia. They speak with sharp erudition of the soothing effects of an Yquem following dinner as well as the architectural additions to the Château d'Yquem as it passed from the Sauvage d'Yquem family to the de Lur Saluces family in the late eighteenth century – through marriage. They are the masters of the rarified airs of stylish exchanges in art galleries displaying their taste for multiple genres of music, literature, poetry, theatre, and film. Yet, their laboriously cultivated aesthetic lives and their highly refined formal sensitivities do not suffice to restrain their angered Jupiterean gaze, their terrible penchant for discord, for petty self-absorption, unbridled self-aggrandizement, and the undervaluing of the work of other architects.[53] They desire fame, and enjoy being applauded for their contributions to culture and the culture of building, for their creativity, their originality, and the complex reasoning they undertook in order to achieve their admirable tours de force. They enjoy the authority of their own reflection in the mirror and vow to seduce the mirror itself. Above all, architects are authorities on themselves.

NOTES

1. II, 1,3, F. Granger (Tr.), (Harvard University Press, 1931).

2. *Treatise of Man*, XI.

3. Conflict and antagonism are here distinguished. The terms of a conflictual relationship are opposed, whereas those of an antagonistic relationship are contradictory. Inside one system of thought, it is possible for a conflict to be overcome. It is also possible that two positions may eventually become complementary once the conflict is overcome. But in antagonism, (Greek: *agon*) the clash will end only if one of the opponents disengages or looses the confrontation.

4. The literature concerning the psychology of aesthetic experience, the explanations and justifications of its diverse facets, occupied the attention of many scholars since the nineteenth century. Some of the principal figures include Robert Vischer, Wilhem Dilthey, Theodor Lipps, Conrad Fiedler, George Santayana, Benedetto Croce, Adolf Hildebrand, Alois Riegl, Wilhem Worringer, Jean-Paul Sartre, Martin Heidegger, Maurice Merleau-Ponty and others. Ranging from Arthur Schopenhauer's passive contemplation of form to Robert Vischer's active imputation of qualities onto form, termed *einfühlung* or empathy, these scholars' work aimed at establishing the psychological explanation as one of the foundations of art theory. Schopenhauer's passive contemplation has been articulated in his *The World as Will and as Idea* (1883), R. B. Haldane and J. Kemp (Tr.), (Routledge & Kegan Paul, 1950). See also D. Jacquette (ed.), *Schopenhauer, Philosophy and the Arts*, (Cambridge, 1996). For a survey of empathy theories, see K. Aschenbrenner and I. Isenberg (eds), *Aesthetic Theories: Studies in the Philosophy of Art*, (Englewood Cliffs, 1965); M. Beardsley, *Aesthetics from Classical Greece to the Present*, (1966), (University of Alabama Press, 1975); W. Tatarkiewicz, *A History of Six Ideas: An Essay in Aesthetics*, (Polish Scientific Publishers, 1980); R. Arnheim, *New Essays in the Psychology of Art*, (Berkeley, 1986); M. Barasch, *Theories of Art*, (Vol.III, Routledge, 1998). The self-indulgent/hedonist approach to aesthetic experience has been developed by G. Santayana in *The Sense of Beauty*, (1896). B. Croce's *Estetica come scienza dell'espressione e linguistica generale* (1902) proposed the notion that art is intuition and cognition. Related to the psychology of perception, the phenomenological approach presented the idea that human making has a metaphysical aspect. This was developed by M. Heidegger, *Poetry, Language, Thought*, A. Hofstadter (Tr.), (Harper and Row, 1971); and M. Merleau-Ponty, *Phénoménologie de la perception*, (1945), (Gallimard, 2002).

5. The notion of the will to make in general, meets Alois Riegl's notion of artistic will (*kuntswollen*), as well as Ernst Gombrich's will to form, or formative will, and Roberto Salvini's art intention. Riegl conceived of the artist being at once determined by the cultural *kunstwollen* as well as being a representative of it. This quasi-historical determinism was later contested by Gombrich and gestalt psychologists. It was also contested during Riegl's life time by Benedetto Croce who considered that art history is rather determined by the personalities of artists. Art history is a history of artists affirmed Leo Tolstoï who held that "geniuses do not derive one from another, they are absolutely independent one from another". According to Riegl, the term *kuntswollen* applies to a particular work of art, to a particular artist, to group of artists, or, at a larger scale, to the artistic orientation of a period or culture; the important element being the personal deliberate effort of the artist. Applied to architecture Riegl's *kuntswollen*, can be said to refer to the architect's purpose behind building, as well as the purpose of a larger architectural tradition within which architects may work. See E. Gombrich, *Art and Illusion*, (Princeton, 1960), and *The Sense of Order: A Study in the Psychology of Decorative Art*, (Oxford, 1979); A. Riegl, *Grammaire historique des arts plastiques*, É. Kaufholz-Messmer (Tr.), (Klincksieck, 1978); M. Olin, *Forms of Representation in Alois*

Riegl's Theory of Art, (University Park, 1992); R. Salvini, *La critique de la pure visibilité et du formalisme*, E. Dickenherr, C. Jatosti, A. Pernet, and A. Real-Charrière (Tr.), (Klincksieck, 2000).

6   "Mon premier mouvement d'esprit a été de songer au faire". Paul Valéry, *L'homme et la coquille*, in *Oeuvres*, I, (Pléiade, Gallimard, 1957), p. 891.

7   A contrary view was held by Spinoza who proposed that "It is … plain … that in no case do we strive for, wish for, long for, or desire anything, because we deem it to be good, but on the other hand we deem a thing to be good, because we strive for it, wish for it, long for it, or desire it". Benedict de Spinoza, *Ethics*, Part III, Prop. IX, (1677) Translated from the Latin by R.H.M. Elwes (1883), (MTSU Philosophy WebWorks Hypertext Edition © 1997).

8   According to Pierre Aubenque in *La prudence chez Aristote*, (Presses Universitaires de France, 1963), pp. 106–19; and Jean-Pierre Vernant in "Ebauche de la volonté dans la tragédie grecque", in *Mythe et tragédie en Grèce ancienne*, I, (Maspero, 1973), pp. 41–74, the translation of boulesis as will, applies primarily to later Greek texts, whereas other meanings of the term such as wish, desire, or intention relate more to Greek philosophy considered as a whole.

9   Aristotle, *De anima*, Bk. III, J.A. Smith (Tr.), Part 10. Italics added.

10 Spinoza, *op. cit.*

11 I. Kant, *The Critique of Practical Reason*, (1788) T. Kingsmill Abbott (Tr.), p. 7.

12 G.W.F. Hegel, *Phenomenology of Spirit*, A.W. Miller (Tr.), (Oxford, 1977), p. 108.

13 Such was A. Schopenhauer's pointed contention that the world has a double aspect, namely as will and as representation. *The World as Will and Representation* (1819), E.F.J. Payne (Tr.), (Dover, 1969).

14 In his *summa*, Aquinas underlined this distinction between the intelligible and sensuous good. "As the Philosopher" says (*Rhet*. i, 11), "concupiscence is a craving for that which is pleasant". Now pleasure is twofold, as we shall state later on (31, 3,4): one is in the intelligible good, which is the good of reason; the other is in good perceptible to the senses. The former pleasure seems to belong to soul alone; whereas the latter belongs to both soul and body: because the sense is a power seated in a bodily organ: wherefore sensible good is the good of the whole composite. " *Summa Theologica*, Article One, Literally translated by Fathers of the English Dominican Province, Second and Revised Edition, 1920.

15 A.C. Quatremère de Quincy, "Art", in *The Historical Dictionary of Architecture, Introductory Essays and Translation* by Samir Younés, (Papadakis, 1999).

16 *Des choses cachées depuis la fondation du monde*, (Grasset, 1978), p. 279.

17 On desire and action, see J. Lacan, "Subversion du sujet et dialectique du désir dans l'inconscient freudien", in Écrits, (Seuil, 1966); J. Baudrillard, *Le système des objets*, (Gallimard, 1968); A.F. Mackam, "The Incredibility of Rejecting Belief–Desire–Action Explanations", in *Philosophy of Science Association*, 2, (1982), pp. 117–26; M. Platts, "The Object of Desire", in *Critica*, 17(50), (1985), pp. 3–28.

18 Next to satisfaction and pleasure, one must reserve a place for the joy of practicing one's vocation, the joy of action that demands no other satisfaction than its own realization, its own production, its own affirmation. This is one difference between Spinoza's *conatus* (endeavor) and Nietzsche's will-to-power.

19 *Poetry, Language, Thought*, Albert Hofstadter (Tr.), (Harper and Row, 1971), pp. 145–51.

20 The desire for objects of art and architecture (as well as their plunder in war) in order to include them within the confines of a single enclosure constitutes a significant basis for the development of the museum and the museal mentality. In fact the museum as a receptacle for critically selected objects of desire bears strongly on socially instituted artistic judgment. Once this phenomenon is extended to the city, it correlates with desires to conserve buildings. These desires are then formulated in conservation policies and laws.

21 Many architects discuss the pleasures of taste in its effects on all the senses. They point to analogies between architectural composition and the compositions of culinary art and its effects on seeing, smelling and tasting. Some *pasticcieri* like Bartolomeo Scappi, the "secret cook of the popes" in sixteenth century Rome, occasionally composed architectural culinary fantasies, see, J. di Schino and F. Luccichenti, *Il cuoco segreto dei Papi*, (Gangemi, Rome, 2007). Few are the architects or artists, however, who have taken the analogy so close as the legendary French *pâtissier–architecte*, Antonin Carême. Carême produced his culinary compositions based on diligent architectural studies of the treatises of Vignola, Palladio, Durand, Ledoux, as well as architectural travel books such as those of Alexandre de la Borde, and architectural descriptive texts such as those of Krafft and Ransonnette. Seeing architecture and cooking as fine arts, he even proposed several architectural schemes for the embellishment of Paris and Saint Petersburg. He designed a project for a triumphal column in the Place du Carousel, presented proposals for the completion of the bridge of the Concorde, a triumphal arch for L'Etoile, and an idea for a new Opéra de Paris. Of his voluminous works, the most important for architecture is *Le Pâtissier pittoresque, précédé d'un traité des cinq ordres d'architecture* (1828), and parts of his posthumous five volume *L'Art de la cuisine française au XIXème siècle*, (1833–44), (Payot–Rivages, 1994). Georges Bernier's study *A. Carême (1783–1833). La sensibilité gourmande en Europe*, (Grasset, 1989), discusses Carême's influence on the "culinary revolution" in late eighteenth century Europe.

22 Sometimes these histories closely follow factual archaeological evidence. Other times, as was the case in J-J. Winckelmann's *History of Art*, they are written based on a fervent desire for an ideal, the Greek ideal, with a limited knowledge of archaeological evidence. Other times still, historical narratives give a false impression of historical happenings.

23 See our previous discussion of the technicist image in Chapter 4.

24 The formation and fomenting of architectural desire is inseparable from the formation and fomenting of desire within the consumer society in which the dazzling effects of photography constantly compel viewers to accept that they too can be like the figures they admire.

25 They were Raphael, Giuliano da Sangallo, Baldassare Peruzzi, Jacopo Sansovino (the latter won the competition for the early scheme without however completing the church), Antonio da Sangallo the Younger, Michelangelo, Giacomo della Porta, Francesco Borromini, Carlo Maderno (who completed the dome by 1634), and finally Alessandro Galilei who finished the *façade* in 1738.

26 J. Hillman, *A Terrible Love of War*, (Penguin, 2004), p. 213.

27 *Roma Antiqua. Grandi edifici pubblici*, (Edizioni Carte Segrete, 1992), pp. 192–9.

28 Vasari suggests that Michelangelo's reluctance to show his drawings stems from the fact that he did not want to reveal the astonishing effort that he expanded in order to complete his works. Before moving to Florence in 1518, Michelangelo burned his drawings in Rome, and shortly before his death he ordered his drawings burned. While most scholars agree that the drawings that can currently be attributed to

Michelangelo number around eight hundred, a recent study, echoing the scholarship around the turn of the twentieth century such as Bernard Berenson's, suggests that the number of drawings that can be attributed to Michelangelo with any degree of certainty is actually much smaller – around 200. See F. Zöllner, T. Popper, and C. Thoenes, *Michelangelo: Complete Works*, (Taschen, 2007).

29 See the Conclusion in this book.

30 G.W.F. Hegel, *Principle of Right*, S.W. Dyde (Tr.), First Section, Purpose and Responsibility, §115, (Batoche, 2001).

31 This parallels F. Nietzsche's notion of will to power, developed in his *Beyond Good and Evil* and *The Will to Power* – the view that all human relations may be interpreted in terms of power relationships intending on expanding their sphere of influence.

32 See Carl Jung's discussion of the psychology of projections in the *Essential Jung*, Anthony Storr (ed.), (Princeton University Press, 1983), pp. 87–125.

33 On identity and incitement, see A. Maalouf, *Les identités meurtrières*, (Grasset, 1998).

34 As a basis for criticism, analysis can be said to fall within three mutually supporting approaches: the formal, mimetic, and genetic. The formal approach examines the intelligibility of a building depending on its individual properties (structure, proportions, materials) and on common properties shared thematically with other buildings. Formal analytical methods can be interpretive (hermeneutics) or descriptive (composition and structure). The mimetic approach designates the capacities of architects to transform the empirical givens of a certain constructional condition, learning the wisdom of a tradition and at the same time contributing to that tradition. This approach places expression and representation as its central focus seeing the work of architecture itself as the reproduction of either expression or representation. Finally, the genetic approach examines the intelligibility of a work of architecture within the external conditions that gave it birth. Here, critical theory in its application to architecture, aimed at situating its discourse beyond the contents of traditional architectural theories in order to examine the position of the theoretical milieu itself, and in order to take a posture toward the ways in which this milieu compartmentalizes architectural expressions. This position practices theory as criticism, and adopts a negative stance toward the idea of system or a given, e.g. historicism, positivism, thus affecting the ways in which theory and history are written.

35 The phenomenon of "mean thought" has been surveyed in two recent studies: V. Azoulay and P. Boucheron, *Le mot qui tue. Une histoire des violences intellectuelles de l'antiquité à nos jours*, (Champ Vallon, 2009); and P. Drachline (ed.), *Le grand livre de la méchanceté*, (J'ai lu, 2009).

36 "Siamo tutti fratelli, ma è difficile stabilire chi sia Caino e chi sia Abele", my translation.

37 "La substance même des rapports humains, quels qu'ils soient, est faite de mimétisme". Girard, *Celui par qui le scandale arrive*, p. 8. My translation. Girard's reflections meet Lacan's conclusions that "man's desire is the desire of the other". See Lacan's "Of the Gaze as objet petit A", in *The Continental Aesthetics Reader*, C. Cazeaux (ed.), (Routledge, 2000), p. 540.

38 The notion of mimetic desire, mimetic rivalry and violence, is developed in René Girard's *La violence et le sacré*, (1972), (Pluriel, 1990), especially Chapter VI, "Du désir mimétique au double monstrueux", pp. 213–49; *Des choses cachées depuis la fondation du monde*, (Grasset, 1978); *To Double Business Bound*, (Johns Hopkins University Press, 1978); *Celui par qui le scandale arrive*, (Desclée de Brouwer, 2001); *La voix méconnue du réel*, (Grasset, 2002); *The Girard Reader*, James Williams (ed.), (Crossroads Herder, 2003),

pp. 9–62; *Les origines de la culture*, (Pluriel, 2004); and *Politiques de Cain*, Domenica Mazzù (ed.), (Desclée de Brouwer, 2004).

39 The words mimesis and imitation are used here in their most elementary sense of "making like", and not in the artistic sense of imitating nature, imitating the principles of a tradition, or stone imitating wood, etc.

40 R. Girard's "Les appartenances", in *Politiques de Cain*, pp. 19–33.

41 One wonders if it was it a mark of mimetic temperance or stylistic adaptability, that compelled architects to more readily adopt Le Corbusier's glasses and bow tie rather than Frank Lloyd Wright's hat, cape, and cane.

42 R. Girard, *Celui par qui le scandale arrive*, pp. 17–18.

43 Some of the most noted studies on the Querelle include: H. Rigault, *Histoire de la querelle des anciens et des modernes*, (Hachette, 1856); W. Folkierski, *Entre le classicisme et le romantisme*, (1925), (Champion, 1969); R. Saisselin, *The Rule of Reason and the Rules of the Heart*, (Press of Case Western Reserve University, 1970); W. Herrmann, *The Theory of Claude Perrault*, (Zwemmer, 1973); F. Fichet, *La Théorie architecturale à l'âge classique*, (Brussels, 1979); A. Pérez-Gómez, *Architecture and the Crisis of Modern Science*, (MIT Press, 1983); A. Picon, *Claude Perrault, La curiosité d'un classique*, (Picard, 1988).

44 G. Bateson, "Double bind", in *Steps to an Ecology of the Mind*, (Ballantine, 1969–72), pp. 271–8.

45 R. Girard, *Politiques* …, p. 24. My translation.

46 Michelangelo's denouncement of Baccio d'Agnolo's arcaded loggia that was to surround the octagonal drum of Santa Maria dei Fiori in Florence as a "cricket cage", sufficed to halt the construction of the project. The famous rivalry between Bernini and Borromini has been recently retold and elaborated in Jake Morrissey's *The Genius in the Design*, (Duckworth, 2005), and Nick Mileti's *Beyond Michelangelo*, (Xlibris, 2005). Rudolf and Margot Wittkower's study, *Born Under Saturn*, (Norton, 1963), of the professional rivalries, jealousies, and ambitions of artists from antiquity until the eighteenth century remains a useful source. For an account of the rivalry amongst figures of modernism see Tom Wolfe, *From Bauhaus to our House*, (Farrar Straus Giroux, 1981).

47 Girard called this phenomenon, the "victimizing mechanism" in *Des choses cachées* …, Chapter 3. The scapegoat closes Girard's notion of the fourfold mimetic mechanism: it begins with mimetic desire, develops into mimetic rivalry, becomes exasperated by a mimetic crisis that eventually necessitates some kind of sacrifice – a scapegoat. *Origines de la culture*, (Pluriel, 2004), pp. 61–102.

48 Sigmund Freud, *Moïse et le monothéisme*, (1939), (Gallimard, 1967). On the stranger from without and within, see Julia Kristeva, *Etrangers à nous mêmes*, (Gallimard, 1991), and Georg Simmel, *Sociologie, études sur les formes de la socialisation*, (Presses Universitaires de France, 1999).

49 I am indebted to psychologist John Paul Younés for references on the shadow side of psychology. See the comprehensive anthology *Meeting the Shadow*, C. Zweig and J. Abrams (eds), (Tarcher/Putnam, 1991), as well as J. Hillman, *The Dream and the Underworld*, (Harper & Row, 1979); S. Keen, *Faces of the Enemy*, (Harper & Row, 1986); R. Bly, *A Little Book on the Human Shadow*, (Harper & Row, 1988); C. Nebel, *The Dark Side of Creativity*, (Whitston Publishing, 1988).

50 K. Wilber, *The Spectrum of Consciousness*, (Theosophical Publishing House, 1977).

51 This may, but does not necessarily lead to J. Derrida's *différance* – his intentional misspelling of the French word *différence* as a punning play on the verb *différer* which can be rendered in English as to differ or defer. J. Derrida, *Speech and Phenomena and Other Essays on Husserl's Theory of Signs*, D. Allison (Tr.), (Evanston, IL, 1973).

52 See for example the transcripts of *The Charlottesville Tapes*, (Rizzoli, 1985); followed by *The Chicago Tapes*, (Rizzoli, 1986).

53 The culture of self-inflation has been clearly examined in C. Lasch, *Culture of Narcissism*, (Norton, 1991); R. Sennett, *The Fall of Public Man*, (Norton, 1992); and K. Wilber, *Boomeritis*, (Shambhalla, 2002).

PART TWO

INTERNAL CRITERIA FOR ARCHITECTURAL JUDGMENT

THE FACES OF CHARACTER

7
Architectural Expression: Form, Quality, and Purpose

> *An edifice, by its composition, expresses as on a stage that the scene is pastoral or tragic, that it is a temple or a palace, a public building destined for a specific use, or a private house. These different edifices, through their disposition, their structure, and the manner in which they are decorated, should announce their purpose to the spectator.*
>
> Germain Boffrand

When we first observe a building we begin by considering whether it coheres as a distinct and identifiable whole. We subsequently examine its composition,[1] the ways in which its volumes, its elements, and materials are arranged. We also note how the elements of the composition are tectonically joined. Composition and tectonics display to us how the building is made. Next, we observe how the building meets a street alignment, how it turns a corner, how it inflects, how it helps to enclose a square, and the hierarchical relationship it has with adjacent buildings. Scrutinizing the façades we can imagine the building's plans and sections, the disposition of rooms, and the sequence in which they may be arranged. We can imagine the utility that the building fulfills. We observe the openings, the moldings, the cornice, the roof, and their proportional relationships. Afterwards, we make mental comparisons to other similar buildings, noting their commonalities, their differences, and their propriety to their context. But this is half of the observation. The other half pertains to how all these elements and their qualities convey to our understanding the building's chief property: its character, and whether this character suits our assumption and expectation of what the building's purpose may be. Architectural expression invites judgment. We judge whether the purpose of a library, a market, a school, or a house has been properly expressed by the architect because we expect each building to have its own identity and because we understand identity to mean, at once, something unique and something commonly shared by buildings of the same kind. This, in brief, is one possible sequence of observations that relates our conceptual understanding of architecture in general, with the empirical experience of examining one particular building.

7.1 Rome from the Gianocolo. *Source*: Photo by Author.

Inherent in these observations is the dual understanding that buildings are composed and that this composition amounts to an expression, a distinct character that makes the building's purpose evident. To modify the composition is to modify the character. Composition pertains to the methods with which architectural form is arranged, involving combination, disposition, diminution, exaggeration, regularity, irregularity, repetition, unity, variety, accordance, contrast, proportions, and dimensions. Character concerns such essential qualities that render a building civic, domestic, grand, modest, elegant, serene, heavy, solid, light, or bold. Composition and tectonics display to us *how* a building is made, while character expresses the *purpose* for which a building is made. *Composition serves character, and character expresses the building's public or private purpose – what writers in the Enlightenment called: the destination of an edifice.* Through the matured experience of cities over millennia, the articulation of public buildings: temples, churches, libraries, theatres, courthouses, was clearly distinguished from the articulation of private buildings: the house, the townhouse, the shop, the villa. This clear hierarchy of public and private buildings – not only in scale and in dimension, but also in architectural character – is evident, for example, when overlooking Rome from the Gianicolo. Character denotes a building's identity, its commonalities or differences with buildings of the same kind. Donato Bramante's tempietto at San Pietro in Montorio in Rome and Gunnar Asplund's rotonda in the Stockholm Public Library share a common typology (a tholos), but their characters differ markedly because the purpose of the first is that of a martyrium, while the purpose of the second is that of a library.

7.2 Tempietto at San Pietro in Montorio, Donato Bramante, Rome, 1502.
Source: Photo by Author.

7.3 Stockholm Public Library, Gunnar Asplund, 1928.
Source: Photo by Michael Lykoudis.

Character bears the imprint of the architect's idiosyncracies and their interactions with local and specific contexts or with the larger visual norms of a region or nation. It may be imposed on a city or a region as when the idealism of the academic tradition introduced massive public buildings of intense uniformity irrespective of the pre-existing local character, or when colonialism imposes a foreign aesthetic irrespective of a given national architectural character(s). Regional character may even become anonymous and almost disappear as when standardized technologies apply their building productions to every country regardless of local architectural characters and material conditions. Character can also be a performance. Because of its analogy with the human character and facial expressions, architectural character is "performed" as if the city were a theatre and the buildings were the actors in a civic play.

Denis Diderot's dialogue dedicated to the paradoxical life of the actor[2] can, with a certain degree of analogy, be applied to the paradoxical life of the architect. Using their own bodies as their instruments for expression, good actors are capable of expressing an emotion they do not feel and convince others of the truth (the artistic truth or fiction) of their expression. Analogically, good architects are capable of expressing the proper character of an edifice; but their own personae are one step removed from that edifice. It is true that architecture is a form of body, as Leon Battista Alberti persuasively argued, but this form of body can have two purposes: it can be its own purpose, and it can serve a purpose other than itself. Architects, as we saw in Chapter 5, are profoundly conscious of their selves in their buildings. They may even equate the purpose of building with the purposes of their self-expression. But like the actors who put aside their personae in order to express another persona, so might architects attempt to put aside their selves in order to realize a patron's private mausoleum or a city's public library. In general, one might say that the more public or civic the building is, the less likely is the architect to use it as a vehicle for self-expression. Even though the architect is responsible for most of the building's composition, and this is especially evident when architects are called upon to express a building's civic purpose with propriety, architectural character is not the sole property of the architect. When architecture serves a civic purpose it includes and transcends the aims of the patron and those of the architect. Qualities that are symbolic of civic, religious, artistic, or moral purposes come to be associated (rightly or wrongly) with architectural forms as these forms are being elaborated by architects and builders, patrons and citizens; and as these forms are passed on to the following generations. At times, such desired qualities are even incised on the friezes of palaces as in Federico di Montefeltro's Palazzo Ducale in Urbino,[3] or above the portals of courthouses, theatres, and schools.

The three tasks: to express a civic purpose, to express a patron's private purpose, and the architect's self-expression, need not necessarily be contradictory, and one of the architect's most delicate tasks resides in knotting together, in overcoming, or at least in reconciling the tensions resulting from this paradox. As we shall see, these concerns converge on the skilled arrangement and alliance of forms that we call architectural character; and this character is composed with a certain psychology and is perceived with a certain psychology. It permeates the rational choice of form in serving civic purposes, on the one hand, and on the other, the critical manifestation of selfhood, or even the gracious effacement of the self. As a corollary to Alberti's affirmation that architecture is a form of body, one might add that this form of body is governed by a certain psychology, by a certain character, by a certain countenance. Naturally, the relationship between the expressions of the face and those of the façade, or those of the body and the building, is only analogical and does not imply a direct resemblance. Just like facial countenance expresses a state of mind, so does the façade analogically express a countenance of the civic or private realms evoking an array of impressions and interpretations to which we attach a name or an adjectival equivalent whether in praise, in disparagement, or even with caricatural intent.

Because naming allows us to call forth an object, a site, or a building's essential quality, it also expresses our reactions to buildings as we respond to qualities that we perceive in them, or qualities that we project onto them. For this reason we use a psychologizing language in order to describe the impression made on our minds, on our aesthetic sensibilities, by a building's personality. Buildings may be *majestic* and *sublime* like the pyramids of Giza; *solid* and *massive* like the Colosseum in Rome. They may possess *commodious* residential quarters and *delightful* gardens, like the Generalife in Granada. They may be *weighty* and *commanding*, like the Palazzo Farnese at Caprarola; *grand* and *sublime* like the Duomo in Florence; *modest*, like the farmer's house in the country side; *imposing* like the Palazzo Pitti in Florence; *stately*, like the Palazzo Panfili in Rome; *tenebrous* and *forbidding* like Piranesi's carceri; *tranquil* and *still* like the Taj Mahal; *somber* like Lenin's Mausoleum; *oppressively big* like the skyscraper, or *oppressively small* like the low ceilings within offices in skyscrapers. Rooms can be *vast* and *magnificent*, like the Sala del Maggior Consiglio in the Palazzo Ducale of Venice; *elegant* and *opulent*, like the Galerie des glaces in Versailles; *small* and *intimate* like a bedroom in a country cottage; or *cold* and *minimalist* like the interior of Mies van der Rohe's Barcelona Pavilion.[4]

We also extend this psychologizing language to tectonic elements like walls, arches, columns and architraves, as well as to ornament. For example, in delimiting a public realm (a city) or a private realm (a villa) walls can be associated with safety. The gates in a city's walls assume either a welcoming or repulsing aspect; and when entering the city's gate, a citizen finds identity and security in familiar streets, squares, and buildings. By way of custom, identity and security come to be associated with the city's architectural characters, even if these characters were not necessarily intended for that reason. Architectural elements made of different materials, proportions and ornaments, come to be associated with different social classes depending on the rarity of materials, their nobility, or their modesty. Tectonic elements too have their associative characters. Columns, for example, have long been associated with gender; and when tall arches separate a church's nave from the crossing, they retain their former associations with military triumph and acquire the symbolism of triumph over death especially when the crossing is spanned by a dome that, in turn, comes to symbolize the heavens. Vegetal ornamental motifs, papyrus, acanthus, lily, corn, or tobacco leaves, gain a variety of references ranging from funereal associations to those related to the fertility of the land.

When compared to the figural forms of painting and sculpture architectural forms are truly abstract. A dominant volume in a house contains a large salon, roofs are raised high and built on an incline in order to shed water, while trabeation and arcuation are two ways of spanning an opening in a wall while carrying an upper load. And yet because of our anthropomorphic projections on all the forms that surround us – a much larger role than the psychology of empathy – we project emotions onto the most abstract forms, and we even expect them to express shades of emotion. Many of these projections take into account the standpoint of the observer, and in order for our understanding to be more comprehensive we need to account for the standpoint of the maker, the architect. Indeed, we are compelled to ask: if the destined character of an edifice was intended to cause a certain impression, then was this impression analogically felt by the architect? If the act of building a family mausoleum results from associating architectural and sculptural forms and qualities with commemorated moral qualities, and if grief is a significant companion to the surviving members of the family, was Michelangelo himself grieving when he built the Medici tombs and the sculptures in San Lorenzo? Conversely, did François Blondel feel elation when he built the triumphal arch of the Porte Saint-Denis in order to celebrate the victories of Louis XIV on the Rhine and the Franche-Comté? Associating architectural form with ideas, with emotions, and their verbal expressions in a psychologizing language, form part of a larger set of associations that we will explore in the next three chapters from the standpoint of the maker and the observer. For good or for ill, architects and observers associate the characters of buildings, as well as their tectonic components and ornaments, with a host of factors that include mythico-religious symbolism, the imitation of nature in her laws (*natura naturans*), the idea of the spirit of the age, political content, or private taste. By contrast, other architects and observers associate character with building rationality or with purely formalist intent. All of these associations pertain to reconciling our experience of architecture either with a set of received meanings or with meanings that we project anew.

"In what style do you build"? is a question frequently asked of architects today. This question does not always receive a welcome response as some architects consider it to be the wrong approach to their art. They invariably explain that there is so much more to architecture than style; or that they do not approach architecture stylistically; or that styles are expressions of the past that have now been superseded and that their architecture is consequently beyond style; or that style is what other architects do, and so on. Architects seek the public's approval, but at the same time, they wish the public to understand their art in the same way(s) they see it. A more apt question might be for architects to ask of themselves: *what should be the proper character for a given building?* Or to place the question within a broader context: *what should be the type, the character, and the style for a given building depending on its civic purpose or its private purpose?* But a more difficult question to ask of architects is: what is more important, *that architecture is the expression of civic culture* or *that architecture is the architect's instrument for self-expression?* Some architects believe that this is a false choice, others openly state that their personal expression as artists is more important, while other architects firmly believe that architecture as a civic art is more important than architecture as personal expression. The latter group affirms that personal expression is inevitable; that it accompanies every work of human making; and that architecture serves at once the interests of the private citizen as well as the larger interests of the polity as a whole: the civic realm. Architectural practice, in the final analysis, emerges as a threefold task addressing the civic realm, the private realm of the patron, and the self-expression of the architect. Herein lies the paradoxical side of the architect's life as an image-maker. But architectural character is no more the invention of one single architect than language is the invention of one single individual. It is a collective invention of many minds that emerges from a place and participates in the broad architectural qualities of this place while sharing many commonalties with other places. In exceptional circumstances certain architects produce unique expressions (e.g. Antonio Gaudì, Frank Gehry), but because of their very uniqueness, they do not participate in building the conventions necessary for architectural character to be established.

As a collective invention character designates the most expressive face(s) of architecture. Its scope, or range, falls between the private (or vernacular) and the civic (or public), while the private and the civic themselves contain their own ranges extending from the most simple to the most elaborate. Character concerns the ways in which buildings come to be endowed with their own distinctive physiognomy, their own identity, and the ways in which physiognomy and identity are diffused by local conventions and larger traditions. Character is shaped by the consecrated use of form that we call convention.[5] *Character also qualifies the region from which it emerges, within which it thrives, and the elements that it retains once it is transported to other regions and once it is transformed by combining with other regional characters. Character brings all the elements of judgment to the fore: form (general composition), quality (proportions, tectonics, materials, colors), and purpose (public or private).*

EXPRESSION AND REPRESENTATION

The word character derives from the Greek: *characteer*, to make an impression, a distinctive mark, such as an imprint on a wax tablet or paper. And because character involves impressing, conditioning, and coloring an object according to artistic intent, *architectural character may be defined as the final result of impressing form and materials according to a building's purpose*. When this purpose is urban, it includes two general categories: public buildings serving civic, religious, or mercantile purposes; and private buildings serving residential, or industrial ends. When the purpose is rural, or vernacular, it comprises mostly private buildings serving residential, agricultural, or mercantile ends. Character is the convergence, the final outcome of architectural conception, order, arrangement, disposition, distribution, commodity, propriety, proportions, scale, materials, and colors. As such, it is one of the most important goals of architectural composition, in the sense that the elements of the composition are used by the architect to express the building's purpose. This describes character as it pertains to individual buildings. When various individual architectural characters are considered and composed collectively, they engender the character of a street, a square, a quarter, a city, a province, or a country. At this level character is regional, and its effects on the observer are known as the sense of place.

Architects analyze the work of exemplary architects in order to improve their compositional skills in expressing their buildings' purposes. Analysis serves

7.4 Piazza del Duomo, Ortigia, Sicily. *Source*: Photo by Author.

composition and composition serves character. Whether they call it style, façade, composition, or even sign, character is a leading preoccupation on the part of architects especially when it comes to judging their own buildings in comparison to those made by others. But whereas many contemporary architects may not use the word character in their evaluative vocabulary, many will generally agree that architectural form is evocative of other architectural forms, that it can be used somewhat metaphorically, that it has certain meanings, that its composition may be likened to syntax, or that it may express something. In effect, many architects may agree that the question of expressiveness is intimately connected to the nature of architecture in general, to the specific purpose of a given building, and to their joint and successful realization assuming that the right constructional means are available. But depending on their formal preferences, their disagreements quickly become evident when it comes to the resulting architectural form, to what and how it expresses, and whether it does so successfully.

To say that a building expresses something implies that architecture encompasses a symbolic function of its own, just like painting and sculpture have symbolic functions of their own. Symbolic thought includes a wide variety of expressions and representations, and both of these qualities apply to painting and sculpture with much ease. Painting and sculpture can denote, refer, and allude. They use allegory and analogy with great facility. They represent the characters of the gods, the characters of kings or peasants, the characters of the Church's cardinals and the character of virtues called cardinal. They can personify continents, nations, and their liberal arts and sciences. They can fully express the complex range of human emotions, joy or sadness, pity or ruthlessness, nobility or shame, grace or clumsiness. When a visual art represents it denotes a relation between an idea and an image, or a relation between an image and another image by virtue of which the image is said to be "of", or to "stand for" that idea or that other image. Representation is adequately known when an individual and a society understand what it represents, and if the artist skillfully executed the work to make the subject of the representation clearly evident.[6] In other words, representation may be said to be successful when the effects intended by the artist (intrinsic properties such as composition) correspond to the effects on the perception of the observer (the level of understanding). Artistic representation requires a deliberate resemblance between a crafted image and a subject.

Some contemporary theories of representation, such as the resemblance theory and the illusionistic theory, share the feature according to which an image of a thing gives the observer the belief of actually looking at that thing, with the difference that illusion implies an intentional fakery. The architectural *trompe-l'œil* – which, as the word suggests, implies fooling the eye – is the closest architecture can get to intentionally providing such an illusory perspective. The resemblance theory, by contrast, implies a certain proximity to the represented thing mixed with a certain amount of fiction. Another theory, the seeing-in theory, implies that an image is a representation of a thing only when an observer sees that thing in the image. But among the contemporary representation theories, the semiotic has found popular currency amongst architects because it holds that an image represents a thing

7.5 Comic scene, Sebastiano Serlio, *The Five Books of Architecture*.

by virtue of it belonging to a system of forms, or symbols, based on an operative set of conventions analogous to language. By being based on these conventions, the image gives meaning to the thing it represents. These short descriptions of representation theories apply straightforwardly to painting and sculpture; but what concerns us most is the extent to which expression and representation apply to architecture. Because in artistic representation medium and message are perceived at once, and because artistic representation carries a certain descriptive element, a narrative element, which fits painting and sculpture perfectly well, and because architecture, by contrast, is an art of abstract forms, representation theories carry a modest degree of relevance in architectural expression. Architecture by itself does not narrate at all; yet with the allusions to narrative provided by sculpture and ornament a building's purpose may be rendered evident. A building's purpose may also be understood with the help of a socio-historical narrative.

Few architects use the word expression today but more of them loosely use the word representation, having transposed it from the other visual arts. Yet expression and representation imply two distinct directionalities. They are two functions of the same image. Expression can be said to *emanate from* works of architecture. It gives to society forms and meanings drawn from within the art of architecture itself (larger conventions) and from within the architect's mind (self-expression). If a building expresses, it means that the architect willed this architectural expression and the observer recognized it. Clearly, this does not negate the reciprocal influence between architectural expression and social meanings. We shall return to this question. Representation can be said to operate in the opposite direction. It *draws from* society forms and meanings with the full expectation that works of art will embody or "stand for" these forms and meanings. If an artwork represents, it means that the artist willed a composition based on meanings drawn from society and that the observer recognized them. Expression and representation have had such a pervasive influence in artistic culture at large that many architects have been quite enthusiastic about applying them equally to architecture while rarely questioning, however, the degrees or range of architectural expression, or the even smaller range of architectural representation. Naturally, expression and representation need not be categorically separated even if they imply different directionalities.

Because architectural expression (character) is understood and judged aesthetically as an object made with artifice, and because judgment inherently compares buildings as they are with an idea of what they could be or what they should be, expression bears the strong influence of concepts of architectural making, concepts of beauty, and the concept termed the Aristotelian "ought". In other words, the aesthetic appreciation of buildings, explanations of how they are made, and suggestions of how they can be improved, invariably entail a transformation in our judgment of architectural expression. We will turn to the Aristotelian "ought" in a moment. But it is important, first, to briefly account for the deep transformations undergone since the Enlightenment by the concept of beauty (as well as aesthetics), and that of artistic making. These two concepts intersect with expression on two levels: the aesthetic properties of buildings and human-made objects as they are perceived (the standpoint of the observer), and the ways in which these buildings and objects are composed or designed (the standpoint of the maker). Beauty pertains, on the one hand, to inherent or objective relationships between the parts of an object and that object as a whole (proportions, outline, and general composition). These relationships are inherent because they have been willed by that object's maker. On the other hand, beauty is also related to the subjective perception of the observer, or to the multiple aesthetic judgments made my multiple observers. Dominating artistic culture between antiquity and the Enlightenment (though not exclusively), the concept of objective beauty came to be displaced by many concepts of subjective aesthetics (though not completely).[7] Put differently, the concept of objective beauty differentiated into multiple forms of subjective aesthetic experiences. The dominance of subjectivity stands behind the present general belief that "beauty is in the eye of the beholder", where judging objects to be beautiful now resides primarily in the individual subject. However, the fact that observers experience different aesthetic reactions to the same object is not sufficient to dismiss the objective properties of this object as less important. If all makers and observers do is to express their aesthetic subjectivities, then the concept of beauty as a sense-in-common is in retreat. Having thus transformed artistic culture, aesthetic subjectivity and relativism, in turn, transformed architectural culture where architecture is understood as the subjective expression of an architect who also happens to fulfill the purpose of a patron, with the tacit understanding that the architect's ultimate aim is self-expression above all else. Architectural judgment has been profoundly influenced by this transformation.

Artistic making was the second concept to undergo profound changes. It concerns on the one hand, the reasons behind formal composition, or the inseparable relation between imitation and invention; and on the other, their understanding and perception by the observer. Imitation and invention differentiated from each other, and then dissociated into smaller concepts that suited the subjective judgments of artists and architects. As a result of these multiple differentiations and dissociations, contemporary architectural judgment frequently uses conceptual clusters such as: precedence, resemblance and reference; simulacrum, allusion and illusion; symbolic function, expression, representation, metaphor, sign, and self-referential sign. These concepts initially developed around the visual arts, literature and poetry in order to account for the multiplying variety of images and the ever-increasing subjective reactions to them, and architects and critics sought to apply these word-concepts to architecture, thereby transforming the ways in which architecture is understood. Much to its detriment, contemporary architectural judgment has abjured and almost abandoned the use of clusters of concepts such as: imitation and invention; fiction and allegory; composition, distribution and disposition; invention, innovation, license and caprice. Few architects today use the dual concept of imitation and invention, preferring instead to use the word creativity with the tacit understanding that to be creative is to be always inventive and never to be imitative. The concept of imitation is consequently dismissed because it is confused with the copy, and because it is erroneously considered to be the opposite of invention. Seldom do architects today use the concept of fiction, or the fictive, in architecture, but many more use that of metaphor and sign.

THE ARISTOTELIAN "OUGHT"

Behind the architectural image, we see the image-maker in ourselves; we see the architect's mind and the builder's hand. Whereas the architectural image (or type, character, and style, as we previously defined it) depends on the skilled arrangement of elements and materials, it also transcends this assemblage. The tree becomes the column and the architrave, both of which in turn become a colonnade; the individual stones become the voussoir and the voussoir becomes a dome; and when refined and ennobled, the ordinary joinery of materials becomes the art of tectonics. Construction becomes architecture. The shapes of stone, brick, walls, doors, windows, moldings, cornices, roofs, derive from practical and poietic considerations of framing openings, of entering, of enclosing, or load-bearing and load-borne, and of shedding water. When composed, these elements become a recognizable and identifiable architectural character that serves with propriety the needs of the *res privata* (e.g. the house) and those of the *res publica* (e.g. the courthouse). The simple character of vernacular architecture becomes distinguished from the articulated character of civic architecture, each of them being justifiable based on social propriety. In this passage from the vernacular to the civic we recognize that the classical grew from the vernacular; that the colonnade grew from the modest porch and that the entablature grew from the simple eave. In the distance that separates the modest house in the country from the opulent palace in the city, composition serves character, but it "ought" to do so with propriety.

In the passage from building to architecture, from the private character of the vernacular to the civic character, we have the Aristotelian distinction – developed in the *Poetics* – between the way things *are* and the ways things *can* be, or the way they *ought* to be.[8] That art imitates (*mimesis*) nature and imitates human actions has been one of the most enduring and far-reaching concepts in the theory of art. It implies that imitation mediates between several realms. It mediates symbolically between the daily realities of human making and ideas about Nature, collective ideals about artistic truth, and the personal idols of individual artistic reality. To produce works of art or architecture as imitations of things as they ought to be assumes the existence of a preceding idea, or physical object, that becomes exemplary by virtue of its superlative qualities – in other words, a paradigm. Imitating a paradigm pertains not only to the work or the building to be imitated, but also to the creative principles behind them; and it is these creative principles of making, of composing with typological clarity, that many thinkers have emphasized in the long history of mimetic theory – with frequent cautions to avoid "the servile copy". Contrary to the Platonic view that considered imitation as a copy, the Aristotelian imitation is a resemblance. It plays a significant role in the production of images. To make or produce an object the way it ought to be assumes a comparison with a paradigm which is then considered as a "truth", an artistic truth. Between artistic truth (universals, architectural types, language) and artistic reality (particulars, direct architectural models, speech) stands the realm of the fictive, which involves selective choice, a selective combination of elements of artistic truth and elements of empirical artistic reality.

7.6 Richmond Capitol building, Thomas Jefferson, Virginia.
Source: Photo by Richard Worsham.

Artists and architects select from their paradigms, their exemplars, what they deem important for expression, or worthy of representation. But this selection is not repeated identically, for that would be a copy. Instead, artists and architects transform the preceding forms made available by their choices, e.g. comparing the Maison Carrée in Nîmes with Thomas Jefferson's and Charles-Louis Clérisseau's Virginia State Capitol, as well as Joseph Hansom's Birmingham Town Hall in Alabama. In the imitation, there is always something different and new. There may be a change in materials, and there is more of a focus on one particular formal aspect than another. Quite significantly, there is a noted artistic distance between the paradigm and the imitation. Recognition of this distance is at the source of the intellectual pleasure that an observer experiences, as he or she recognizes what the artist or architect has deemed worthy of selection and transformation from the paradigm. This recognition also invokes criticism regarding the judgment exercised by the artist or architect both in the act of selecting and in the act of transforming. The selection is never neutral, never an innocuous choice, it requires the intervention of personal judgment with a new composition in mind. Much in artistic meaning derives from the selection, the transformation, the distance; and naturally, the skill in execution. If the distance is too narrow, artistic or architectural imitation comes dangerously close to the copy (e.g. Palladio's Villa Capra and Burlington's Chiswick House). If the distance is too wide, rupture is imminent. (e.g. Le Corbusier's Villa Garches and its improbable relation to Palladio's Villa Malcontenta).

The act of imitating exemplary precedents and exemplary figures, and transforming them, is not only formative of the intellectual and manual skills of the artist or architect. It also invites invention, or the composition of edifices based on selective combinations of pre-existing elements, and the making of new compositions based on the demands of site-specific building problems. By imitating and inventing, artists and architects become authors – an endeavor that is at once an individual's personal practice as well as a collective regional practice. Regional schools are formed and conventions are agreed upon, thus forming larger traditions which, in turn, are transformed by influences from other traditions. Taken additively, conventions become traditions. In establishing traditions, in departing from them and in establishing new ones, there is imitation and invention, and there is a presiding idea: *the will to make and remake the world as architects think it ought to be*. Architecturally speaking, imitation and invention serve to make and remake the countenance of the public realm, the City, by making and remaking architectural character.

Having differentiated the concept of beauty and that of artistic making, the move toward full subjectivity also eclipsed the Aristotelian ought and its logical corollaries: imitation and invention. Consequently, questions such as what should architectural character be in relationship to building purpose, what should it express, and what are the limits of its expression, are usually avoided today. It is useful then to consider how architects justified architectural character in the past.

NOTES

1 From the Latin *compositio*, composition – in music and in architecture – implies the order, ordonnance, arrangement, disposition, and structure of architectural elements into a coherent or synthetic whole.

2 D. Diderot, *Paradoxe sur le comédien*, (Sautelet, 1777), published posthumously in 1830.

3 On linking patronage and architectural form, with a focus on columnar orders, see J. Onians' study, *Bearers of Meaning*, (Princeton University Press, 1988).

4 At times also, observers attach a caricatural name to a building, famously, in Rome: the Vittoriano has been known as la *torta nuziale*, the wedding cake, or *la macchina per scrivere*, the typewriter; the Palazzo della Giustizia is known as the *Palazzaccio*, the big and overbearing palace; and more recently, the new pavilion to house the Ara Pacis has been called *la stazione di servizio*, the petrol station.

5 To consecrate, here, is understood in the sense of building a common framework.

6 Theories of representation have explicitly dealt with intention, content, and perception in art. Among them are the illusion theory, the resemblance theory, the seeing-in theory, and the semiotic theory. See R. Wollheim, *Art and its Objects*, (Harper and Row, 1968); N. Goodman, *Languages of Art*, (1969), (Hackett, 1976); E.H. Gombrich, J. Hochberg and M. Black (eds), *Art, Perception and Reality*, (Johns Hopkins University Press, 1972); A.C. Danto, *The Transfiguration of the Commonplace*, (Harvard University Press, 1981); M. Baxandall, *Patterns of Intention: On the Historical Explanation of Pictures*, (Yale, 1985); K.L. Walton, *Mimesis as Make-believe: On the Foundation of the Representational Arts*, (Harvard University Press, 1990); P. Alperson, *The Philosophy of the Visual Arts*, (Oxford University Press, 1992); N. Carroll, *Philosophy of Art: A Contemporary Introduction*, (Routledge, 1999).

7 See W. Tatarkiewicz, "Objectivity and Subjectivity in the History of Aesthetics", in *Philosophy and Phenomenological Research*, 24(2), (1963), pp. 157–73; and "Two Philosophies and Classical Art", in *Journal of Aesthetics and Art Criticism*, 22(1), (1963) pp. 3–8; and "The Great Theory of Beauty and its Decline", *Journal of Aesthetics and Art Criticism*, 31(20), (1972), pp. 165–80.

8 "The poet being an imitator, like a painter or any other artist, must of necessity imitate one of three objects – things as they were or are, things as they are said or thought to be, or things as they ought to be". *Poetics*, XXV.

8
**Character, Imitation, and Invention:
A Discussion of Three Historic Moments**

In order to address the question of judging architectural character the following general contention will be made:

1. the extent to which architecture is expressive depends on the extent to which it is imitative.

To judge if this contention is true, it is important to

2. examine the ways in which architecture is imitative in order to answer;
3. what is imitative in character; and
4. in order to assess the limits of expression in architecture.

As per our earlier discussion of the limits between the arts, the word limit is here used to designate the natural boundaries of expression proper for each of the visual arts; that is, the realm of painterly, sculptural, and architectural expressions. It is closely allied with the concept of propriety, suitability, aptness, the Vitruvian *decor*, the French *convenance* and *bienséance*.

How have architects justified architectural character and its intertwining with the concepts of imitation, invention, and propriety? Conversely, how have other architects justified the separation of these concepts? And upon what bases still, do other architects propose to re-connect them? We briefly look at selected texts from three historic moments: the Italian Renaissance, the French Enlightenment, and the period of Modernism and after Modernism.[1] From the Italian Renaissance, we will examine the dual concept of imitation and invention in relationship to Nature and to antiquity. From the French Enlightenment – when the concept of character began to be comprehensively elaborated – we will examine character in relation to a cluster of concepts that include: imitation and invention, Nature and antiquity, theories regarding the origins of architectural form, meaning arising from social contexts, and personal taste. From Modernism, we will examine the rupture

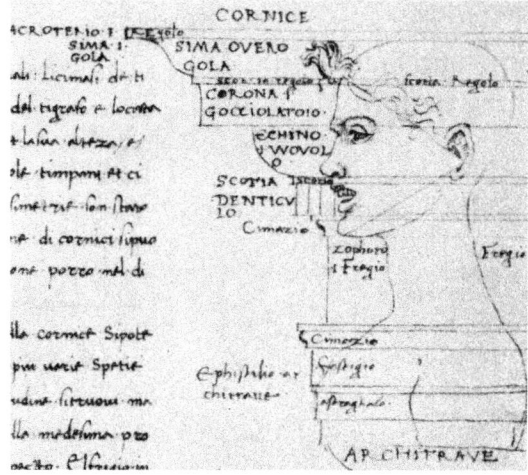

8.1 Face and entablature, Francesco di Giorgio, *Trattati di architettura, ingegneria e arte militare.*

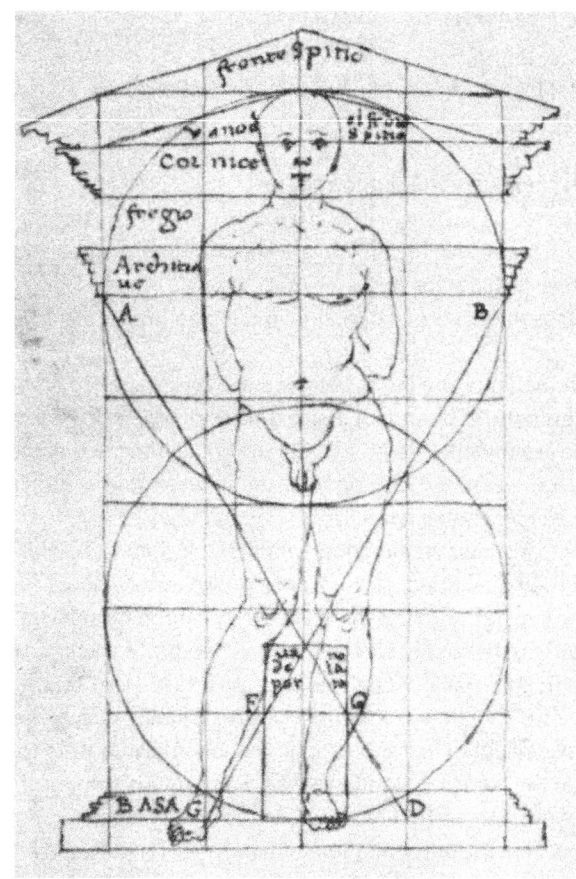

8.2 Superposition of human figure and building, Francesco di Giorgio, *Trattati di architettura, ingegneria e arte militare.*

between imitation and invention, the replacement of the natural paradigm by the paradigm of *technique*, and their effects on architectural character. From after Modernism, we will examine the association of architecture with different theories of meaning, and the new practice of architecture as an evolving tradition based on the paradigm of imitation and invention. In discussing the following selections, as they pertain to architectural character, we shall not assume that each of the three historic moments necessarily presented a complete aesthetic unity. Rather, we shall consider them from the standpoint of common themes addressed by various groups of architects whether in agreement or in opposition. Two of these historic moments, however, the Italian Renaissance and the French Enlightenment, do exhibit broad aesthetic agreements, while the latter period exhibits widespread fragmentation and opposition. For example, the enduring classical principle of *unity through variety* obtained, although in an ever-diminishing role, well into the nineteenth and early twentieth centuries, while *diversity at the expense of unity* has been acquiring an ever-increasing role since the late nineteenth century. Common theoretical positions exhibit much internal variety, and although they come to be codified in practice or institutionalized in academies, they are frequently engaged in exchanges with other theoretical positions. The artistic climate since the Renaissance may be characterized by a gradual increase in the clusters of theoretical positions, reaching a significant multiplicity during and after the Enlightenment and attaining a considerable proliferation since the latter half of the twentieth century. Theoretical themes vary in duration and in emphasis, and because architectural thought invariably involves previous architectural thought, themes may re-emerge long after their assumed disappearance, long after being supplanted by temporarily more dominant events.

A BRIEF CONSIDERATION OF IMITATION AND INVENTION IN THE ITALIAN RENAISSANCE

That imitation is a cognitive practice is duly conveyed in the treatises on artistic and architectural theory since the rise of the Renaissance in Italy where Vitruvius' *Ten Books* played a central role. For the architects of the Renaissance in search of founding principles, the Vitruvian text offered several important observations about architectural imitation which can be organized into four general categories:

1. architecture imitates natural law;
2. the column and the temple imitate the human body in its two genders;
3. the idea of tectonic imitation, of stone imitating wood, of mutules and dentils imitating rafters; and
4. the notion of imitation as simulation, in wall paintings, in tragic scenes, in the imitation of materials, and in the imitation of colors.[2]

As to architectural invention, Viruvius' remarks can be classified into two general categories:

1. the invention of tectonic elements such as the three columnar orders and the elements of the entablature; and
2. a brief definition of invention linking it to imagination in the arrangement, or disposition, of architectural form.

These three, (plan, elevation and perspective) arise from imagination and invention. Imagination rests upon the attention directed with minute and observant fervour to the charming effect proposed. Invention, however, is the solution to obscure problems; the treatment of a new undertaking disclosed by an active intelligence. Such are the outlines of arrangement.[3]

In one of his most sweeping statements, Vitruvius declares that:

Since men were of an imitative and teachable nature, they boasted of their inventions as they daily showed their various achievements in building, and thus, exercising their talents in rivalry, were rendered of better judgment daily.[4]

Thus, imitation and invention, for Vitruvius, were mutually supportive qualities for making and improving architecture; they are sharpened by professional rivalry, which also serves to enhance the architect's judgment.

Broadly speaking, the concept of imitation, with respect to architecture, received its solid theoretical foundations in the work of Leon Battista Alberti (1404–1472) and Francesco di Giorgio (1439–1501). It gained greater justification toward the end of the fifteenth century with the work of neo-platonist thinkers, and throughout the sixteenth and seventeenth centuries with the influence of paradigmatic texts such as Aristotle's *Poetics* and Horace's *Ars poetica*. The concept of imitation in the Renaissance had a two-fold scope: the imitation of Nature, and that of the ancients. More specifically, imitating Nature passed through the imitation that the ancients made of Nature. Transposing the proportions and measures of the human body into architecture was an example of imitation deduced from natural law, enriched by the imitation of ancient buildings. But the excellence achieved by this double imitation extended also to the work of some contemporary Renaissance architects whose exemplary work gained them the merit of being considered as ancients.

Alfred N. Whitehead's remark about the European philosophical tradition consisting of a series of footnotes to Plato can analogically be applied to Renaissance architectural theory as a series of elaborated footnotes to Alberti. Nature, for Alberti is the source of both the paradigms and the materials for the realization of architecture, painting and sculpture. The mind is the discoverer of paradigms already present in Nature. The column had its origin in the tree, and every type of column imitates the tree in that the top is always slenderer than the base.[5] According to Alberti, the art of building is the result of human reasoning over a natural product: matter, achieved by craft. Building the architectural "form of body"[6] consists of lineaments (line, form, outline, and the ways of joining the building components) and structure (the practice of building). Analogically, a city is composed of members, a ship should follow the lineaments of the fish's skeleton; while in building vaults, architects imitate nature as if they were interweaving the bone, flesh, and nerve structures of an organism.[7] Architects imitate Nature by imitating her laws, and not by copying the appearances of her products. These imitative qualities, Alberti held, were well known to the ancients who considered that "the building is very like an animal".[8]

The architecture-body analogy was one of the most enduring themes of Renaissance theory. Filarete's (1400–1469) *Trattato di architettura* identifies in Adam the threefold task of being humanity's progenitor, its first architect, and of being the very image through which buildings were made. Building proportions and their distributions were akin to the human body, and columnar proportions were measured in human heads – although Filarete inverts the Vitruvian columnar proportions. In many treatises, discussions of the body-column analogy and the body-building analogy were occasionally accompanied with compelling, and sometimes farfetched, illustrations of the human facial profile in direct comparison to the profiles of entablatures, or the columnar proportions in comparison to those of the full human body. However, with the notable exception of F. di Giorgio, and later Pietro Cataneo (1510–1571?) and Juan Bautista Villalpando (1552–1608), very few were the *trattatisti* who superimposed an illustration of the entire human body over a complete building plan, or section, or façade, so that the full extent of the imitative analogy between architecture and the human body can be duly appreciated. F. di Giorgio is also rare among the *trattatisti* to make a drawing analogy between the human body and the plan of a town, superimposing the feet and elbows on the fortified towers, the piazza on the navel, the heart on the plan of the church, while the fortress adorned the head.

Returning to Alberti. By admiring the ancients who knew how to extract architectural principles from Nature by retracing her steps, and by considering that imitating the ancients was akin to imitating Nature herself, Alberti did not intend for a passive imitation of Nature or the works of the ancients. Nature, as the ancients had duly realized, produces the beautiful and the ugly, the well-formed and the malformed. It is the task of art to select and generalize from Nature's disparate beauties in order to produce works of art that Nature herself did not intend.[9] In Alberti's view, imitation involves a selection from and an improvement over the upheld model, be it natural or human-made. Anticipating the late seventeenth century *Querelle des anciens et des modernes*, Alberti saw no necessary obligation to follow ancient precedents, contending that contemporary works of architecture can rival and even surpass them.[10] In taking this stance, he expressed for his contemporaries, and for posterity, that drawing on antiquity is not only meant to retrieve, but also to imaginatively reconstruct knowledge and virtues for contemporary practice.[11] Implicit in this position was the distinction between the copy and the imitation.[12] Giorgio Vasari (1511–1574) was to reformulate a similar view in his notion of art triumphing over nature – a feat realizable by the talented few.[13] For Alberti and Vasari, the natural order of things can no longer be passively contemplated, as the artist and architect wished to be vital protagonists whose works improved on Nature and surpassed the ancients. For Vasari, artistic progress meant the progressive perfection of the imitation of Nature, and the artistic imitation of Nature meant to imitate the processes that Nature follows by virtue of her own intrinsic creative qualities. Thus art becomes a second nature – a very important concept for later theorists whose task it was to consolidate the notion of architecture as an imitative art.

Imitation in the *arti del disegno* – the arts of design: architecture, painting, sculpture, in the appellation of Vasari and Vincenzo Danti (1530–1576) – provided the intellectual discipline, the theoretical foundations that enabled the architect, painter, or sculptor to judicially select and unify the best aspects of precedents with the expressions of personal invention.[14] The work of exemplary figures in the arts of design demonstrated that renewal within tradition operated based on a two-fold process: the retrieval of precedents based, on the one hand, on a critical comparison between the Vitruvian text and archaeological evidence, and on the other, on imitation and invention. Imitation and invention underlined the operative concepts of the arts of design such as: *espressione*, expression; *composizione*, composition; and *proporzione*, proportion; as well as the inward, or psychological concepts such as: *idea*, idea; *ingegno*, genius; *giudizio*, judgment; *licentia*, license, and *maniera*, manner.[15] While all of these concepts implicitly converged on architectural character, the concept of character itself only became a theoretical pursuit during the Enlightenment.

Vincenzo Scamozzi (1548–1616) affirmed that there are no "nobler effects" than order and ornament in the products of Nature. Order in the sciences and the "noble arts" is but the transposition of order in Nature, the rational principle without which there is Chaos. The columnar orders are the reflections of order found in Nature as evidenced by ancient architects who imitated Nature.[16] With reason accompanying their art they perfected by imitation the examples offered by natural products.[17] Columns, in imitation of human or animal legs, are always paired, properly proportioned to their kind (*loro specie*), and conveniently show that the building is entered from the middle. Arches and doors imitated the openings and entries of caves that appeared to be masterfully designed by nature. Windows recalled the light shafts needed to introduce light and air into caves, and so did niches recall sea conches.[18] "It is clear ... that in all the parts of architecture, Nature offers examples well-fitted to our needs ...".[19] Similarly, Gian Pietro Bellori (1613–96), in agreement with many his predecessors, prefaced his *Lives of Modern Painters, Sculptors, and Architects*, with an essay that justified imitation based on a threefold reasoning:

1. the theological analogy with God the architect of Nature;
2. humanity's deduction of ideas found in Nature; and
3. the ancients' surpassing of Nature by imitating her processes.

Italian soil offered direct ancient models especially for architects and sculptors. Through measured drawings and attempts at full reconstructions, many a Renaissance architect dedicated much erudition to the task of acquiring as thorough a knowledge of ancient architecture as possible, but imitating ancient buildings still did not rest on a comprehensive archaeological knowledge. The few remains of ancient buildings in the provinces North of Rome, or South of Rome in Campania and Sicily, were known to few local artists and architects. In Rome, few ancient buildings were known in their entirety, that is, as whole compositions, e.g. the Pantheon, the Colosseum, the Baptistery of Constantine, the triumphal arches, the aqueducts; whereas sufficient parts of other ancient buildings remained erect so as to allow for reasonably informed assumptions of their whole compositions, e.g. the Theatre of Marcellus, the Basilica of Maxentius, the Temple of Antonino and Faustina, the Septizodium. What was more readily available to Renaissance architects, however, was an abundance of fragments of columns, of entablatures, of vaults, of pavements, and many different kinds of wall construction. In inventing the characters of new classical buildings architects of the Renaissance imitated antiquity, but their invention was based, to a considerable degree, on the knowledge of fragments of ancient buildings and on assumptions regarding their previous complete states. Selections were made from pre-existing fragments and new wholes were constructed out of the same. By imitating and inventing at once, Renaissance architects answered the need for different building purposes and societal exigencies than those of the ancients. Composition – the combination and recombination of pre-existing elements – produced buildings that were imitative of antiquity, and yet Renaissance architects produced no identical copies of ancient buildings. The important distance between a paradigm and its imitation allowed the new buildings to evoke their ancient paradigms while, at the same time, detaching themselves from them.

A BRIEF CONSIDERATION OF CHARACTER, IMITATION, AND INVENTION IN THE FRENCH ENLIGHTENMENT

To the double imitation of Nature and antiquity, and the recent principles enunciated in the Renaissance, architects and architectural theorists in the French Enlightenment added the deepening pursuit of several guiding concepts. Chief among these were the concern with a theory of origins, as well as a theory of expressive qualities, in other words, architectural types and characters. The search for originating principles, such as the various forms of primitive huts, became a recurring preoccupation. Architects compared the linkage between the discovery of fire, language, architecture, and the formation of early settlements, already implied in the Vitruvian text, with the new anthropological accounts penned by historians and by missionaries to contemporary primitive cultures.[20] The principle of origin(s), or causality, answered the vital intellectual need of identifying the architectural forms closest to nature. It also shed light on the ways in which architectural historical experience built its layers around assumed origins or assumed beginnings.[21] Understanding the distance traversed between a myth of origin and subsequent historical experience, at least in theory, explained the many architectural traditions and their differentiations within various regions and countries. The qualitative assessment of architecture, however, was always measured against the paradigms offered by what scholars considered as "the most enlightened nations and centuries" which usually designated the Greek, Roman, and then Italian architecture since the fifteenth century. Additionally, the principle of origin assisted architectural judgment by virtue of its relationship to architectural rules. It also played a rectifying role, as a guarantee against the decline of architecture and the vagaries of taste.

Expressive character, the second guiding concept, included linguistically based analogies such as symbolic architecture and speaking architecture (*l'architecture parlante*). Contrary to the concept of type – which was in part understood in connection to a historical sequence, and in part understood as abstracted from such a sequence – expressive character anchored architectural meaning both to a history and to a social context, and hence to social propriety and mores. Type and character pertained to essence and appearance in architecture, and imitation and invention were intimately connected to their production. Published within a few years of each other, the abbot Marc-Antoine Laugier's *Essai sur l'architecture* (1752), *The Essay on Architecture*, and Germain Boffrand's *Livre d'architecture* (1745), *Book of Architecture*, respectively launched the debates on type and character. It was also around the same time that the abbot Charles Batteux published his *Les beaux-arts réduits à un même principe* (1747), *The Fine Arts Reduced to a Single Principle*, in which architecture was indirectly classified as a fine art.

Nature's alternating clement and harsh conditioning, according to Laugier (1713–1769), compelled primitive humans to rationally use and assemble natural materials by necessity:

> *Some fallen branches in the forest are the right material for his purpose; he chooses four of the strongest, raises them upright and arranges them in a square; across their top he lays four other branches; on these he hoists from two sides yet another row of branches which, inclining towards each other, meet at their highest point. He then covers this kind of roof with leaves so closely packed that neither sun nor rain can penetrate ... Such is the course of simple nature; by imitating the natural process, art was born. All the splendors of architecture ever conceived have been modeled on the little rustic hut I have just described. It is by approaching the simplicity of the first model that fundamental mistakes are avoided and true perfection achieved.*[22]

Like Batteux who modeled the fine arts on the single overarching principle of imitation, Laugier modeled architecture on a single overarching type, a generating principle valid for all of architecture: the primitive hut. Since the hut derived from the use of natural materials, and since humans added the rational imitation of nature as a "supplement" to natural processes, in Laugier's words, the hut could be considered as a natural and hence universally applicable principle. The hut is to the house what the forest is to the city. Speaking as a legislator who truly believed that architecture can be reformed through his admonitions, Laugier did not wish architecture to run too far astray from the essential elements that were potentially present in the hut.[23]

His tenacious and essentialist approach to composition – which allowed the use of few architectural elements: the column, the architrave, the pediment, while austerely condemning pilasters, arcades, niches – depended on a distinction between the essential, the necessary, and the capricious. "The parts that are essential are the cause of beauty, the parts introduced by necessity cause every license, the parts added by caprice cause every fault".[24] In order to avoid capriciousness and mistakes Laugier expects architects to be mindful of *commodité*, commodity, and *bienséance*, aptness.[25] By commodity he designates three things: a building's proper *situation* or siting, the logical and comfortable *distribution* of rooms, and the *dégagements*, or internal connections of rooms. By aptness, he designates a twofold scope: that of public buildings (churches, royal palaces, town halls, court houses, and religious houses) and that of private buildings (private houses). Without using the term, Laugier addresses architectural character by concentrating instead on the proper decoration that fits the exteriors and interiors of public buildings and private buildings. Churches should be dignified, majestic, magnificent, simple, virile, solemn, and serious – all qualities, in Laugier's opinion, aptly fulfilled by the choir of Notre Dame de Paris.[26] Royal palaces should be grand, spacious, and magnificently decorated. Hospitals should be solid and simple, but not opulent, because "Buildings intended to house the poor must retain something of poverty".[27] He reserves little discussion to private houses except to note they should clearly reflect the owner's rank within social hierarchy, e.g. it is improper for wealthy owners to build houses that surpass those of the nobility.

Laugier dedicates some of the last sections of his *Observations sur l'architecture* (1765), *The Observations on Architecture*, to architectural invention, dealing specifically with the invention of a new columnar order as well as ways to invest such an order with a French character. It would be humiliating, in his view, if the Greeks had the "exclusive privilege" of inventing columns.[28] New columnar orders can and should be invented, but they should be characterized by a "very marked" difference in the base, capital, and entablature, because changes in the proportions of an entablature do not necessarily make for a new order. According to Laugier, there are two ways of producing novelty in architecture: the making of new moldings or a new combination of old moldings.[29] For an order to be French, it should be clearly distinguished from those of antiquity, its capital should resemble a Corinthian capital, and its proportions should range between a "heavy" ten to one, and a "light" eleven to one. "It is just that a French order participates in the character that all of Europe attributes to us; and being regarded as the nation possessing the most delicate mind and refined mores, the French order must be the lightest of all orders".[30] Laugier then declares that he proposed this idea in order to show that it was not impossible to invent new columnar orders, and he asks the reluctant Académie royale d'architecture to oversee and encourage such inventiveness.[31]

The project of inventing a "new" columnar order and of simultaneously linking it to national character occupied the minds of many other architects before and after Laugier, with most of these orders being variations on the Corinthian.[32] But it was in Ribart de Chamoust's *L'Ordre français trouvé dans la nature* (1783), the *French order found in nature*, that nature and national character were closely associated to architecture. Imitating the Greeks was insufficient an enterprise, affirmed Ribart; one must imitate Nature, the very source behind the types, the originating principles that animated Greek architects. In an emotional narrative Ribart relates how Nature had, as if by chance, planted trees in his garden in groups of three, two sets of which had formed a hexagon, a "natural room".[33] Ribart then recounts how after having trimmed the tree-tops, laid lintels between the trees, and constructed the skeleton of a roof over his natural room, he left his garden to nature's own devices for a period of one year. Upon his return, he found that Nature was already forming capitals and a roof, thus completing the work that he had begun earlier. Nature and the human-made, or rather French nature and the French architectural mind, were qualified by a unity of purpose, a partnership. The French architectural order could naturally grow from the French soil and the French mind just like the Doric and Ionic orders grew from the Dorian and Ionian soils and minds.

Nature, in Germain Boffrand's (1667–1754) Dissertation sur ce qu'on appelle le bon goût en architecture, the Dissertation on what is commonly known as good taste in architecture, originated the "germ of all the arts", but it was genius that was responsible for extracting artistic principles from nature, while thinking and experience developed, nourished, and validated them.[34] Thus could artistic principles appear as "natural consequences". Thus could Classical and Gothic architecture claim their natural origins. Like the Greeks who transformed the tree into a column, the Druids transformed branches, twigs, and leafs into tall columns, assembling these members in order to make vaults shaped like "curvilinear triangles, in imitation of the branches of trees which rise to intersect at an angle", forming the ogival arch.[35] In his praise of Gothic architecture, especially its high proportions, Boffrand assumes that Gothic architects extracted some of their principles from those of Greek and Roman architecture, which remained the overarching paradigms to imitate. But he was keen to add that there is an architectural character that fits every nation, and what is beautiful and right for one nation is not for another.[36] The same applies to individuals, and to individual buildings as Boffrand makes the parallel between the character of a house and the character of its master who sets the tone for the architect to follow. If the master's character is "sublime and modest, his house will be distinguished more by elegance of proportions than by rich materials".[37] If the master has an ill-tempered character, the house will be made of disparate parts that do not go well together. Judging the character of the owner by the character of the house assumed that the architect had the capacity to successfully express the analogy between architectural character and human character. But this did not necessarily mean that Boffrand's architect was a neutral figure who self-effacingly produced architectural expressions of human character. For Boffrand, the architecture of private dwellings, whether hôtels particuliers or châteaux, converged three characters: that of the owner, that of the house, and that of the architect. Their successful union demanded a thorough knowledge of propriety, of refined taste, and of the difference between the mediocre, the good, and the excellent, e.g. how excellence for a prince is not excellence for a merchant.[38] By closely linking human character with architectural character, Boffrand suggests that architecture can transparently and faithfully express social mores and personal taste. Furthermore, he asserts that architectural principles can be derived from those of poetry, and in a clever transposition from poetry to architecture, he proceeds to amend passages from Horace's Ars poetica, substituting the word architecture to the word poetry.[39]

Boffrand's distinction between the mediocre, the good, and the excellent, was continued by Jacques-François Blondel (1705–1774) and applied to a diversity of building characters. His Cours d'architecture (1771–1777), Course on Architecture, contains an intricate classificatory system that distinguishes between many desirable and even some undesirable architectural characters.[40] In addition to the long-established characterization of buildings according to the columnar orders,

Blondel enumerates over sixty architectural qualities that include the noble, sublime, and terrible; masculine, solid, and virile; feminine, light, and elegant; as well as the servile, licentious, dissimilar, ambiguous, frivolous, barbarous, cold, sterile, poor, and the flat. Blondel's classificatory system of characters becomes a criterion for architectural judgment, an instrument for directing and reforming architectural taste through the correct use of the elements of composition. Following the example of Boffrand, all buildings, affirms Blondel:

> *must have a character that determines their general form, and that announces the edifice for what it is. It is insufficient that this distinctive character be only designated by the attributes of sculpture.*[41]

In separating between distinctive character and the added sculptural attributes, Blondel appeals to architects for a certain specificity to the art of characterizing in architecture – one that did not have to rely on sculpture. General massing and the choice of forms endow each edifice with:

> *a way of being suitable to it or to other edifices of its kind: only architecture has the right to fix the rules of propriety; without it, the architect cannot guide his genius, nor determine the judgment that he must proffer on the beauty or the mediocrity of his works.*[42]

Propriety, or convenance, in the right use of forms and materials was the predominant concern in Le génie de l'architecture ou l'analogie de cet art avec nos sensations (1780), The Genius of Architecture; or the Analogy of that Art with our Sensations[43] authored by Nicolas Le Camus de Mézières (1721–1789). Le génie de l'architecture was dedicated mostly to the architect's sensibility for convenance, for propriety, in the context of the French hôtel, the private residence par excellence of urban noble families. It emphasized the ways in which the proper architectural forms related to the proper social class and evoked the proper feelings and sensate reactions in the observer and the inhabitant. Thus, a hôtel intended for a nobleman, a palace for a bishop, a town house for a magistrate, a house for a military man or a wealthy private citizen, should each have its own character. Le Camus urges architects to know the causes for which forms affected our sensations, and these causes, he proposes, were best understood by a combined understanding of painting, sculpture and architecture. Arrangement in the forms of the visual arts offers:

> *an inexhaustible source of illusion. We must start from this principle whenever we intend to arouse emotion through architecture, when we set out to address the mind and stimulate the soul ... Effects and sensations spring from the considered intention that governs the ensemble, the proportions and the agreement of various parts.*[44]

Arousing the proper emotions in the observer demanded the architect's skill in endowing buildings with grandeur, nobility, grace, and simplicity. With the appropriate use of line, contour and ornament, and with the exact relations between the parts that make good proportions, harmony is then produced – a characteristic learned from Nature.[45] At the same time as he was emphasizing the arousal of proper emotions or sensations and the resulting intellectual pleasure, Le Camus mentioned the work of the painter Charles Le Brun (1619–1690) whose Méthode pour apprendre à dessiner les passions, Method for learning to draw the passions, was posthumously published in 1698. This reference to Le Brun implied a continuation of the body and face analogy with architecture, an analogy between human character and architectural character, because both were apt to produce the intended sensation within the interlocutor or the observer. Architectural character, for Le Camus, is intended to serve the proper sensations, the art of pleasing, in the observer and the inhabitant.

> … a building that is well lit and well aired, when all the rest is perfectly treated, becomes agreeable and cheerful. Less open, more sheltered, it offers, a serious character; with the light still more intercepted, it becomes mysterious or gloomy.[46]

Architectural character, in the context of the hôtel, concerned the interiors in particular; and Le Camus insisted on the importance of endowing rooms with their particular character and on the sequences in which rooms are arranged expressing the anticipated satisfaction in which "each room makes us desire the next".

Le Camus's emphasis on sense-based apprehension of architecture was fervently shared by Etienne-Louis Boullée (1728–1799) in his *Essai sur l'art*.[47] But contrary to Le Camus who dealt primarily with the *hôtel particulier*, Boullée directed his attention to public buildings on a grand scale, to the pump and magnificence in national libraries, theatres, basilicas, national palaces, and cenotaphs dedicated to famous men. In his chapter on character, Boullée defined the word as:

> the effect that results from [an] object causing within us a certain impression … To put character in a work [an object, a building] is to accurately use all the proper means to make us experience no other sensations than those that must result from the subject.[48]

Boullée's method for endowing buildings with character passes through an enthusiastic and poetic observation of nature's varied forms and colors and their varied emotive effects on the senses. He advises architects to look at the landscapes offered by nature in order to understand how "we are forced to express ourselves based on their actions on our senses". Springs and summers evoke "sweet harmony", "resplendent light"; autumns evoke "gaiety" and the "picturesque" (the painterly) in the observer who becomes "drunk with joy" in appreciating these "celestial pleasures". Agreeable sentiments shape one's taste, and taste in turn is but the art of refining the things that please. In order to analogically imitate gaiety and lightness in nature, architecture must diversify its forms and use svelte proportions. Conversely, winter light evokes sadness and somber effects, forms appear hard and angular, and the earth resembles a "universal sepulcher".[49] In order to analogically imitate these natural qualities the architecture of funerary monuments must be characterized by naked walls, low proportions, and dark colors. It must be delineated by shadows and offer the image of a "buried architecture" – a discovery, Boullée proudly affirms, is all his own. Boullée treats invention by discussing the imagination that "disguises and singularizes picturesque forms" and contrasts light and shadow, producing ingenious combinations that strike with their novelty. Character for Boullée is the impression or the effect caused in the observer. It is produced by an analogical imitation between the desired architectural forms and the known desired effects that result from them. Its direction proceeds from the building toward the observer.

Claude Nicolas Ledoux (1736–1806) briefly mentions character in two contexts: mores and legislation on the one hand, and decoration, on the other. Written from the standpoint of the architect as a reforming legislator, his *L'architecture considérée sous le rapport des mœurs et de la legislation* (1804), *Architecture Considered in Relation to Mores and Legislation*, links national mores, laws, and architectural form. Architecture renders in physical form the "mutual need and reciprocal affection" upon which society is founded, while "the character of monuments, as well as their nature, serve to propagate and purify mores".[50] Thus the benefits of a courthouse, (an enlightened temple of justice in Ledoux's words) counteracts the dark places where crime lurks in the city; while the very presence of a police building (a *prétoire* in Ledoux's words) causes a feeling of public serenity. Since each building needs to be endowed with its proper character architecture must attend to a wide variety of characters; and Ledoux encourages variety because it facilitates multiple architectural physiognomies in their adaptations to adjacent buildings. Architectural character then is shaped by the building's own purpose as well as the influence of its context. But he warns that variety has its limits, stating: "I am far from believing that it must rest on the mobile bases of caprice".[51] As a corrective to capriciousness, he recommends correct distribution for forms and propriety with respect to a building's purpose, purified by taste. The second context in which Ledoux discusses character is in connection with decoration in order to assert that both character and decoration are extensions of one another. "Decoration is the expressive character … of each edifice … it enlivens surfaces, immortalizes them, imprints them with all the sensations, all the passions".[52]

If many architectural theorists validated architectural character in relation to the passions and the effects on the senses, Antoine Chrysostôme Quatremère de Quincy (1755–1849) justified character based on a synthetic rational approach. In one of the most extensive essays of his *Dictionnaire d'architecture*, (1788–1825), the *Dictionary of architecture*, Quatremère begins by clarifying that an object, a human being, or a work of art, can be said to have character, or to have *a* character, without however having *its own* character.[53] The latter distinction, that of a work having its own character, decisively invoked the notion of propriety. That a building, or work of art, has its proper character is a phenomenon linked to its nature, its essence. The formal qualities of different edifices or different works of art were necessarily linked to their nature. "An architecture has character when therein reigns in a sensible manner a certain quality that became its tone, and its dominant mode".[54] Quatremère distinguished between three general categories of architectural character: the distinctive, the essential, and the relative. Distinctive character, or the character of originality, is to "architecture what physiognomy is to the face".[55] It is subject to historical contingency, to social mores, to different building conventions, to climatic and national variations, all of which can be either favorable or unfavorable. The distinctive character of Egyptian architecture is solidity and massiveness, while that of Chinese architecture is lightness. The distinctive character of Greek architecture is grace and harmony, while opulent luxury and vanity belong to the Roman. Thus a distinctive physiognomy is imprinted onto each national architecture, a quality that reflects the distinctive moral character of nations".[56] But the fact that an edifice has a distinctive character, or physiognomy, which might be considered original is not necessarily a mark of praise. Originality, Quatremère argues, is usually praised because society values rare objects; but originality by itself is no guarantee of quality. Whereas every innovation has something new, everything new is not necessarily inventive. Nevertheless, an architectural character is distinctive only because of the talent and the taste of the architect. "Without a doubt, a monument will have as much character – that is, an original physiognomy – as the artist [architect] himself possesses".[57]

If distinctive character was subject to national mores and historical circumstances, essential character, the second category, is an irreducible quality that reflects the very nature of buildings. This quality endures irrespective of the changing circumstances of history, and Quatremère saw it as synonymous with strength, solidity, and grandeur – three qualities that usually qualify the early development of societies.[58] Of the three columnar orders, the Doric has the most character because it is "the primitive order, where the expression of carpentry and the constitutive types of the art is enunciated and manifested with more strength and evidence".[59] For this reason Greek architecture, where the Doric predominates, has more character than Roman architecture as it begins to loose such essential character. The persistence of this loss, according to Quatremère, continues to the point of becoming "unrecognizable" in modern architecture. In order to rectify this deficiency, and in a manner reminiscent of Laugier's admonitions, he recommends to architects to always:

> *have your eyes fixed on the model, whether real or ideal, that gave being to architecture. Let all the constitutive parts of your edifices be pronounced following this intention to make them conform, as much as possible, to the parts of the model that they represent. Never lose sight of their origin, the needs that motivate their formation, and finally the reality of the objects of which you only render the image. This primitive model, of which you are but the copyist, will save you from all these oddities in the whole and in the details [of composition] that diminish and weaken the appearance and the effects of edifices ...*[60]

Additionally, an edifice might not appear solid and yet be solid, and vice versa; but it is the architect's task to ensure that the essential character of solidity is rendered evident in the building's composition.[61]

The third category, or relative character, is synonymous with propriety according to Quatremère. It operates on the architect's "instinct for propriety".

> *The art of characterizing, that is to say, to render sensible through material forms the intellectual qualities and the moral ideas that can be expressed in buildings, or to make known through accord and propriety between all the constitutive parts of an edifice, its nature, its properties, its use, its purpose; this art, I say, perhaps of all the secrets of architecture, is the subtlest and the most difficult to understand.*[62]

Within relative character, Quatremère saw two divisions: the ideal genre and the imitative genre. The ideal genre concerns architectural qualities of an abstract and intellectual level. Based on the Vitruvian text Quatremère uses the Greek term *Thematismos* (implying both customs and nature) as an example of the ideal genre that endows temples with the qualities of particular divinities.[63] Such characterization is easily achievable in sculpture or in painting, yet the architect possesses no direct model, no rules that enable the imitation of the qualities of the gods in buildings. "His imagination must at once create the model and its imitation". Relative character bears the "great influence of natural causes on the genius of a people, of the mores propitious for its development, and the reciprocal accord between a people and its artists …".[64] The purpose of the imitative genre, which Quatremère insists is not separate from the ideal genre, is to convey through the composition the nature and the destination of an edifice. The imitative genre is a "manner of expressing or painting".[65] But contrary to the ideal, the imitative genre can be "subject to uniform observations and stable rules".[66] It concerns a large variety of buildings in different contexts, including the variations in propriety, in mores, in the kinds of construction, in the gradation of materials and proportions.

Considered generally, architectural character, for Quatremère, is analogous to a set of signs, and twice in his extensive essay *Caractère* in the Encyclopédie Méthodique, he mentions the analogy between character and sign. Character is "an indicative sign of what an edifice is or must be"; it is a "skillful blending of signs that this art [architecture] can use in order to speak to the eyes".[67] The signs of character – in its threefold classification: essential, distinctive, and relative – express abstract ideas or concrete social conventions. Character, when skillfully executed by the architects and well understood by society, operates based on resemblance, based on transparency between ideas and forms, in other words: imitation. The domain of imitation for Quatremère is twofold: those arts that have in nature a direct and tangible model, for example: painting and sculpture, and those that have in nature and intellectual or abstract model, for example: architecture and rhetoric. Contrary to the other arts, architecture, then, does not have a direct model in nature; no model that can be termed an origin or a beginning.[68] Architecture's model is not materially tangible within physical nature. To remedy this lack of a direct model, the human mind instituted another model that is deduced from the understanding of Nature in her laws. This model is fictive in the sense that it operates on the level of artistic truth, on the level of paradigm. The hut for example is a fictive type (origin) and not a material or direct physical model (beginning). The success of the hut as a type, and later the art of carpentry, resides precisely in the metaphorical transformation of wood into stone. Stone construction, according to Quatremère, developed after a prolonged experience in wood construction, which although solid was less permanent than stone or brick. Wood offered the imitative mind a vast array of "analogies, inductions, and free assimilations".[69] Architraves, dentils, brackets, and cornices, received their forms in stone precisely because of their imitation of wood. But in recalling the precedents in wood tectonics, stone tectonics is not a direct transposition, not a direct copy, but rather an imitation in another material.

The imitating mind, according to Quatremère, analogically transposed the idea of order in nature into the idea of order in architecture, for example: the type (the universal) and the model (the particular); unity through variety; symmetry and harmony. Architectural making imitates natural making by being based on a theory of essences. Architectural types are the ideas behind the individual appearances of buildings. Architectural types are Platonic Forms from which an infinite number of individual buildings derive. Types reside in the realm of essences, the realm of the true, while the models regard individual buildings, the realm of the real, the factual. Even if the type is imitated and the model copied they are inseparable, for the model is one of many possible realizations of the type. Imitating the order in nature also implies the imitation of an important product of nature: the human body. Observing the human body directly or through the study of sculpture reveals the necessary relationship between the parts of one whole. It revealed general laws of proportions and the various characters of the human body which were analogically adapted to the various characters in architecture. Analogical adaptation is not a direct resemblance; and Quatremère considers the Vitruvian analogy between the Doric, Ionic and Corinthian columnar orders and the male and female bodies to be a reasonable proposition. But he parts company with Vitruvius when the latter accepts a literal parallel between the baseless Doric column and a man's naked foot, or between the ornate base of an Ionic column and women's elegant footwear, or their headdress and the Ionic volute, or the folds of their robes and fluting.

Central to Quatremère's thought is that imitation produces the resemblance of an object in another object that becomes its image. The imitation reveals one object within another. This imitative representation implies a distance between a type and an object or building, it affords the kind of intellectual pleasure that precisely derives from understanding this distance. The imitation is a resemblance, but it is an incomplete resemblance. It is rather a selection of qualities from one object, hence the notion of the fictive which serves another kind of truth: artistic truth. Such an imitation is categorically distinguished from the copy which repeats the reality of an object. The copy implies repetition, sameness, counterfeit; it is an object's double. In his influential essay *De l'imitation* (1823), *On Imitation*, Quatremère elaborates on the vital distinction between the copy and the imitation, between "similarity by means of identity" and "resemblance by means of an image".[70] The copy, Quatremère concluded, applied to the mechanical arts, while imitation applied to the fine arts.

The French Enlightenment produced several understandings of the concept of character in its relation to the concept of imitation, which can be summarized in the most salient nine points:

1. Although it does not have a direct model in nature, architecture imitates natural order. Originating principles, such as various theories of types, come to be considered "natural" by the architectural mind in search of paradigms. The architectural character of stone showed its derivation from wood construction.
2. More accurate archeological knowledge was becoming available for the architects of the Enlightenment, but imitating the ancients was insufficient

by itself. Architectural thinkers wanted to reach much further, urging other architects to imitate the very principles in Nature that inspired the work of the ancients. And although conventions have a double origin, in Nature and in historical experience, the truest principles were rationally discovered after superfluous historical accretions had been removed.
3. Architectural character expressed and represented national character.
4. Architectural character expressed social mores and national laws, and it also played a reformatory role in purifying social mores by virtue of the same expressive qualities.
5. Architectural character also expressed the personal taste of the patron as well as that of the architect.
6. In expressing social mores and personal taste character operates based on propriety. Architectural forms and their multiple compositions corresponded to certain consecrated uses that suited public and private buildings, different social classes and vocations, urban or rural contexts. When used with propriety architectural character educates and reforms personal taste.
7. Character is also a mode of classification based on the propriety of composition and the intended purpose for a building. Character can fall into three categories: the essential, distinctive, and relative.
8. Character is appreciated by the educated taste: the intellectual pleasure that derives from the impressions received by the senses. The proper use of character depends on the proper correspondence between architectural form, reason, and the desired sensations, all of which operating on a convergence of taste between patrons and architects. Many theorists shared the assumption that a building's effects on the sensations or perception of the observer corresponded directly to the effects intended by the architect.
9. Finally, many theorists also concurred on the general belief that architectural form can imitate (express) natural order, social order, urban and architectural hierarchies, as well as social taste and personal taste. Paradigms derived from Nature, ultimately, and from the consecration of architectural forms dedicated to civic or private social purposes as proven by various building traditions.

A BRIEF CONSIDERATION OF INVENTION, *TECHNIQUE*, AND TRADITION IN MODERNISM AND AFTER MODERNISM

During much of the twentieth century modernism exerted the most dominant influence on architectural form and discourse, and despite several notable challenges that served to weaken its hold many of its tenets still pass for granted. The term[71] covers a cluster of positions elaborated by several artistic and architectural movements that include Constructivism, Futurism, De Stijl, Expressionism, the Bauhaus, Functionalism, the International Style, the declarations of ten C.I.A.M. congresses (1928–1956), and others. But it also applies to subsequent positions (onward from the 1960s) whose stated objectives signaled, on the one hand, a departure from early modernism, while on the other, their expressions still continue as transformations of modernist forms and materials. Where the Renaissance and the Enlightenment shared the belief in the transparency between Nature, architectural tradition and present architectural making, modernism presented an opacity with respect to the idea of imitation in its dual scope: the imitation of Nature and the imitation of architectural tradition. Yet although the unity between the nature-made and the human-made was mostly rejected, a few of the leading protagonists of modernism, such as Le Corbusier, did indeed make an analogy between natural order and the works of the engineer and those of the architect. The law of economy, mathematical calculation, and the engineer's operation, Le Corbusier asserts, "puts us in accord with universal laws. He achieves harmony"; while through the use of formal arrangements, the architect "gives us the measure of an order which we feel to be in accordance with that of our world".[72] In Le Corbusier's thought, however, nature was understood in the most mechanical sense, taking the machine as a paradigm. But what characterizes modernism goes beyond the architectural use of mass-produced industrial forms. It is rather a way of conceptualizing architecture, indeed much of the world, according to the efficiency and rationality that distinguished technological processes – the phenomenon that French philosopher Jacques Ellul called: *la technique ou l'enjeu du siècle*, technique or the wager of the century.[73] Other figures of modernism, such as H-R. Hitchcock and P. Johnson, apprehended technological efficiency and rationality as an aesthetic, but this aesthetic consideration of technological products was not equally shared by all modernist architects. Some of the most fervent proponents of functionalism and the belief in scientific and technological dominance over artistic culture, such as Swiss engineer and art historian Sigfried Giedion, expressed a greater concern with architecture's role in answering practical problems than with the aesthetic appreciation of proportional relationships.

Modernist art and architecture rejected imitation, or anything that it considered as deriving from a-priori rules, in favor of individual experimentalism and making anew, always anew, based on the supposed unique ability shared by artists and architects to incarnate in their works the all-informing spirit of the time – the kind of spirit that S. Giedion called a "unity, a secret synthesis in our present civilization".[74] Denying imitation, historical continuity, and proscribing the influence of previous traditions – such as the opposition to academic teaching – necessitated a spirit of transgression that served the aims of an extraordinary rupture with received tradition. Walter Gropius called for "a breach", and Le Corbusier called for a "crusade, or the twilight of the academies".[75]

> *'Styles' no longer exist, declared Le Corbusier, they are outside our ken; if they still trouble us, it is as parasites. If we set ourselves against the past, we are forced to the conclusion that the old architectural code, with its mass of rules and regulations evolved during four thousand years, is no longer of any interest; it no longer concerns us: all the values have been revised; there has been a revolution in the conception of what architecture is.*[76]

The antagonistic rupture with previous traditions, the righteous suppression of ornament, the espousal of increasing levels of abstraction and minimalist aesthetics in the service of functionalism, and the conception of buildings as separate aesthetic objects, were some of the more notable tenets of modernism. With regards to urbanism, the idea of the city as a large solid from which streets and squares were carved as a system of spaces came to be replaced by a conception of the city as a collection of object-buildings inhabiting a ubiquitous space.

Swiss architect Le Corbusier (Charles-Édouard Jeanneret, 1887–1965), one of the most prolific figures of modernism, held two positions regarding style, both of which he understood in a historical sense: the "styles" of past traditions, and the style of the present time. Beginning with his polemical articles in *L'Esprit Nouveau* he repeatedly and categorically admonished his readers that "Architecture has nothing to do with 'styles'" and that "styles are a lie". But he also saw style as a "unity of principle animating all the works of an epoch, the result of a state of mind which has its own special character. Our own epoch is determining, day by day, its own style".[77] Even though he did not use the phrase architectural character, a theory of character in Le Corbusier's thought may be said to take shape around three sets of considerations:

1. his observations regarding the effects of form on the sensations;
2. his "Threefold Reminder" to architects; and
3. his "Five Points".

In the early pages of *Vers une architecture* (1923), *Toward an Architecture*, Le Corbusier links the engineer's aesthetic with architecture along with the clear directive that for architecture to be successful it needed to emulate the efficient forms of engineering. Both engineering and architecture were associated with natural order. Because of its bases in the law of economy and mathematical precision engineering "puts us in accord with universal laws", while architecture "gives us the measure of an order which we feel to be in accordance with that of our world …".[78] Architectural forms exerted a profound role on our sensations and the resulting sense of beauty. The architect "realizes an order which is a pure creation of his spirit; by forms and shapes he affects our senses to an acute degree and provokes plastic emotions; by the relationships which he creates he wakes profound echoes in us, he gives us the measure of an order which we feel to be in accordance with that of our world, he determines the various movements of our heart and of our understanding; it is then that we experience the sense of beauty".[79] Repeatedly, in his most influential polemical text, Le Corbusier returns to the sensations that architectural form causes in the observer. In this sense he is aligned with some of the previously discussed architectural theorists of the Enlightenment, especially the link between reason and sensation, that is, the link between architecture as a product of reason and the effects on the sensations caused by architectural character. Although, as we said, he does not use the phrase "architectural character", Le Corbusier insists on the undeniable effects of architectural form on the sensations as these quotes demonstrate:

> *[It is the] business of architecture to establish emotional relationship by means of raw materials.*[80]
>
> *Architecture is a thing of art, a phenomenon of the emotions lying outside questions of construction and beyond them. The purpose of construction is to make things hold together, of architecture to move us. Architectural emotion exists when the work rings within us in tune with a universe whose laws we obey, recognize and respect. When certain harmonies have been attained, the work captures us. Architecture is a matter of "harmonies", it is a "pure creation of the spirit".*[81]
>
> *The elements of architecture are light and shade, walls and space. Contour and profile are the touchtone of the architect ... they call for the plastic artist.*[82]
>
> *... architecture, which is a matter of plastic emotion ... should use those elements which are capable of affecting our senses, and of rewarding the desire of our eyes, and should dispose of them in such a way that the sight of them affects us immediately by their delicacy or their brutality, their riot of their serenity, their indifference or their interest; these elements are plastic elements. Forms which our eyes see clearly and which our mind can measure. These forms, elementary of subtle, tractable or brutal, work physiologically upon our senses (sphere, cube, cylinder, horizontal, vertical, oblique etc.), and excite them. Being moved we are able to get beyond the cruder sensations; certain relationships are thus born which work upon our perception and put us into a state of satisfaction (in consonance with the laws of the universe which govern us and to which all our acts are subjected), in which man can employ fully his gifts of memory, of analysis, of reasoning and of creation.*[83]

Central to Le Corbusier's judgment is his distinction between lower and higher sensations, between the physiological effects on the senses and the psychology of "being moved" to a state of resonance with universal laws. Such as state compelled him to admire the temples of the Athenian Acropolis on the same level as the most significant products being rapidly developed by the forces in process of building the technological society. Regarding the character of the Parthenon's corner trabeation, he exclaims:

> *Here is something to arouse emotion. We are in the inexorable realm of the mechanical. There are no symbols attached to these forms: they provoke definite sensations; there is no need of a key in order to understand them. Brutality, intensity, the utmost sweetness, delicacy, and great strength.*[84]

As to the moldings of the Parthenon, he considers them to be:

> *infallible and implacable. In severity they go far beyond our practice or man's normal capacities. Here the purest witness to the physiology of sensation, and to the mathematical speculation attached to it, is fixed and determined: we are riveted by our senses; we are ravished in our mind; we touch the axis of harmony.*[85]

And yet, quite significantly for Le Corbusier, these forms did not owe their effects to a certain idea of representation, to a symbolism or an iconology, but rather to their highly precise relationships where:

> the fraction of an inch comes into play ... All this plastic machinery is realized in marble with the rigor that we have learned to apply in the machine. The impression is of naked polished steel.[86]

Although no other architecture affected Le Corbusier's sensations to the extent that the Athenian Acropolis had, he still admired the Egyptian and Roman architectures, but the object of his admiration concerned the prisms, cubes, cylinders, pyramids, and spheres inherent in these architectures.[87] Architectural form was valued in its most abstract geometrical properties. In this sense, the manifestation of architectural character for Le Corbusier might be said to reside in abstract geometry and the play of light and shadow.[88] It is in this abstract sense that his three reminders to architects – adumbrated in the first issue of *L'Esprit Nouveau* (October 1920) and elaborated later in *Vers une architecture* – might be seen. But this abstraction has a double scope: the one historical, the second architectural. The new architecture was to be decisively abstracted from all the previous "styles", and its abstract character and analogy to still-life paintings will consist of volumes wrapped by smooth surfaces and generated by the plan.[89] One important difference exists between his two expositions of the "Threefold Reminders" in 1920 and in 1923 in that in the former case the plan is said to carry "within it the essence of sensation" – a note that is omitted in the latter case.

His "Five Points of a new architecture" (1926), the pilotis, the roof-garden (*le toit-jardin*), the free plan (*le plan libre*), the horizontal window (*la fenêtre en longueur*), the free façade (*la façade libre*), were offered as a set of new rules for architectural composition and as "the means that bring a solution to the great ills of present cities".[90] These new rules reversed the previous uses of these elements in traditional architecture in favor of developing an architecture whose character is decidedly technological. The pilotis inverted the notion of meeting the ground with a solid base by proposing that the building meets the ground with rows of thin concrete columns. Where there was a solid previously, Le Corbusier proposes a void, a transparent ground floor whose origin ultimately derives from the hypostyle type, e.g. the Italian tradition of the *broletto* with a colonnaded or arcaded ground floor surmounted by a town hall. The advent of central heating, according to Le Corbusier, invalidated the need for the traditional sloping roof. Even in cold climates, he suggested, roofs no longer needed to shed water toward the outside, but rather toward the inside. The elimination of the traditional roofs was also accompanied by the elimination of cornices that supported these roofs and allowed water to be shed away from the building. The flat roof could therefore accommodate terraces and gardens accessed by ramps. These two elements alone, the pilotis and the flat roof, radically transformed the ways in which buildings met the ground and the ways in which they met the sky. In opposition to the load-bearing tectonics of traditional architecture that generally required the superposition of walls and columns, Le Corbusier's free plan separated the structure from the wall enclosures which can now be arranged at will inside the increasingly widening structural spans. The thin horizontal ribbon windows, that came very close to the building's corner, reversed the previous vertical aedicule window with projecting sill, jams, and architrave; and in addition to the horizontal roof line the horizontal window accentuated the horizontal proportions of the façade. Finally, the free façade too overturns the previous integration with structure. Façades are now considered as "none else than light membranes" around the building, as envelopes that are independent from the structure; indeed the columns step back from the façade toward the interior of the building.

The five new rules for architectural composition operated as an inventory of elements and were seen as the symbol-products of the technological society. Influential technological products like factories, grain silos, or ocean liners, were not only the symbols of the modern age and of the technological society, they were not only evoked or used in a metaphorical way in Le Corbusier's buildings, (e.g. the ocean liner imagery on the roof of L'unité d'habitation in Marseille, the factory smokestacks in the Assembly Building in Chandigarh, or the church of Saint-Pierre in Firminy) rather they were technological images directly transposed into architecture and associated with a particular functional role in the building's composition. The products of the technological society, in the final analysis, were to become the very referential system of architectural forms, the only répertoire of forms suitable for that society based on the practical necessities embodied in the work of engineers.

The understanding of style as a collective determination of an epoch rather than a place compelled American architectural historian Henry-Russell Hitchcock (1903–1987) and American architect Philip Johnson (1906–2005) to identify the emerging modernist architecture as an *International Style*[91] (1932) and to demonstrate its international coherence. Hitchcock and Johnson saw this "single new style" in opposition to the stylistic revivals of the nineteenth century which they considered to be a "decorative garment to architecture, not the interior principles according to which it lived and grew".[92] Extreme individualism on the part of architects assured the avoidance of what the authors considered the "imitation and sterility" inherent in previous architectural traditions, but they allowed for the possibility to learn from the architecture preceding that of the nineteenth century in a way that they termed scientific and not imitative. This same opposition to imitation was expressed in their understanding of "the idea of style as the frame for potential growth, rather than a fixed and crushing mould".[93] The International Style was characterized by three principles: the conception of architecture as a composition of volumes as opposed to masses, that architectural composition is characterized by regularity as opposed to axial symmetry, and the widely diffused opposition to ornament and decoration.

Conceiving architecture as a composition of volumes depended on a gridded structure of thin vertical supports and horizontal reinforced concrete slabs enveloped by non-load-bearing smooth surfaces. The character of solidity expressed by solid brick buildings has been replaced by "an effect of volume, or more accurately, of plane surfaces bounding a volume".[94] Hitchcock and Johnson recommend that where the character of traditional architecture appeared more solid on account of the façades being more wall than windows, the continuous surfaces of International Style buildings should reduce the contrast between solid and void.[95] Within their discussion of volumes Hitchcock and Johnson contrast the characters of different epochs, stressing that Greek architects endowed their buildings with the "plastic somatic character of their sculpture" while Gothic architects "emphasized the impression of height and of orderly multiplicity of organically related parts".[96] With respect to the architecture of the International Style they affirm that:

> *Style is character, style is expression ... The architect who builds in the international style seeks to display the true character of his construction and to express clearly his provision for function.*[97]

By identifying style, with character and both with the expression of function, Hitchcock and Johnson posit that volumes and the plane surfaces that wrapped them constituted the main elements of an architectural composition that fits the present age. The roof is considered a roof plane, because all roofs are meant to be flat as if by definition. The roof is also the "bounding surface of a volume" and any roof projections were condemned as a "lack of feeling for contemporary style".[98]

Regularity, the second principle, is an aesthetic ordering that corresponds to the structural consistency and regularity in modern standardized construction. Bilateral symmetry is thereby superseded. "Asymmetrical schemes of design are actually preferable aesthetically as well as technically ... Function in most types of contemporary buildings is more directly expressed in asymmetrical form".[99] But asymmetry ought not be arbitrary or used for "decorative reasons", and the mark of a good architect resides in the ability to adapt standardization and regular parts to irregular functional demands. The absence of ornament, which they do not distinguish from decoration, is the third principle to govern the architectural composition of the International Style. The very craft traditions that produced the applied ornament in previous traditions, Hitchcock and Johnson declare, were no longer compatible with the new methods of standardized mechanical production. If there was to be any ornament to the new style, it was in the architectural detailing and joinery.

Prior to modernism, imitation meant that objects are made out of combinations of other objects, cities and buildings out of combinations of other cities and buildings, while invention sought to improve the rational choice made from exemplary precedents. Whereas skepticism regarding the practice of imitation as part of a historical continuity began to be voiced in the eighteenth century, it is important to note that imitation and invention, in general, were considered as two facets of the same coin well into the nineteenth century and beyond. With modernism, however, invention became an end in itself. The different facets of the coin: imitation and invention, now became two identical facets: invention and invention. Artistic and architectural production was now considered to be *all invention* at the same time that imitation and invention came to be understood as antagonistic rather than complementary concepts. To be inventive meant that artists and architects were to practice *creatio ex nihilo*, the making of objects out of nothing, following their subjective expressionism. Yet, despite their fervent wish to be unique and produce the previously unseen, and despite their determination to separate imitation from invention, modernist architects still learned, appropriated, and practiced their preferred architectural forms through undeniable imitative acts for two important reasons. First, any collective construction of architectural values and forms and their transmission over several generations means that a tradition is being elaborated; second, artistic and personal identities are inextricably connected to those of other architects who share the same world-view. For these reasons modernism itself became a tradition. At one point, even a renewed avant-gardist urge toward continual change passes from being a transitory phenomenon to becoming an established practice, even if only for the duration of a few decades.

The idea of technologically remaking the world, the complex sets of phenomena that J. Ellul called *la technique*, was conflated by modernist architects with the uncertain belief in architecture as a scientific discipline. This idea operated on the assumption that science (understood as technology), architecture and art, were linked by the *same* idea of progress. Whether it is cities, buildings, ocean liners, automobiles, aircraft, or kitchen utensils, the technological society was to be made with technological products and be represented by these same products. Every product must be qualified by a technological character. This unassailable belief exerted some far-reaching influences on architectural character, on symbolic thought, and on the architecture-language analogy. Because technology was both the symbol and the product, the true and the real, the signifier and the signified, the artistic idea and its representation converged or rather collapsed into each other. Because *technique* as a mentality presented an opacity to meanings outside of itself, meaning was internal to *technique*. When meaning becomes enclosed within a self-organizing and self-referential system that accepts no external feedback it becomes non-dialectical, a presentational immanence, a spurious infinity. In the technological order that permeates society, the idea of making always resembles itself and replicates itself. It became its own ends. For this reason *technique* became monistic. It also eclipsed the symbolic ends, forms, meanings, and cultural conventions that previously allowed architecture to express a civic character or a private one. And yet, although modernist architects enthusiastically embraced the non-dialectical modes of the technological order, they still wished their forms to symbolically represent this order because they still retained the traditional idea that any object acquires a symbolic function simply because it was made. They justified their architecture as a *reference* to technology, while in reality *it was* technology. So the problem was not that there was a lack of correspondence between "image and substance", as Robert Venturi suggests,[100] but rather that the image and content were equal. Thus, what is usually considered to be one of modernism's strongest points, that is, the view that architecture symbolized the technological society and its informing zeitgeist, is actually its weakest. A symbol that symbolizes itself is a spurious infinity, in other words, a vicious circularity.

The symbolic function received another setback with modernism's attempts to eliminate imitation; and this act also meant removing the difference between the imitation and the copy while producing numerous identical repetitions of technological buildings and products in every continent irrespective of the character of place. Eliminating the difference between imitation and the copy also meant eradicating the distinction between the type and the model. The type became the standard and the *maison domino* was meant to be the standard underlying the very idea of every modern building. Because any architectural character can be attached to this structure, structural form can be dissociated from character and meaning which in turn become removable attributes, thus displacing the issue of artistic truth.

It has often been repeated that modernism operated an artistic tabula rasa, by which is usually meant a decisive rupture from tradition. And although this dualistic opposition between tradition and modernism is to a large extent true, it needs to be assessed with respect to the idea of artistic making. Modernism's attempts at eliminating imitation served its hallowed aim of *creatio ex nihilo*, which it described as giving free reign to inventiveness, imagination, and intuition. Only, artists and architects do not create in the elementary sense of creation from nothing as their forms are invariably based on older forms even if they are the inversions or abstractions of previous forms. Instead modernist forms have been made, situated, evaluated, and judged with respect to *technique* as the value that outweighed all other values. The big contradiction resided in the modernist claims to freeing the imagination and invention while wholeheartedly accepting technological determinism.

That product and symbol can converge and that building structure and architectural character can be separated precipitated a crisis of meaning. In the symbolic vacuum left by modernist architecture, American architect Robert Venturi (b.1925), and others, searched for a kind of architectural symbolism that communicated and carried messages, including the signs of commerce and mass advertising displays used by the consumer society and exemplified especially in the American Main Street. In this case, meaning was sought within the framework of a society based on mass consumption, mass media, and mass popular taste. "Each medium, Venturi argues in his second influential book *Learning from Las Vegas* (1972), has its day, and the rhetorical environmental statements of our time – civic, commercial, or residential – will come from media purely symbolic, perhaps less static and more adaptable to the scale of our environment. The iconography and mixed media of roadside commercial architecture will point the way, if we will look".[101] The great transformation of architectural character by the commercial sign is to a large extent authored by the consumer society, by forces external to architecture and whose influence on architects, Venturi suggests, is a given. His two most quoted expressions: the "decorated shed" and the "duck", respectively stood for a symbolic content to architecture, which he favored, and for opposing the building that conforms to one single image, itself a sign that stands for certain formal associations given to it by society. Venturi's acute criticism of the lack of correspondence between "image and substance" in modernism derived from his observation that where modernism wished to achieve symbolism through functionalism, the functional aspect of such elements was frequently found to be deficient, e.g. "glass walls for western exposures" or "the impressions of wooden framework in the concrete of high-labor-cost economies".[102] The kind of symbolism that Venturi championed depends in part on previous forms and associations of meanings with these forms, and he compellingly argues that an "architecture that depends on association in its perception depends on association in its creation".[103] But the symbolic content that Venturi spoke of was not only linked to the meanings derived from traditional architecture in general. Symbolic content also derived from a semiotic relation between architectural form and the forms of consumer society with strong links to Pop Art. The Gothic church is considered as a building preceded by a façade which announced or advertised the content much like billboard advertising. Deriving ultimately from the pioneering work of Ferdinand de Saussure, semiology considered both the word and the image, the verbal and the visual, as systems of signs containing linguistic and aesthetic functions.[104] Its application to architecture derived in part from theories of perception and in part from the crisis of meaning pertaining to a "referential content" in architecture.[105] Considering architecture as a system of signs depended on the analogy between visual and verbal systems. That consideration played an important role in hastening the continuing differentiations of architectural forms.

Architects, and philosophers, who brought architecture into the semiotic sphere, beginning in the 1960s, shared the belief that the visual and the verbal, or any human expression, are collections of signs that carry meaning. This implied that the visual and the verbal, or the image and the word, can analogically stand for the same meaning; and at this level, the proposition appears reasonable. To provide a discourse on the value of harmonic proportions in buildings can analogically stand for composing proportionate relationships between the parts of a building. The words harmony or proportion can be expressed in many different formal combinations and meaning arises from the similarities and from the distinctions. This concerns a semantic analogy between word and image, or text and building. However, the syntactic analogy presents different problems from the standpoint of the makers and the observers of verbal and visual forms. Writers and architects syntactically assemble (Greek: *suntassein*, to put together) words and forms according to a system, to a structure, and on that general level the analogy obtains; but the experience of the word in syntax is unlike the experience of the image in visual art. The relationship between a writer and a reader or two people communicating in the same language, is not the same as that of the architect and an observer's perception of the architect's building. It is one thing to say that the word can define, explain, represent, and evoke images; but it is another to imply a transparent equivalency between the word and the image or to suggest that they share the same dialectical structure. If that were the case, then the verbal and the visual are reducible to each other. They come to be considered as arbitrary but conventional signs that lead an independent existence until a pre-conceived meaning is later attached to them. From here derives the larger deduction that not every carrier of message can necessarily be considered a language. The linguistic analogy is useful precisely if kept on the level of analogy.

In this context Peter Eisenman's (b.1932) work enters in force because of his opposition to an ideal structure that gives meaning to architectural form. His houses and writings pursue the possibility of achieving a syntactic structure to architecture that did not carry a previous meaning. To put it in Saussurian terms, Eisenman intends to achieve an architectural syntax (a structure or formal system) without architectural semantics (meaning arising from distinctions between words, symbols). That objects have meaning, Eisenman affirms, does not mean that all objects are to be likened to texts, or that all objects necessarily exhibit a textual structure.[106] For this reason he distinguishes between the formal analysis, the symbolic analysis, and the textual analysis of architecture. Formal analysis pertains to composition, order, or symmetry, while symbolic analysis is concerned with the received meanings associated with architecture as in the metaphorical association between the face and the façade. But neither the formal nor the symbolic can lead to revealing what Eisenman called the textual structure of architecture. Textual analysis reveals "a structural meaning, not a metaphoric one. A structural meaning is one in which there is a differentiation and not a representation. Symbols are metaphoric: they are objects that represent other objects. Signs, however, are textual in that they differentiate one element from another in a set of structural, rather that formal of metaphoric, relationships. Signs are notational devices that will not yield to formal or symbolic analysis and, therefore, are self-referential: that is they do not participate in a formal of symbolic whole".[107] Textual analysis, or textuality, presents a different path than the one presented by language because signs, according to Eisenman, can be separated or extracted from their formal or symbolic elements. Only in such a way can the resulting architectural form be considered a text. Separating architectural form from symbolic imitation allowed for the sign to sever its connection with traditional representation as exemplified, in Eisenman's view, by Mies van der Rohe's Barcelona Pavilion and Tugendhat House. Eisenman continues this project of separation of form and meaning in order to arrive at what he calls "the end of the classical". To that end, he undertakes to build a theory that avoids or rather suspends three of the tenets of classicism which he considers as fictions: the concept of origin, that of representation (e.g. imitation), and that of rationality.[108] Since there is no distance left between a symbol and a product, a reality and its representation, representation no longer becomes a source of meaning. Representation, in Jean Baudrillard's opinion, gives way to simulation. Representation gives way to dissimulation, in Eisenman's expression. Here, the collapse of the theory of imitation is complete, and Eisenman searches for a non-representational architectural form, one that is not connected to previously expressed values and by extension value judgments. Eisenman pursues what he calls a "timeless" architecture, not in the sense of an architecture that is enduringly valid across time, but rather an architectural form that is neither connected to an idealized past nor to determinist forces that will lead architecture to an idealized future. By "timeless" architecture he means an architecture that is disconnected from cultural history. He imagines the possibility of architectural forms as systems of *traces*, which are fragments of signs, that are "unconcerned with forming an image which is the representation of a previous architecture or of social customs and usages; rather, it is concerned with the marking – literally the figuration – of its own internal processes. Thus the trace is the record of motivation, the record of an action, not an image of another object-origin".[109] The observer could then approach such a building ostensibly without any previous association. Eisenman's aim is clearly the avoidance of architectural characters related to the layers of meanings associated with classicism as well as modernism. But the question as to whether it is even possible to realize an architecture without character remains unresolved since some form of expression will inevitably accompany human-made objects. This question also begs another: why should such a project be pursued in the first place?

The rupture between form and meaning had its antecedents, in part, in the proliferation of styles and their consumption in the late nineteenth century and their near dissolution in the twentieth. A pumping station could be endowed with the character of a villa; a house of parliament, a school, or a museum, could receive the character of an industrial factory or warehouse; a museum could be given the amorphous shape of a vase; and an office building could be shaped like a kidney bean. In this confusion of genres, the links and boundaries between architectural characters, indeed the very nature of the architectural object itself, were eroded by a series of transfers between form and meaning followed by a rupture between form and meaning. The disconnection between forms and established social meanings participated in the dissolution of forms. Dissatisfied with modernism's proscription on the use of traditional forms and enlivened by the multiple formal possibilities offered by the architecture-language analogy, some architects, collectively known as protagonists of post-modern classicism, experimented with the elements of architectural character from the standpoint of signs and their manipulation using arches, trabeations, and pediments in compositions that took their inspiration from the wealth of architectural traditions.[110] These compositions were criticized on historical grounds on two accounts. First, because their present uses were contrary to their originating compositions, and second, because these forms did not originate in the present time and were therefore judged inadequate on that basis. But an increasing number of architects that emerged from that multifaceted set of experiments loosely called post-modernism began to use the elements of traditional architecture according to their genuine tectonic logic. Arches, trabeations, pediments, load-bearing walls, brackets, pitched roofs, ornament, are rationally-derived tectonic elements that cannot be discarded just because they originated in the past, or just because of the modernist aim to break with tradition. In the reformatory spirit of the Aristotelian "ought", these modern traditional architects took up again the link between character (architectural expression) and instrumentality (building use).[111] But they had to first clarify that the practice of modern traditional architecture was not a revival in the stylistic sense of the term.

Demetri Porphyrios' (b.1949) essay *Classicism is not a Style*[112] underlined that traditional architectural forms do not owe their validity to historical classificatory schemes, but rather to their tectonic rationality of load-bearing and load-borne construction, to the finite nature and formal properties of materials and their joinery, to the visual statics of formal arrangements, and to the rational imitation (not the copying) of exemplars whose very enduringness across the centuries testifies to their success. Imitation, Porphyrios argues in *Classical Architecture* (1998):

> raises the question of how art and architecture can be meaningful. Architecture as one of the aspects of civilization is concerned with images which afford the recognition of the world. The roof, the truss, the portico, the column, the ochre

> or white-washed wall, the brick pergola opening up to the garden, all connect
> one building to another and help make intelligible our architectural experience
> of the world. Through the fictional images of imitation architecture raises itself
> above the mere contingencies of building and sets symbols for recognition. These
> symbols are composed, varied and recomposed in an ever-changing chain of
> transformations.[113]

Because the symbolic mind elevates artifacts, building forms and their construction to a mythos, objects of human making have their own character that speaks of their purpose while at the same time transcending their usefulness, their instrumentality. Character, Porphyrios continues, not only reveals the hand of its maker, "it is rather an attribute that assigns proper and typical features to artifacts so they may speak of their purpose, rank, immediate context or distant ancestors".[114] Continuing the reflections of ancient thinkers Porphyrios reminds that character depends on four considerations: *symmetria*, *rhythm*, *akribeia*, and *ornament*. Symmetria concerns the relationships between the parts to a whole; rhythm establishes a syncopation of the elements of the overall composition; and akribeia means the quality of the skill in executing a work of art or architecture, and it is closely related to the *techne* that produces them. As to ornament, it pertains to profiles of moldings that derive from construction or from the ritualized transformations of natural objects. The *torus*, for example, expresses the weight that is carried by the column and transferred to the building's base, the *scotia* separates two adjacent elements of different geometries, while ornamental motifs such as the acanthus leaf or the garland derive directly from nature.

> Ornament speaks always of a mythic animation which is bestowed upon
> construction and upon natural phenomena and social customs. Ornament, like
> language, is originally bound up entirely with myth. It is only much later that it
> achieves its purely representational, purely "aesthetic" role.[115]

Architectural character, according to Léon Krier (b.1946), suffered from two major factors since the advent of modernism. First is the lack of a hierarchical distinction between the private realm (*res privata* and *economica*) and the public realm (*res publica*) to which correspond two sets of characters, the one private or personal, the other civic and collective. This first important factor to harm architectural character, Krier argues in *Architecture of Community* (2010), is precisely the lack of distinction that has prevailed over several decades now between the vernacular or private realm, and the classical or civic realm.

> Vernacular building is the artisan culture of construction ... classical or
> monumental architecture is the artistic culture of vernacular building. It is
> concerned with the symbolic language of construction, with the decoration of
> public structures ...[116]

No building character betrays such a lack of clarity than that of the contemporary monument, a character that has been in retreat since buildings erected to extol private power and interests (e.g. the skyscraper) have been consistently overwhelming civic buildings (e.g. the city hall, the library, the church) in scale, in dimension, in prominence. The former essential hierarchy between civic architectural character and private architectural character has been inverted.

The second factor is the disconnection between building technology and architectural expression. Whereas in traditional architecture a building's character was inseparable from its load-bearing masonry, in modern building technology a building's structure stands separate from its façades. The evaluative methods employed by the American Institute of Architects and the National Architectural Accreditation Board in the United States, for example, take it as a given that the façade is but an envelope that surrounds the building. Such an understanding of structure as a skeleton upon which any character can be grafted facilitated the phenomenon of kitsch. The result is the transformation of "traditional-looking buildings into authentic fakes".[117] But it is not only traditional buildings that suffer from the separation between structure and façade because the industrial appearance of modernist buildings themselves is now "seldom the outcome of true industrial processes".[118] Furthermore, the thin veneers that expand or contract separately from their bearing structure necessitate frequent high maintenance and waste of materials and funds. But this rupture between structure and façade, Krier underlines, is now an ontological rupture because it concerns the nature of the architectural object itself, a rupture between the physiognomy of buildings and what makes buildings stand. For this reason Krier urges the adoption of a typological and morphological clarity and a clear terminology that explains them.

> *The configuration of external volumes ought to be a logical expression of interior spaces. In any case, the architectural composition should be the coherent and simple realization of a typological organization in plan and in section in a symmetrical or asymmetrical order. Uniformity or complexity, regularity or irregularity must always be grounded in a typological order. This is a necessary principle in architectural composition in order to avoid all gratuitousness in matters of uniformity or complexity, of the regular and irregular. Without typological rigor architectural composition degenerates into arbitrary games, into chimera.*[119]

Krier's call for a typological rigor concerns architectural making and architectural character in a broad sense. It assumes that imitation and invention are means to rationally use and rationally improve traditional cities and buildings, and that architectural character corresponds to a hierarchy of public and private purposes.

> *If factories have the façades of cathedrals and houses resemble royal palaces, if museums look like assembly lines and churches like industrial warehouses, a basic value of the body politic is threatened, the very nature of its public realm is in peril.*[120]

This rigor, Krier hopes, is meant to rescue architectural composition from being subject to the daily zealous innovations of architects. It is also meant to clarify that architectural invention is not a proposition of unlimited expansion that is disconnected from the civic or private expressions of architecture. The zealous pursuit of innovation produces only the transitory and is itself bound to disappear ephemerally, while impairing architectural character in the process. Contrary to what some architects may think, the general public is quite sensitive to the character of buildings. Thus, when ordinary citizens engage in caricatural naming of buildings, Krier admonishes, architects ought to listen because naming calls forth the object in its nature, in its character. Naming lays bare the object's artistic truth. Designating the Centre Pompidou in Paris as an "oil refinery" or the new museum for the Ara Pacis in Rome as a "petrol station" shows an indelible sense of what architectural character "ought" to be even if the general public may not necessarily know the exact form this character may take.

In broad summary, the period of modernism and after modernism produced three positions on architectural character. Firstly, modernist architects championed *technique* as the central new paradigm to replace the natural paradigm as well as the historical paradigm, and considered architectural character to be at once the product and the symbol of a technologically made world. To be judged valid, architectural character was to be a technological character. It is meant to primarily express the age irrespective of place, irrespective of regional architectural characters. Technological character outweighed the previous characters that expressed the civic and the private realms. Because imitation and invention were seen as opposite concepts, modernist architectural character was to be disconnected from previous architectural characters; while the pursuit of abstract and minimalist aesthetics entailed the suppression of ornament as one of the components of character. Yet, despite vigorous opposition to orthodox modernism on the part of some, and a wholesale reassessment of modernism on the part of others, modernist tenets still dominate the teaching, practice, and judgment of contemporary architecture.

Secondly, critics of modernism who were dissatisfied with its closed system of expression, opened their répertoire to other traditions and saw architectural character as a system of signs that is analogous to syntactic permutations. Of these critics, a smaller group wished to associate architectural syntax with meanings derived from the products of consumer society, while an even smaller number wished to dissolve the linguistic analogy altogether, questioning the very idea of meaning in architecture by suggesting that it can be separated from syntax. The linguistic analogy has been debated either by populist theorists or by thinkers whose philosophical writings proved a deterrent to architects who are little versed in theoretical matters. Both groups expounded more on linguistic theories than on architectural character and unconvincingly argued for the proper application of these theories in relation to architectural character. The result has been a general and vague reference in everyday parlance that architecture is a language.

Thirdly, another group of architects rejected the ruptures instituted by modernism and justified architectural character in relationship to a place, to an evolving tradition of building typology and urban form, and to the architectural propriety in expressing the public and the private realms. Modern traditional architects re-connected the concepts of imitation and invention with respect to the practice of traditional architecture based on reason, while avoiding the justification of architecture as an imitation of Nature. Modern traditional architects re-linked the concepts of regional character with building propriety and building purpose. All of these positions co-exist uneasily in the present pluralist-relativist context.

****

From the aforementioned three historic moments we have briefly examined architectural character in relation to imitation and invention, yielding the following six categories of expression and meaning:

1. Architecture imitates Nature in her laws in two ways, the one direct, the other indirect. The symmetries of the human body are an example of a direct model whose laws can be transposed into architecture. The idea of type is an example of an indirect model (because in contradistinction to the other arts architecture does not have a direct model in nature) that operates as a paradigm that informs architectural form.
2. Architecture imitates its previous traditions and their conventions. Architectural character is influenced by its reference to an origin and a beginning, which we respectively described in Part One, Chapter 2 as a *principle from which* and *a point from which*. Although the difference between origin and beginning was not sharply demarcated, the Renaissance used antiquity as a reference point, the Enlightenment used both antiquity and the Renaissance as reference points, while, modern traditional architecture draws on the wealth offered by all these traditions.
3. Architectural character expresses and represents national character, social mores, and personal taste with propriety (*decorum, convenance*). Character speaks to reason and to the senses.
4. Architectural character can be associated with the spirit of the age, and this spirit, in turn, has been associated with the idea of *technique*.
5. Architectural character has been also considered as a system of signs that carry messages.
6. Architectural character expresses the civic and the private realms in relation to the rational practice of tradition.

These categories show that the causes for architectural form are not confined to architecture itself, that in addition to serving its own purpose, architecture has a purpose other than itself. They show that meaning in architecture arises from the dialectic between these two sets of purposes, and that architectural character is molded by the complex demands of imitation and invention. Theory may be said to have emerged from the simultaneous demands that imitation and invention placed on the architect's poietic mind facing the many exigencies of practice. In other words, theory begins to emerge as architectural conventions are being elaborated; and it comes to be established and modified as conventions themselves are established and modified. A close examination of a multitude of architectural characters suggests that not a single building is completely original, nor is a tradition, rooted as it is to a place, ever the work of one single architect. Architectural character is a group elaboration. Compositional elements are shared between buildings within well-established genres and variations on them. Since the eighteenth century, and especially after Romanticism, originality has been considered as a superlative aesthetic category, and hence a criterion for judgment, leading architects, artists, and historians to regard it as the main condition to assure excellence.[121] In pursuing originality as a major artistic goal architects elevated self-expression above the other two tasks of serving the civic and private realms with an appropriate character. To be original meant to be original with one's use of architectural character. Architectural character became subservient to self-expression. Pursuing architecture as a project of originality also led to depreciating the value of tradition as a whole, discarding at once what in tradition works very well and what does not. Whereas artistic invention implies something new, every novelty is not necessarily inventive, reminded Quatremère de Quincy, nor is it necessarily an assurance of excellence. Invention appears when inherited conventions need improvement, or when the problems of practice present the architect with the necessity to invent a new combination of forms that answered a given purpose. Whereas invention might begin by operating outside of conventions, or in parallel to these conventions, it eventually takes its place among these very conventions when it finds itself validated by the collective approval of many reasoning architects. *In our recurrent association between convention and imitation, we tend to overlook the fact that many conventions used to be inventions.* Between imitation and invention theory arises as *ratio*, as the architect's reasoned judgment between the practice of architecture as a civic art and the practice of architecture as personal expression.

NOTES

1   Given the vast area covered by this topic, we leave for another study the eclecticism of the nineteenth century and the work of Augustus Welby Pugin, John Ruskin, Eugène-Emmanuel Viollet-le-Duc, and Gottfried Semper. For comprehensive surveys of architectural theory see H-W. Kruft, *A History of Architectural Theory from Vitruvius to the Present*, (Princeton Architectural Press, 1994); and H.F. Mallgrave (ed.), *Architectural Theory, An Anthology, From Vitruvius to 1870 and 1871–2005*, 2 Vols., (Blackwell, 2006).

2   *The Ten Books*, respectively: 1) V,1,3 and X,1,4; 2) IV,1,8; 3) II, 2,1; IV,2,2; IV, 2, 3; and IV, 2, 5; and 4) V, 6, 9 and X,1,4. F. Granger (Tr.), (Harvard University Press, 1931).

3   *Ibid*, respectively: I,1,9; IV, 1,7; IV, 2,2; and I,2,2.

4   *Ibid*, II, 1,2.

5   *De re aedificatoria, On the art of building in ten books*, J. Rykwert, N. Leach, and R. Tavernor (Tr.), (MIT Press, 1988), I, 10, p. 25, and VII, 6, p. 201. For Alberti's comparative discussion of columnar types and their details (e.g. the borrowing of tectonic details; the temporal succession of columnar types from the Doric to the Corinthian; the origin of the Ionic volute in the rolled bark of a tree). See VII, 6–15.

6   *Ibid*, Prologue, p. 5. "… building is a form of body, which like any other consists of lineaments and matter, the one a product of thought, the other of Nature; the one requiring the mind and the power of reason, the other dependent on preparation and

selection; but we realized that neither on its own would suffice without the hand of the skilled workman to fashion the material according to the lineaments".

7   Respectively: I, 9, p. 24; V, 12, p. 136; and III, 14, p. 86, "... with very type of vault, we should imitate Nature throughout, that is, bind together the bones and interweave flesh with nerves running along every possible section ... When laying the stones of a vault, we should, in my opinion, copy the ingenuity of Nature".

8   *Ibid*, IX, 5, p. 301.

9   In his treatise *On Painting*, J. Spencer (Tr.), (Yale, 1956), p. 93, Alberti recounts the celebrated story of Zeuxis making a new composition of Helen, based on a selection of the disparate beauties of several women from Croton. See also *De re-aedificatoria*, IX, 7, p. 310.

10 *Ibid*, I, 10, p. 24. "Although other famous architects seem to recommend by their work either the Doric, or the Ionic, or the Corinthian, or the Tuscan division as being the most convenient, there is no reason why we should follow their designs in our work, as though legally obliged; but rather, inspired by their example, we should strive to produce our own inventions, to rival, or, if possible, to surpass the glory of theirs".

11 Although Alberti had some direct knowledge of ancient buildings and undertook some excavations in Rome, most of the buildings mentioned in his treatise are from literary sources. See J. Rykwert, "Theory as Rhetoric: L.B. Alberti in Theory and Practice", in *Paper Palaces*, V. Hart and P. Hicks (eds), (Yale, 1998), pp. 33–50.

12 The imitation and the copy would gain a sharper differentiation with the theorists of the eighteenth century, where the copy was qualified as servile.

13 See the passage in Vasari's biography of Raphael where he mentions nature being vanquished by art at the hands of Michelangelo as well as Raphael. "Di costui fece dono al mondo la natura quando, vinta dall'arte per mano di Michele Agnolo Buonarroti volle in Raffaello esser vinta dall'arte e dai costumi insieme", *Le vite*, Vol. 4, (Edizione Giunta e Torrentiniana, 1999), p. 155.

14 See Alina Payne's discussion of *imitatio* and *inventio* within the Renaissance treatise *The Architectural Treatise of the Italian Renaissance*, (Cambridge, 1999).

15 For a comprehensive survey of artistic terminology and classification, see W. Tatarkiewicz, "Sixteenth century theory of the visual arts", in *History of Aesthetics*, Vol. 3, (1970–74) (Thoemmes Press, 1999), pp. 192–221.

16 *Dell'idea dell'architettura universale*, Part II, Book Six, Chapter I, pp. 1–3, and Chapter V, p. 15, Centro Internazionale di Studi di Architettura Andra Palladio, (Edizioni Colpo di fulmine, 1997).

17 *Ibid*, Part I, Book One, Chapter XXIII, p. 69.

18 *Ibid*, Part II, Book Six, Chapter IV, pp. 12–14.

19 *Ibid*, p. 13.

20 For the historical context of theories of origin in the eighteenth century see J. Rykwert, *On Adam's House in Paradise*, (Museum of Modern Art, 1972); *The First Moderns*, (MIT Press, 1980); A. Vidler, *The Writing of the Walls*, (Princeton Architectural Press, 1987); R. Dripps, *The First House*, (MIT Press, 1997).

21 See Part One, Chapter 2, for our distinction between origins and beginnings.

22 *Op. cit.*, Translated with an Introduction by Wolfgang and Anni Hermann, (Hennesey and Ingalls, 1977), p. 12.

23   "Let us judge severely the good works of our artists. Let us overlook no defect. Let us demand that they explain the forms, the proportions, the ornaments ..." *Observations sur l'architecture*, Avertissement, (Desaint, 1765), pp. xj. My translation.

24   *Essai*, p. 12.

25   *Ibid*, Chapter III, Article II and III.

26   Like M. de Frémin, *Mémoires critiques de l'architecture*, (1702); the abbot J-L. de Cordemoy, *Nouveau traité de toute l'architecture*, (1706); and J. Germain Soufflot's "Mémoire sur l'architecture gothique" (1741), Laugier was relatively well disposed toward Gothic architecture.

27   *Essai*, p. 98.

28   *Observations*, Sixième partie, p. 251.

29   *Ibid*, p. 265.

30   *Ibid*, p. 276. My translation.

31   *Ibid*, pp. 279–80. Prior to the publication of Laugier's *Observations*, the Académie, in 1763, had condemned the search for a "sixth order".

32   The history of a "French order" goes back at least to Philibert Delorme's (1514–1570) adaptation of Doric, Ionic, and Corinthian columns for the Tuileries, and illustrated in his *Le Premier tome de l'architecture*, (1567). In direct imitation of nature, Delorme also proposed tree-trunk columns like D. Bramante's earlier columns in the Canonica cloister in Milan. But the official thrust to invent a French order was given strong impetus by Jean-Baptiste Colbert's cultural policies, and specifically the 1671 competition to design a French order intended for the Louvre's attic level. The competition attracted the attention of François Blondel, Claude Perrault, Antoine Desgodets, Charles-Augustin D'Aviler, Sébastien Leclerc, (who also provided a Spanish order in his *Traité d'architecture* of 1714), and other architects. For a history of the "French order" see J-M. Pérouse de Montclos, "Le sixième ordre ou la pratique des ordres suivant les nations", *Journal of the Society of Architectural Historians*, 36(4), (1977), pp. 223–40; see also his *Philibert Delorme, architecte du Roi*, (Mengès, 2000); R. Chitham, *The Classical Orders of Architecture*, (London, 1985); A. Izonis and L. Lefaivre, *Classical Architecture: The Poetics of Order*, (MIT Press, 1986). J. del Prado and J. Bautista Villalpando proposed the Tyrian or Hierosolymitan order in their *In Ezechielem ... templi Hierosolymitani* (1596–1604); and in his *Erste Ausübung* of 1699 Leonhard Christoph Sturm proposed a German order. A British order was proposed in the *Works of Robert and James Adam*, (1773–1778), and an American order with tobacco leaves and corn was designed by Benjamin Latrobe for the US Capitol Building in Washington, DC, in 1803.

33   *L'Ordre français trouvé dans la nature*, (Paris, 1783), pp. 2–7. Monique Mosser and Anthony Vidler drew attention to the Masonic influence in Ribart's conception of the garden. For the wider context of Nature, the Revolution, and Freemasonry, see the catalogue *Les fêtes de la Révolution*, J-P. Bouillon, M. Mosser, and D. Rabreau, (Clermont-Ferrand, 1974); and *The Architecture of Western Gardens*, M. Mosser and Georges Teyssot (eds), (MIT Press, 1991); A. Vidler, *op. cit.*

34   G. Boffrand, *Book of Architecture* (1745), C. van Eck (ed.), David Britt (Tr.), (Ashgate, 2002), p. 4.

35   *Ibid*, p. 5.

36   *Ibid*, p. 6.

37 *Ibid*, p. 7.

38 *Ibid*, p. 4.

39 See the section entitled "On the principles of architecture derived form Horace's Art of Poetry", *Ibid*, pp. 8–12. On rhetoric and architecture see the relevant sections in C. van Eck's *Organicism in Nineteenth Century Architecture*, (Architectura & Natura Press, 1994); and her *Classical Rhetoric and the Visual Arts in Modern Europe*, (Cambridge, 2007).

40 *Cours d'architecture, ou traité de la décoration, distribution & construction des bâtiments; Contenant les leçons données en 1750, & les années suivantes*, 8 vols., (Paris, 1771–77) – (the last two volumes were written by Pierre Patte), Tome II, pp. 229–32.

41 *Ibid*, p. 229. My translation.

42 *Ibid*, p. 230. My translation.

43 Introduction by Robin Middleton and translation by David Britt. (The Getty Center for the History of Art and the Humanities, 1992).

44 *Ibid*, pp. 71–2.

45 *Ibid*, p. 87.

46 *Ibid*, p. 87.

47 Written between 1796 and 1797, the *Essai sur l'art* remained unpublished until 1953. See Helen Rosenau's translation of the *Essai* as *Boullée's Treatise on Architecture*, (Tiranti, 1953); J-M. Pérouse de Montclos (ed.), *Etienne-Louis Boullée: Architecture, Essai sur l'art*, (Paris, 1968), and Étienne-Louis Boullée, (Flammarion, 1994); W. Szambien, "Notes sur le recueil d'architecture privée de Boullée, 1792–1796", in *Gazette des Beaux-Arts*, (xcvii, 1981), pp. 111–24; A. Jacques, *Les Architectes de la Liberté*, (Gallimard, 1988). The integral text is also available at the Bibliothèque Nationale de France. Available at: http://expositions.bnf.fr/boullee/index.htm

48 *Ibid*, my translation.

49 Werner Szambien suggests that Boullée's association of the four seasons with varied architectural characters may have been influence by A.C. Quatremère de Quincy's discussion of gardens in the first volume of the *Encyclopédie méthodique* of 1788. See Szambien's *Symétrie, goût, caractère*, (Picard, 1986), p. 194.

50 *L'architecture considérée sous le rapport des mœurs et de la legislation*, (Paris, 1804), p. 3. My translation.

51 *Ibid*, p. 11. My translation.

52 *Ibid*, pp. 12. My translation.

53 *Dictionnaire d'architecture*, 3 vols., *Encyclopédie Méthodique*, (C.J. Panckoucke, 1788–1825), pp. 427–521. See Chapter 1 for our discussion of character according to Quatremère.

54 *Ibid*, p. 498. My translation.

55 *Ibid*, p. 498. My translation.

56 *Ibid*, p. 499.

57 *Ibid*, p. 499. My translation.

58 *Ibid*, p. 500.

59 *Ibid*, p. 500. My translation.

60 *Ibid*, p. 500. My translation.

61 *Ibid*, p. 501.

62 *Ibid*, p. 502. My translation.

63 *Ibid*, pp. 503–4.

64 *Ibid*, p. 505. My translation.

65 *Ibid*, p. 503.

66 *Ibid*, p. 505. My translation.

67 *Ibid*, pp. 502 and 503 respectively. My translation.

68 See "Imitation", in S. Younés, *The True, the Fictive, and the Real: The Historical Dictionary of Architecture of Quatremère de Quincy*, (Papadakis, 1999), pp. 175–9.

69 *Ibid*, see "Architecture", and "Wood".

70 *De l'imitation*, (1823), (Archives d'architecture moderne, Bruxelles, 1980), pp. 21–8.

71 See our earlier discussion of the ambiguity of the term in Chapter 2. For surveys of the history of modernism see: N. Pevsner, *The Sources of Modern Architecture and Design*, (Oxford University Press, 1968); N. Pevsner, *An Outline of European Architecture*, (Penguin, 1972); M. Tafuri and F. Dal Co, *Modern Architecture*, (H.N. Abrams, 1972); C. Jencks *Modern Movements in Architecture*, (Anchor Press, 1973); K. Frampton, *Modern Architecture, A Critical History*, (Thames & Hudson, 1985); C. Rowe *The Architecture of Good Intentions*, (Academy Editions, 1994); M. Hays (ed.), *Architectural Theory since 1968*, (MIT Press, 1998); S. Williams Goldhagen and R. Légaut, *Anxious Modernisms*, (MIT Press, 2000); S. Kwinter, *Architectures of Time*, (MIT Press, 2001); A. Colquhoun, *Modern Architecture*, (Oxford, 2002); H. Mallgrave, *Twentieth Century Architecture; Modern Architectural Theory*, (Cambridge University Press, 2005).

72 *Towards an Architecture*, (1923), F. Etchells (Tr.), (Praeger, 1927), p. 1.

73 See our discussion of *technique* in Part One, Chapter 4.

74 *Space, Time, and Architecture*, (1941), (Harvard University Press, 1967), p. vi.

75 See Le Corbusier's *Croisade, ou le crépuscule des académies*, (Editions G. Crès, 1933).

76 *Towards an Architecture*, pp. 286–8.

77 *Towards an Architecture*, p. 3.

78 *Ibid*, p. 1.

79 *Ibid*, p. 1.

80 *Ibid*, p. 4.

81 *Ibid*, p. 19.

82 *Ibid*, pp. 5–6.

83 *Ibid*, pp. 16–17.

84 *Ibid*, p. 211.

85 *Ibid*, p. 220.

86 *Ibid*, pp. 214, 216, 217.

87 *Ibid*, pp. 29–31. He does not extend his admiration to the Gothic cathedral because only the nave, he held, is an expression of simple geometry while the rest is a complex

system of arcuations. For this reason he does not consider a cathedral "very beautiful" as "we search in it for compensations of a subjective kind outside plastic art. The cathedral is not a plastic work; it is a drama; a fight against the force of gravity, which is a sensation of a sentimental nature".

88 *Ibid*, p. 26.

89 *Oeuvre complète, 1910–1929*, (Septième Edition, 1960), p. 33.

90 *Ibid*, pp. 128–9.

91 The phrase International Architecture had previously been used by Walter Gropius in his first *Bauhausbuch*, 1925. Erich Mendelsohn and Bernhard Hoetger used the phrase World Architecture in 1928, and Buckminster Fuller, the term Universal Architecture in 1932.

92 *The International Style*, (Norton, 1932), p. 34.

93 *Ibid*, p. 36.

94 *Ibid*, p. 56.

95 *Ibid*, p. 66.

96 *Ibid*, p. 56.

97 *Ibid*, p. 57.

98 *Ibid*, p. 83.

99 *Ibid*, p. 72.

100 R. Venturi, D. Scott Brown, and S. Izenour, *Learning from Las Vegas*, (MIT Press, 1972), p. 137.

101 *Ibid*, p. 131.

102 *Ibid*, p. 137.

103 *Ibid*, p. 131.

104 On architecture and semiotics see G. Klaus Koenig, *Analisi del linguaggio archittetonico*, (1964); R. de Fusco, *Architettura Come Mass Medium*, (1967); U. Eco, *La struttura assente*, (1968); R. Barthes, *Eléments de sémiologie*, (1968); M. Luisa Scalvini, *L'architettura come semiotica connotativa*, (1975); C. Jencks, *The Language of Post-Modern Architecture*, (1977); G. Broadbent, R. Bunt, and C. Jencks (eds), *Signs, Symbols and Architecture*, (1980).

105 Referential content is an expression used by Joseph Rykwert in *The Necessity of Artifice*, (1982).

106 *Eisenman, Inside Out. Selected Writings 1963–1988*, (Yale, 2004), pp. 190–93.

107 *Ibid*, p. 191.

108 *Ibid*, "The Representation of Doubt", pp. 144–51, "The End of the Classical", pp. 153–65.

109 *Ibid*, p. 163.

110 See R. Venturi, *Complexity and Contradiction in Architecture*, (Museum of Modern Art, 1966); A. Rossi, *A Scientific Autobiography*, L. Venuti (Tr.), (Oppositions Books, 1981); C. Jencks, *The Language of Post Modern Architecture*, (Rizzoli, 1977).

111 Collectively, the work of these architects has been known as Modern Classicism, Modern Tradition, the Other Modern, or more generally: traditional architecture. For the more recent surveys see: R. Economakis (ed.) *Building Classical*, (Academy Editions,

1993); N. Crowe, R. Economakis, and M. Lykoudis, (ed.), *Building Cities*, (Artmedia Press, 1999); G. Tagliaventi (ed.), *L'altra modernità 1900–2000*, (Dogma, 2000); A. Sagharchi and L. Steil (eds),*The New Palladians*, (Artmedia, 2011).

112 D. Porphyrios (ed.), *Classicism is Not a Style*, (Architectural Design, 1982).

113 *Classical Architecture*, (Papadakis, 1998), p. 26.

114 *Ibid*, pp. 58–9.

115 *Ibid*, p. 67.

116 *Architecture of Community*, (Island Press, 2010), p. 51.

117 *Ibid*, p. 36.

118 *Ibid*.

119 *Ibid*, p. 46.

120 *Ibid*, p. 29.

121 On originality, see R. Mortier, *L'originalité, une nouvelle catégorie esthétique du siècle des lumières*, (Droz, 1982); R. Krauss, *The Originality of the Avant-garde and other Modernist Myths*, (MIT Press, 1985); E. Gazda (ed.), *The Ancient Art of Emulation, Studies in Artistic Originality*, (University of Michigan Press, 2002).

9
The Limits of Architectural Expression

The vital question of the limits of architectural expression gains special value when seen against the backdrop of the successive removal away from paradigms external to architecture toward paradigms that are internal to it. Thus Nature as a paradigm gave way to history as a paradigm, to tradition as a paradigm, to social mores as a paradigm, to *technique* as a paradigm, to the linguistic analogy as a paradigm, to the paradigm of the city as a receptacle of experience-tested types, characters, and styles. Very few architects today operate on the basis of imitating the laws of Nature, although the relationship between globally detrimental building practices and severe ecological disturbances may eventually compel an earnest reconsideration of this paradigm. Few architects associate specific architectural forms with social mores, although many architects reflect with concern on the sociological impact of their buildings. Architectural character is justified today mostly on the basis of four competing paradigms. First is modernism. Operating under the assumption that modernist artistic abstraction definitively replaced the imitation of Nature and the imitation of conventions, modernist architects directly relate architectural representation to the abstraction in modernist painting and sculpture. Indeed compositional strategies such as volumetric organization, spatial definitions, spatial transparencies, relations between solids and voids, tensions between context and frame, are considered as common compositional devices shared by architecture, painting, and sculpture. Second, is the continuing strong influence of *l'architecture parlante* and versions of the linguistic analogy. Architects who adhere to this paradigm expect architecture to always communicate a degree of expressive content, e.g. that the character of a hospital, a bank, or an art gallery somehow communicates something about healing, about securing material wealth, or about displaying art. Third, there are architects who seek to produce an architecture that is conceived as a set of fragments of previous fragments, that distorts and destabilizes established meaning.[1] They use the new means offered by digital technologies developed for automobile, aircraft, and defense industries, in order to bring together complex, ambiguous, contorted, and unrelated forms with different tectonic purposes and different textures. Some, explain their complex non-linear geometries and folded forms as direct presentations of the complex socio-cultural conditions of the post-Cold war era, of the rends in social fabric, of gender ambiguity, or a resistance to rampant consumerism. Other architects still, search for forms devoid of any meaning and representational value whatsoever. Fourth, is the architectural paradigm based on established conventions that range hierarchically from the private to the civic. Columns, piers, arches, windows, doors, hipped or gable roofs, and domes, are shared by private and civic buildings alike, but these elements find themselves further ennobled, articulated, and built of more refined and enduring materials when answering the purpose of civic architecture. In turn, private buildings and civic edifices each have a hierarchical and unambiguous range of expression that distinguishes between the character of a hospital and that of a hotel, between the character of a church and that of a house.

With faithfulness to their positions adherents to these four positions project their understanding on contemporary buildings. And, In their efforts at achieving historical justification they also proceed to project these same understandings onto buildings of the past, claiming for instance that the linguistic analogy always formed a part of architectural expression, or conversely, that architectural expression is not and was never about expressing social meanings. However, with the exception of architects who reject representational value, other architects of differing ideologies still agree – with varying degrees of conviction – that architecture should express private and civic purposes in ways that are justifiable by architects and understood as such by society. But this conviction is confronted by the widely accepted opinion that in the present pluralist milieu architecture must be open to formal influences from many other fields and that architectural character is somehow meant to reflect these influences, raising the problem of limits or links and boundaries between architecture and the arts that we discussed in Chapter 5. That architects entertain concerns about a society swarming with upheavals is one thing, but that they should transform, deform, or fragment architecture as a way to reflect these upheavals, or to resist them, is quite another. The essential questions, with respect to the visual arts in general, are:

1. which art is used for which ends; and
2. which art is a more fitting vehicle to express social concerns?

Put differently, are not painting and sculpture more appropriate vehicles to express social concerns than architecture? Architects certainly have the freedom to use architecture as a vehicle for their private concerns. They certainly have the right to raise their self-expression over and above the civic task of architecture. But should they?

As we saw earlier, many contemporary architects are likely to conflate the *limits* of architectural expression with what they erroneously see as the *limitation* of their personal expression, of their intellectual freedom. For this reason many architects are likely to reject the difficult question of the limits of architectural expression. Yet,

9.1 Pumping station, Friedrich Ludwig Persius, Potsdam.
Source: Photo by Dieter Brügmann.

when confronted with a building that demonstrates a clear confusion of genres they may conclude that architectural expression is inseparable from propriety. Consider, for example, the case of the water-pumping station servicing the fountains of the Sanssouci Park in Potsdam. Built between 1841–45 by Friedrich Ludwig Persius (1803–45), the water-pumping station has the character of a mosque with the minaret serving as its chimney. The same may be said when a church is indistinguishable from a warehouse, or when a museum or school are barely distinguishable from the forms of an industrial factory.

The confusion of genres immediately calls forth the question of limits by the very transgression of these limits. Yet there is a fictive dimension in architectural composition that cannot be separated from the limits of architectural expression. Its range covers the artistic distance that allows either a reference to a model or a departure from it. Fiction in architecture occurs when a model is imitated and inventively modified. There is no fiction in the copy as it is by definition a double. There are several kinds of fiction in architecture. A fictive dimension is at play when stone construction imitates the formal characteristics of wood construction but with a transformation that is appropriate for stone. Such, for instance, are the stone column flutes that stylize the grooves previously present between clustered circular wooden posts. Another kind of fiction allows for the stylized transformations of what used to be ritualistic implements such as votive tripods into tectonic elements of architectural composition, namely: the triglyph.[2] A different kind of fiction in architecture is required when an established architectural element is applied in ways and meanings that differ from its originating context in order to enhance a building's civic presence – not always a successful endeavor. For example, the appropriation of the temple front for the purposes of a private residence (Andrea

Palladio's Villa Capra, 1560s), medical school (Jacques Gondoin's École de Chirurgie in Paris, 1775), a banking institution (Thomas Cooley's Royal Exchange in Dublin, now the City Hall, 1779), a theatre (Karl Friedrich Schinkel's State Theatre in Berlin, 1821), or a library (Thomas Jefferson's Rotunda at the University of Virginia, 1827). There is also a kind of fiction that approaches the literal to the point that there is a confusion between the limits of architecture and those of sculpture. For example, C.N.L. Ledoux's proposal for a house for the inspector of the waters of the Loue river in the shape of a water conduit. An altogether different kind of fiction, this time a fictive narrative external to architecture, allows different nations to associate the same architecture with their national identities. An illustration of such narrative is the coeval claims made in France, Germany, and England for the Gothic as a national architecture, whereas this claim might be more appositely stated as the different ways in which the Gothic tradition is expressed in each of these countries. For there are French, German, and English sensibilities of expressing the Gothic, and for that matter the Classical. Fiction then is of different kinds and it occurs in several steps. It begins on a causal level, when an architectural form is beginning to develop; it continues when the same architectural form begins to be applied in similar conditions and for the same building purpose; and it is later modified not only on formal levels, but also in its application for different building purposes than those that saw its birth. If architectural character is said to be expressive, accepting various degrees of fiction ranging from purely abstract tectonic factors to those of social concerns, then the limits of architectural expression relate to the limits of fiction that architecture is capable of. The problem of judging the limits of architectural expression becomes clear: can architecture truly express all that is expected of her?

To illustrate the range of architectural expression, we now examine a small selection of civic buildings from antiquity to the late twentieth century. We shall not, however, examine these buildings from the standpoint of a survey of art-historical categories. Nor shall we seek to emphasize differences in expression as architectural history surveys have commendably displayed the rich varieties architecture can assume. Rather, we shall be examining the following buildings from the standpoint of the propriety of external expression in relation to the building's purpose; and when applicable, the role played therein by sculpture and ornament. Few building purposes are called to express character more poignantly than the civic purpose, whether it is judicial like a courthouse; votive like a temple or church; commemorative like a memorial to national reconciliation or to a war; or cultural like a museum, a library, a theatre. Because civic monuments converge civic purposes, they become urban and cultural landmarks that converge the full cultural attention of a city, a region, a nation. They anchor in a place a set of ideas that are either general and abstract or quite tangible and specific. In a most general way courthouses are buildings where social justice is administered irrespective of country or region, but in a very tangible way the courthouses of the American Midwest draw on a definite set of architectural compositions that become anchored in a region, e.g. grand staircases, podia, arcades, grand halls, pediments, domes, and civic towers. Churches shelter religious services in many countries and regions,

THE LIMITS OF ARCHITECTURAL EXPRESSION   203

but the Baroque churches of Rome or the Romanesque churches of Normandie are firmly anchored in a place because of their use of definite sets of compositions. The buildings we shall examine are a temple, a church, a mint, a national mausoleum, a sculpture gallery, an academy, pavilions for world fairs, an opera house, a museum dedicated to a national art, a university quadrangle, and an open-air theatre and pavilion.

OBSERVATIONS ON A FEW BUILDING CHARACTERS

Standing at the foot of the Roman Capitol, below the Tabularium, near the Temples of Saturn and Vespasian, was a site that had long been consecrated by three temples dedicated to Concord. The first temple, from the fourth century BC, was dedicated to the reconciliation between the plebeians and the patricians. The second temple of Concord, from the second century BC, was built to celebrate the victory of aristocratic power over the reforms sought by the Gracchi. This temple, which burned down in nine BC, was replaced by the third temple (ten AD), this time dedicated to Concordia Augusta. The third temple was built by Tiberius, in his name and in the name of his defunct brother Drusus, in order to celebrate the return of civil peace. Funds for the erection of the temple had been collected from their share of the booty from their German campaign. The third temple

9.2 Temple of Concord, Rome. After Constant Moyaux. From Hector D'Espouy, Fragments d'architecture antique, Vol.2, Paris, Ch. Massin, 1905.

occupied the former temple's podium, except that its new Corinthian hexastyle pronaos engaged the long side of the cella making a T-shaped plan, and facing the Forum. Flanking the impressive flight of steps that led to the pronaos stood two statues, the one of Hercules carrying his club, to the left, the other of Mercury holding his caduceus, to the right. Profiles of the club and the caduceus were also carved on the stone slabs in the threshold of the temple's door. The moral strength and physical might represented by the statue of Hercules were balanced by the reasoned temperance of Mercury, leading some scholars to consider the two statues as the veritable entrance to the temple, to Augustan Concord.[3] A coin from the time of Tiberius shows that the temple's pediment was crowned with statues of three female divinities: probably Concord in the center, flanked by Peace (*pax*) and Health (*salus*). The pediment also displays two male figures with lances, alluding presumably to Tiberius and his brother Drusus.

From the standpoint of expressiveness, how were the architects of the Temple of Concord to express civil concord, the return to civil coexistence, when the typological components are: a grand staircase, a tall stylobate, a pronaos with six Corinthian columns and a pediment, and a cella? Conversely, how would an observer conclude, by considering these components, that this temple was built to Concord? Architectural composition can vary the components' proportions ranging from the heavy to the slender, but it does not express the idea of concord architecturally, nor does it express the qualities of Hercules or Mercury architecturally. Rather, political concord, the state's strength, and the desire for tempered reason, are associated with the temple by a mythico-historical narrative represented with a sculptural program. Naturally, one does not expect Roman architects to have necessarily thought in terms of what later came to be known as *l'architecture parlante*. Rather, they would have dedicated the votive act of building the temple to the idea of concord. And yet, the Vitruvian text clearly contains recommendations on associating divine and moral qualities with architectural qualities. But contrary to Vitruvius's recommendations (e.g. the use of the Doric as the proper columnar order for divinities of virile strength such as Minerva, Mars and Hercules,[4] and the use the Corinthian for delicate divinities such as Venus, Flora, and Proserpina) archaeological evidence has shown that temples to Hercules can be Corinthian. Their dimensions can be small and their shapes can be round like

9.3 Temple of Mars Ultor, Rome. After Louis Noguet. From Hector D'Espouy, Fragments d'architecture antique, Vol.2, Paris, Ch. Massin, 1905.

9.4 Santa Maria della Salute, Baldassare Longhena, Venice. *Source*: Photo by Ettore Mazzola.

the temple of Hercules Victor (and Olivarius) in the Forum Boarium, or rectangular like the large sanctuary dedicated to Hercules Victor in Tivoli. The architectural composition of the Roman temple can provide hexastyle, octastyle, peripteral, dipteral, or prostyle Corinthian temples of varying sizes, proportions, and materials, but it does not express martial avenging qualities as in the case of the Temple of Mars Ultor, anymore than it can express the refined mores of the deified emperor Antoninus Pius and his wife Faustina. Dedicated in two BC, the temple of Mars Ultor[5] was set within a rectangular forum, flanked by two long Corinthian porticoes surmounted by an attic storey with Caryatids and shields with the ram-horned face of Jupiter Ammon, and with an exhedra in each portico containing niches and statues connected to the Julian family as well as various statues personifying the peoples conquered by Augustus.

The temple was used by the Senate and military commanders for debates regarding military campaigns, while the porticoes were used as courts for legal deliberations. The temple has a Corinthian octastyle made of white Luna marble crowned by a pediment with bas-reliefs and sculptures and raised on a podium. Instead of volutes, the capitals had winged Pegasus motifs. The pronaos and cella floors were paved with Numidian yellow, Phrygian purple, and Lucullan red and black marbles, while the apse contained the focus of the cult, the marble statue of Mars. Votive intention provided the purpose for building the temple whereas its sculptural program conveyed the military dedication.

Building the Venetian church of Santa Maria della Salute[6] followed another votive act, this time expressed by a city to the Virgin after the terrible loss of life resulting from the plague of 1630.[7] Situated prominently near the Dogana where the Gran Canale, the Bacino di San Marco, and the Giudecca meet, Santa Maria della Salute occupies the site of a former church dedicated to the Trinity. Built of white Istrian stone, La Salute was completed in 1687, five years after the death of its architect, the Venetian Baldassare Longhena. Like the Baptistery of Constantine and the church of Santa Costanza in Rome, as well as San Vitale in Ravenna, the church is typologically an octagonal tholos, an octagonal plan with an internal ambulatory surmounted by a double-shelled dome and dominated by a statue of the Virgin standing on a crescent moon with a crown of twelve stars. Six sides of the octagon contain chapels which are expressed on the exterior as pedimented aedicules with large thermal windows. The other two sides differ. The side that faces the Gran Canale is a tall tetrastyle triumphal arch with pediment and a tall arched door that allowed an uninterrupted axial view to the chapel of the high altar, itself surmounted by a smaller dome. This last feature is particularly important because the church was to be the culmination of the annual procession from San Marco. It satisfied the commission's requirement that the High Altar as well as the other altars be easily visible as one moved into the church. It also gave a clear axial directionality to an otherwise centralized plan. Mediating between the lower and upper octagons are twelve very large scroll-buttresses adorned by statues of the Apostles and also corresponding to the twelve stars of the Virgin's crown. In the text accompanying his competition entry Longhena had commented on the rotund form of the church "being in the shape of a crown, since it is dedicated to the Virgin".[8] The date of the founding of the Salute was associated by the Venetians with legendary founding of Venice on the feast of the Assumption, giving an added meaning to the votive dedication to the Virgin and her protection against the plague. To this association many scholars have recalled the long-established tradition in Italy of raising round churches to the Virgin (previously to Vesta). But from the standpoint of architectural expressiveness, how does this church express gratitude to the Virgin, or health, or salvation? Indeed if the statues of the Virgin as well as the apostles were to be removed the votive purpose would not be evident, even though the civic purpose of the Salute is unmistakable.

Still in Venice, across the Bacino di San Marco, stands the Zecca, built between 1536 and 1545 by the Florentine architect Jacobo Sansovino (1486–1570) in order to accommodate the city's edifice for minting coins. The Zecca accommodates foundries, workshops, and administrative offices. It is composed of nine bays in two storeys, the third storey was added in 1558. The rusticated ground floor with

9.5 The Zecca, Jacobo Sansovino, Venice.
Source: Photo PAVDW.

voussoirs, included the Procuracy's cheese shops and is surmounted by a second storey with rusticated Doric columns. Spanning the windows at a height occurring toward the top third of the Doric columns are weighty projecting lintels which, when coupled with the boldly projecting mutules in the entablature give the building a top-heavy aspect. Rustication and strong tectonic projections, as many historians have observed, are closely associated with the character of fortifications such as those built by Michele Sanmicheli (1484–1559) in Verona. The analogy has been made between the solidity and amplified strength required by fortified walls and gates, and the sense of economic and political stability and military impregnability that the Venetian state wished to portray to citizen and foreigner alike. Portraying strength gives confidence to the citizen, while conveying the appearance of military might invokes respect if not fear in the minds of the enemies of the state. Like the Roman Tabularium and the buildings of the Procuracy on the Piazza San Marco, the Zecca's principal façade is composed almost exclusively of openings, arches, columns, and entablatures. But contrary to a palazzo's façade, which, as a comparison between solids and voids, is usually more wall than openings, the Zecca's façade contains more openings than wall. In fact, the wall is almost absent – a quality that also characterizes Sansovino's neighboring Biblioteca Marciana, as well as the Procuracies in the Piazza San Marco. In the Zecca the character of solidity and the scalar elements of the composition undeniably express the character of a public building that undoubtedly houses administrative offices. But with the absence of sculpture and bas-relief, the façade does not express that the building is a mint.

9.6 The French Panthéon/ Ste. Geneviève, Jacques-Germain Soufflot, Paris. *Source*: Photo in public domain, Cornell University Library.

The relation between sculpture and architectural character played a significant role in the secularization of the church of Sainte Geneviève in Paris. Located on the Montagne Sainte Geneviève – in part over the ruins of the Roman thermae as well as the former abbey of Ste. Geneviève – the church was designed by Jacques-Germain Soufflot (1713–1780), the foundations being laid in 1758.[9] The slightly elongated nave of an otherwise Greek cross plan, is preceded by a hexastyle Corinthian portico whose height surpasses that of the nave. The crossing is crowned by a tall tempietto with thirty columns raised on a drum. In 1791, the *Directoire* commissioned A-C. Quatremère de Quincy to secularize the church, transforming it into the French Panthéon, a national mausoleum for the burial of France's great national figures. Quatremère's architectural modifications consisted in isolating the church from the urban fabric in which it was integrated and removed the two bell towers that flanked the apse, effectively making the church an object building. In order to achieve an austere, sepulchral, and somber aspect in the interior, Quatremère denuded the walls and closed the fenestration in the cupola so as to admit light only from the lantern in the manner of ancient temples. The interior could then acquire the enclosed character of a grand tomb, for unlike sculpture and painting, architecture cannot convey admiration or grief for the loss of pivotal national figures.

Quatremère's sculptural modifications aimed at replacing all the religious sculptures and bas-reliefs by ones that symbolized and celebrated the state's public virtues. For the tympanum, for example, Quatremère removed the sculptural group *Triumph of Faith* and replaced it with a new grouping executed by Jean Gillaume Moitte: the *Motherland Crowning the Civic Virtues* (later changed again under the *Restauration* by David D'Angers). Much has been written about Soufflot's attempts to balance the heaviness (*pesanteur*) of the Classical with the lightness (*légèreté*) of the Gothic, and his lecture to the Académie des Beaux-Arts in

Lyon on Gothic architecture attests to his genuine appreciation of both systems.[10] The larger project undertaken by the *Directoire* and the architects who worked on secularizing the church has significant implications for the notion of architectural character. Passing from a church dedicated to the patron saint of Paris to a national mausoleum dedicated to illustrious leaders by virtue of the previously mentioned modifications, implies that the civic destination of the monument still obtained, even if one were to remove the sculptures altogether. Yet, if the monument is still identifiable as a church, it is only because of the long-established convention – dating back from Santa Maria dei Fiori in Florence, to St. Peter's in Rome, St. Paul's in London, and the domes of the Val de Grâce and the Invalides in Paris – that associates a pedimented portico, a great hall, a Greek or Latin cross plan, and a dome, with a church. In fact the Panthéon was briefly changed back to a church before becoming definitively a secular monument. But the French Revolution's monument *par excellence* conveys that the same architectural character, with slight modifications and a new sculptural programme, served the purpose of a church to the patron saint of Paris and that of a mausoleum to Mirabeau, Voltaire, Rousseau, Marat, Portalis, Cabanis, and many others including Soufflot himself. This experiment of divesting the portico, the pediment, and the dome, of their religious associations paved the way for the secular use of these same elements[11] in the various national and state capitols as well as universities in the Americas, e.g. the United States Capitol in Washington, or El Capitolio in La Havana, Cuba.

The Munich Glytothek and the Academy of Athens are two examples of the adoption of the same architectural character by two countries based on a fictive common narrative. Designed by Leo von Klenze (1784–1864) the Glyptothek sculpture gallery (1816–1830), in the Königsplatz complex in Munich, was commissioned by Crown Prince Ludwig of Bavaria as a great homage to ancient Greek culture. This homage includes the city's Propylea, also by von Klenze, in 1862. The Glyptothek was built in order to house the acquired Aegina Marbles as well as other Greek and Roman antiquities. Its main façade consists of a Greek octastyle Ionic portico whose capitals are a variation of the fifth-century BC Ionic capitals of the Erechtheion in Athens, while the pediment is crowned by an anthemion and two griffin-acroteria at the corners. The portico is flanked by two solid wings

9.7 Munich Glyptothek, Leo von Klenze. *Source*: Photo Chris73/Wikimedia Commons.

each containing three pedimented niches sheltering ancient Roman sculptures. That the Glyptothek has no windows, and that it is only entered from the portico helps to express a self-contained character, the idea that this building encloses and shelters valuable art within solid forms, and that this art is further ennobled by associating it with a Greek temple form. Doubtless, the building's details show von Klenze's considerable archaeological knowledge, but far from being Greek the general composition of the Glyptothek bears the influences of his training with Charles Percier, Pierre F.-L. Fontaine, and J.N.-L. Durand in Paris. Nonetheless, von Klenze's Glyptothek inscribes itself within Ludwig's larger idea of a German Athens championed also by architects Friedrich Gilly and Karl Friedrich Schinkel. Such assumed oneness of cultural purpose compelled Schinkel to propose a new royal palatial complex on the Acropolis, where a new Greco-German Classicism would combine with the ruins of the Parthenon and the Erectheion. In their attempts at forging a new German architectural character these architects eclectically converged compositional elements culled from local as well as Greek, Roman, and Italian Renaissance sources, producing a German classicism that obtained well into the 1940s. Following Greek independence, Ludwig's son, Otto, initiated a similar forging of a new classicism in Greece along the lines of German romanticism, beginning in the 1830s with a new master-plan for Athens by Friedrich von Gärtner and a modest number of buildings realized by several German architects including von Klenze and Ernst Ziller. But it was with the work of Danish architects Hans Christian Hansen (1803–1883), his brother Theophil Edvard Hansen (1813–1891),

9.8 Academy of Athens, Theophil Hansen.
Source: Photo by Michael Lykoudis.

and their Greek pupils that the new classicism exerted its widespread influence on the architecture of modern Greece. Their most important commissions in the newborn Greek state are the three architectural ensembles of the Athens University (1839–1889) by C. Hansen, and the National Library (1885–1892) and the Academy of Athens (1859–1897) by T. Hansen.

The Academy is organized around a central hall conceived as a tall marble amphiprostyle temple with a hexastyle Ionic portico. The volutes, architraves, soffits, and other tectonic details are rendered in the polychromatic tradition while the central tympanum contains haut-reliefs, by the sculptor Leonidas Drosis, that depict the birth of Athena. Hierarchically, the central hall is raised over the adjacent wings that face it at ninety degrees. Although the classical had one of its initial sources in Greece, and although it had been an established tradition in Germany, the new essentialist pursuit of the classical (Neo-classicism) was reintroduced to both countries as an "import". Assured by the cultural program of one dynasty that ruled both countries, this import became the shared bi-national architecture (with the Gothic in Germany being the other national architecture). Indeed, this new Greco-German classicism became inseparable from the architecture of Greek identity, influencing even the character of modest houses.

No other architectural setting was called to display national architectural character(s) than the early World Fairs, or Universal Expositions, that began in the

9.9 The Italian Pavilion, Exposition Universelle 1900, Paris.
Source: Photo by Joseph Hawkes.

middle nineteenth century. World fairs assigned to architects the difficult task of summarizing within one choice – usually one pavilion that housed national products – what might be considered the most expressive national architectural character. Painfully reductive though such an architectural exercise may have been, it was charged with the task of becoming an instant national monument thrust onto the world scene. In a sense, the World Fair pavilions played the role of temporary embassies where one building was called upon to express one national character. In the 1900 Exposition Universelle in Paris, for example, Italy's pavilion was closely based on the church of San Marco, and some of the patterns selected from the Dodge's Palace. The pavilion was a rectangular hall entered on four sides through high arches and Gothic tracery, surmounted by a tall dome modeled on San Marco's central dome. Italy was represented by Venice. The United States' pavilion was a centralized plan entered through a triumphal arch surmounted by a quadriga guided by Liberty and a crowning dome loosely based on that of the Invalides.

9.10 The United States Pavilion, Exposition Universelle, 1900, Paris.
Source: Photo by Joseph Hawkes.

The US pavilion continued the grand Beaux-Arts triumphalism that had been launched in 1893 by the World's Columbian Exhibition in Chicago. Surpassing its predecessors by its extravagant scale where Roman Forae, baths, Baroque palaces, massive colonnades, and tall domes defined the edges of vast artificial lagoons and canals, Chicago's Columbian Exhibition played a significant role in the future of American architecture.

Although the buildings were a temporary and perishable scenography made of wooden scaffolding, plaster, and canvas, they marked the American imagination in an enduring way by elaborating a civic character in the grand manner that was later adopted in many American cities as a manifestation of their city-state consciousness and pride. Its most visible effects were the City Beautiful Movement, most notably the McMillan plan of Washington, as well as civic complexes in Chicago, Cleveland, Madison, Denver, San Francisco, and other cities. However, as World Fairs multiplied and as modernist architecture came to dominate, the architectural characters of the pavilions gradually became less identifiable with a country and more with abstractions such as the future, or progress. e.g. the French Pavilion or Soviet Pavilion in the Brussels Exposition of 1958. The universality these forms enjoyed was due precisely because of their abstraction from a previous place or tradition.

THE LIMITS OF ARCHITECTURAL EXPRESSION   213

9.11   The World's Columbian Exhibition, 1893, Chicago, Illinois, Machinery Hall.
Source: Photo from *The Columbian Exposition Album*, Rand, McNally & Co.
Publishers, Chicago and New York, 1893.

9.12   Sydney Opera House, Jorn Utzon.
Source: Photo by Karina Lizzi.

Built at Bennelong Point, a site that reaches prominently into Sydney Harbour, the Sydney Opera House (1957–1973) was one of the most discussed buildings of the twentieth century. It was designed by Danish architect Jorn Utzon (1918– 2008), who had won the international competition, although the building was completed, with modifications, by other architects in 1973 after Utzon's resignation in 1966. The Opera House is mainly composed of a low rectilinear masonry-clad base contrasted by the hovering white-tiled precast concrete roofs that have been described as sails, shells, and even a family of swans. Dominating the overall massing, the two most important halls, the Concert Hall and the Opera Theatre, inflect slightly one from the other. Each of them is surmounted by three shells that face the harbor while the single shells, built over the entrances, face the city. There is little façade, in the conventional sense, as the building is primarily made of a base and roofs. Admiring architects frequently describe it as an expressionistic monumental sculpture, citing a "poetic factor" that considers the base and the roof as symbolic representations of the earth and the heavens, with the sails or shells being likened to cloud canopies. Parallels have also been made to similar preceding structures such as the Radiohaus (1933–45) in Copenhagen by Vilhelm Lauritzen, the Los Manantiales restaurant (1958) at Xochimilco in Mexico City by Felix Candela and J. Alvarez Ordonez, and the TWA Terminal at the John F. Kennedy International Airport in New York by Eero Saarinen (1956–1962).[12] The Sydney Opera house is a national monument that has become synonymous with national identity, indeed a declaration by the Australian government exclaims that the opera house is "as representative of Australia as the pyramids are of Egypt and the Colosseum of Rome".[13] The purpose of the New South Wales' government to erect a civic monument dedicated to the performing arts certainly galvanized the civic consciousness toward finding a fitting architectural image that several competing proposals tried to express. Yet, beyond general comments about observing nature, appreciating elegant animal forms, as well as his indebtedness to the work of Alvar Aalto, Utzon rarely explained the direct influences behind his chosen forms or the reasons for developing his scheme as the proper expression for an opera house that was also meant to be a national monument. Doubtless, the unique, bold, and vast forms he produced show his interest in the distinctive silhouettes resulting from assembling segments of precast concrete parabolic shapes that may be evocative of ship's sails or animal shells. If the roofs were indeed representations of sails, or shells, presumably because of the building's site in the harbor, then it would be indeed fundamental to know how the relationship between sails concert halls are justified architecturally and sculpturally. There is no question that the building's unique expression, and complicated engineering, made for its renowned fame linking it to buildings such as Rudolf Steiner's second Goetheanum at Dornach (1928), Le Corbusier's Notre Dame du Haut at Ronchamp (1954), and Frank Gehry's Guggenheim Museum at Bilbao (1997). Yet in each of these cases respectively, it is difficult to see the character of the building as an expression of Goethe's thought, of the divine qualities of the Virgin, or of the Guggenheim's art collections. But it is relatively evident to see these buildings as deeply subjective expressions especially when compared to their estrangement from their contexts. Whereas the character

9.13 Yale Centre for British Art, Louis Kahn, New Haven. *Source*: Photo by Anthony Younés.

of monuments previously emerged from within the forms of local architectural culture, the Sydney Opera House show that the character of a monument is now considered successful precisely because of its abstract expression. The paradox presented by buildings such as the Sydney Opera House is its astonishingly rapid association with a national identity notwithstanding the fact that it is an intensely personal expression that bears no connection to the architecture(s) of Sydney. Indeed had it been built on the waterfronts of Tokyo, Rio di Janeiro, or New York, it would have been as distinct from the architecture of all three cities. The same may be said of Frank Lloyd Wright's Guggenheim Museum in New York (1956–59) and the new cities of Brasilia in Brazil (inaugurated in 1960) and Chandigarh in India (1952–59).

Housing one of the most extensive collections of British art in the world (ranging from the late eighteenth to the middle nineteenth century), the Yale Centre for British Art was completed in 1974 following the death of its architect Louis Kahn (1901–1974), who had also built the neighboring Yale University Art Gallery in 1953. The Yale Centre for British Art was established by American philanthropist Paul Mellon "to reflect the humane and orderly world of the paintings it was to house, and it was to be an unassertive presence in its urban setting".[14] Occupying a corner block and maintaining the street edge, the building contains a wide two-bay corner entrance and museum shops on the ground floor, while the galleries occured on the upper levels. Kahn's choice of expression for the façades is a grid of rectangular concrete bays enclosing glass and stainless steel panels. This expression, met with widespread professional approval, with occasional dissenting remarks about the building's lack of connection to its architectural context.[15] If, in the most general sense, museums are great containers of art, then Kahn's building, because of its

9.14 Magdalen College, Demetri Porphyrios, Oxford. *Source*: Photo by Porphyrios Associates Architects, © D. Porphyrios.

enclosed system of bays and occasional windows, does indeed express self-containment. And unlike the repetitive and undifferentiated gridded façades of many contemporary structures, the Yale Centre's grid is differentiated into smaller divisions of panels. This compositional device notwithstanding, the fundamental three-part question concerns the relationship between the museum's abstract industrial character, the art that it is supposed to shelter, and the local architectural character into which it is inserted. An observer will find difficulty in deducing that the building contains British, African or Japanese art, or that the building forms part of the campus of Yale University that contains a significant number of Collegiate Gothic buildings many of which had been completed only forty years before.[16] The Yale Centre results from Kahn's preference for the universal applicability of an industrial character over the threefold issue of building character, the art it contains, and the context. Accommodating this threefold issue, however, is no easy matter, even if it was the architect's intention to do so. Robert Smirke's British Museum is well inserted within the immediate urban context of London's Great Russell square on the level of scale and its hierarchy as a civic building. Yet, like von Klenze before him, Smirke's preference for the Greek Revival as the most apposite architecture to house Egyptian, Greek, and Asian art also signaled his belief in the universal applicability of the Greek Revival irrespective of urban context.

Built by Demetri Porphyrios (b.1949), Magdalen College at Oxford (1994–98) provides new student residential quarters and an auditorium. Based in part on the Oxbridge tradition of quadrangles, Magdalen College is organized around a three-sided rectangular space with the fourth being open to the neighboring park. Rather than surrounding the quadrangle with one single continuous building, Magdalen College is composed of five buildings, four of which serve residential uses, with the last building being the auditorium. The smaller residential buildings, standing side by side, assure the spatial definition of the quadrangle while facilitating hierarchy between them and with respect to the auditorium. As it is primarily a

9.15 Pritzker Music Pavilion, Frank Gehry, Chicago, Illinois. Source: Photo by Author.

building dedicated to lectures or small performances, the classical auditorium has few openings except for the round clear-storey windows. It's simple geometry, a single volume built of yellow Ketton stone surmounted by a gable with copper roof, serves to distinguish it hierarchically from the residential buildings which are built in the Magdalen Gothic and articulated with arcades, flat ogival arches, tripartite windows, and stone roofs with oak dormers. The auditorium is located at the shorter end of the rectangular quadrangle, thus perspectively emphasizing its hierarchical position. By treating the new quadrangle as a square, and providing a clear distinction between the public and the private characters, a new complex of buildings was inserted within a preexisting architectural context with decorum, maintaining urban and architectural continuity.

Completed in 2004, the Pritzker Music Pavilion in Chicago was designed by Frank Gehry (b.1929) as the central element of a larger urban proposal that links two parts of Grant Park, on the shore of Lake Michigan, that are presently separated by a multi-lane highway. The Pritzker Pavilion was built to hold outdoor musical performances, accommodating four thousand fixed seats, and many more on the lawn. It is composed of two principal parts: the slightly sloping seating area, and the ensemble of forms that includes the stage area. Facing the stage, a trellis network of steel pipes supports a speaker system that diffuses the music into the broad lawn facing the stage. The most distinguishing feature of the Pavilion is the undulating forms that surmount the stage and project over it in the direction of the audience. These undulating forms are folded aluminum ribbons coated with an outer layer of stainless steel and are carried, projected, and suspended, by a structural system of steel members. A description by the Guggenheim Museum states that this project "suggests musical qualities", that the forms projecting over the stage shell are "reminiscent of brass horns", and that the trellis network "suggests sound waves washing over the audience".[17] Another, more architectural, description called the project a "Baroque bandstand" presumably by associating Gehry's undulating forms with the convex and concave forms present in Baroque buildings, but also in reference to Gilles Deleuze's book *Le pli: Leibniz et le baroque*, *The Fold: Leibniz and the Baroque*, in which he sees Baroque folding forms not in a historical sense, but rather as an ahistorical formal sensibility that manifests in architecture or clothing.[18] These attempts to explain the Pavilion by analogies with the art of music, with instruments that produce music, and with the plastic sensibilities of Baroque architecture, show the observers' search for meaning and justification from outside of architecture as well as from inside of it. Proposing that the Pavilion suggests musical qualities and a reminiscence of brass instruments, implies a belief in a certain imitative transparency, even on a weak level, between music, the crafting of musical instruments, and architecture. Calling the Pavilion a Baroque bandstand assumes that behind the architect's decisions were Baroque sensibilities with immediate emotional appeal such as mannerist folds, profound capriciousness, vertical and lateral movement, expressionistic theatricality, and even a "painterly" affinity (to use Heinrich Wölflin's term). The Pavilion fulfills at once the requirements of a bandstand as well as the architect's ardent interest to surmount and surround the bandstand with his folded sculptural forms, displacing the idea of planes, of verticality, horizontality, and enclosure. If the building seems grounded, the idea of roof has been avoided. Much has been said about the contrast between the large curvilinear forms against the backdrop of even move massive and vertical skyscrapers, and by virtue of this contrast and its singular presence in the park, the Pavilion assumes the aura of a landmark. Yet like the Sydney Opera House, it is paradoxically considered a fitting civic monument not because of its participation in a sense of place or because it emerged from established traditions, but precisely because it is an expression of intense individuality and abstraction. With respect to the limits of architectural expression, Pritzker Pavilion is a fusion between sculpture and architecture stemming from the belief that the same expression applies to both arts.

****

Because of the multiple associations we project onto architectural character, we sometimes overlook that the number of elements available for architectural composition is remarkably small. Most of the volumes and geometries are usually derivative of the cube (square), the sphere (circle), or the pyramid (triangle). Most of the tectonic elements derive from ideas of enclosing, covering and spanning; from which we derive walls, openings, stairs, trabeations, arcuations, trusses, and roofs. Most of the materials are stone, brick, mud, wood, plaster, tile, glass, and metal. A vast range of buildings serving the civic and the private realms can be produced with a finite number of elements and their numerous combinations. At the heart of the issue of character lies the multiplicity of associations that we make between expression and purpose. As we have seen, architects and historians have labored at associating architectural character with Nature, with history, social mores, social classes, personal taste, the patron's taste, *technique*, the spirit of the age, the rupture with history, the linguistic analogy, personal expression, and regional traditions. Architects who strive for clarity of expression expect buildings to unambiguously identify their purpose by the very composition of their volumes, façades, and ornaments. Only, with conflicting associations and multiple compositions, confusions may arise.

For that reason we have distinguished between two kinds of confusions. The first is a confusion between artistic genres, the second is a confusion in the use of architectural elements. The first confusion consists in expecting architecture to express the same set of ideas, mores, feelings as the other arts. This error began when earlier theorists tried to elaborate a unitary theory of the fine arts that evolved, as an unintended consequence, the belief that the same general theory of composition is somehow applicable to all the arts. *L'architecture parlante* and its derivatives continued the expectation that architectural and artistic expression can draw very close and may even fuse. That is why we argued for keeping the clarity between the limits or bounds of expression proper to each of the arts, differentiating between the limited artistic fiction available to architecture and the wider range of fiction available to the other visual arts. The second confusion results from using the same architectural element for widely different purposes thus harming the clarity of association between expression and purpose. When the pedimented portico comes to be indiscriminately applied to civic buildings such as the church, the courthouse, the state capitol, the bank, the stock exchange, the library, the museum, and private buildings such as the town house and the villa, this element looses its civic as well as its private associations. Additionally, we contended that it is possible to avoid the confusion of genres without harming artistic freedom of expression. And as the artistic freedom of expression is linked to the artistic limits between the arts[19] we cautioned that the notion of limits should not be confused with the notion of limitation on artistic freedom, on self-expression. We noted that although artistic freedom of expression is to be enthusiastically encouraged, (otherwise we cannot make claims to democratic pluralism) such a freedom does not operate by itself. Self-expression is a partial cause for architectural character. The other two tasks are civic purpose and the patron's private purpose, and the architect's difficult charge resides in reconciling the three. Hard though this charge may be – as many architects are unwilling or unable to reconcile the three tasks – it is not impossible to realize.

Achieving clarity between expression and purpose extends also to the collective gathering of individual building characters that amounts to a regional character, whether that region is a quarter, a city, or a nation. But that desired quality is in dire retreat today because of the widespread disagreement amongst architects regarding what constitutes architectural character. For this reason, few cities for the foreseeable future – except those with disciplined conservation policies – will exhibit a coherent regional character. And yet, we hold several contradictory positions on this issue. On the one hand, we strongly desire the sense of place that is assured by a coherent set of architectural characters, and we acclaim it in international organizations, such as World Heritage, and in local conservation organizations. On the other, we exalt self-expression to such a point that it outweighs the previous sense of place as a matter of daily practice. In fact, it is no exaggeration to state that many architects today believe that their self-expression overrides the sense of place. If architectural practice means self-expression to the exclusion of civic decorum, then the City is condemned to be the haphazard accumulation of competing private tastes. The private realm can then overwhelm the civic realm, and the City reverts to its beginnings as a settlement. Many architects equate self-expression with their will and their right to differ, even though on a propositional level, self-expression also includes the will to agree with others on a common set of principles in view of a larger good. Despite the occasional advocacy for contextualism (a term that has been given widely different interpretations) we are a long way from arriving at a resolution that satisfies at once our admiration for the sense of place with our exaltation of self-expression. This does not imply that for architects to participate in the sense of place, they must engage in widespread copying of existing buildings. We already distinguished between the copy, on the one side, and the inseparable couple: imitation – invention, on the other. Revivalist architects and conservation movements make the historical mistake of assuming that once regional character is formed then it should remain fixed once and for all. Yet, the life of cities shows that regional character undergoes internal transformations and accepts external additions which later come to be considered as local. With time, they may even be considered native. Of course, not all external interventions are created equal. Some of them willfully harmonize with their context, while others produce jarring, violent, and shocking results. Political pluralism justifies the right of expression to both approaches. Artistic pluralism, however, compels judgment as to which is the more decorous approach based on a set of evaluative criteria, such as the ones discussed in this book. This is the difficult essence of the Aristotelian "ought" as applied to architectural judgment.

NOTES

1   J. Kipnis, "Toward a New Architecture", in *Architectural Design*, 102, (London, 1993).

2   There have been several alternative explanations to the Vitruvian theory of petrification according to which triglyphs are stylized tectonic elements in stone recalling their origins as the ends of wooden beams – most notably was E-E. Viollet-le-Duc's explanation of triglyphs as stone piers. The recent explanation that places the tripod as the origin of the triglyph has been advanced by Mark Wilson-Jones. See his "Tripods, Triglyphs and the Origins of the Doric Frieze" in *American Journal of Archaeology*, 106, (2002), pp. 353–90.

3   See I. Kagis McEwen's discussion of the Temple of Concord in *Vitruvius: Writing the Body of Architecture*, (MIT Press, 2003), pp. 104–12.

4   I, 2, 5.

5   Octavian (Augustus) had vowed to build the temple at the battle of Philippi where Caesar's assassins were defeated in 44 BC.

6   Latin: *salus*; Italian: *salute*, designating at once physical health as well as spiritual salvation.

7   Other churches had also been previously dedicated to healing the victims of the plague such as the church and *scuola* of San Rocco.

8   Quoted in D. Howard, *The Architectural History of Venice*, (Yale, 2002), p. 216.

9   For a history of Ste. Geneviève and its transformations, including the praise and the disputes surrounding its construction, the stability of its dome, see A. Braham, *The Architecture of the French Enlightenment*, (University of California Press, 1980); *Soufflot et l'architecture des lumières*, Actes du colloque à Lyon, (Ecole Nationale Supérieure de Beaux-Arts, 1986); *Jacques-Germain Soufflot*, Jean-Marie Pérouse de Monclos, (Monum, 2004).

10 See "Mémoire sur l'architecture gothique" in *Esthétique du XVIIème siècle. Le modèle français*, Baldine Saint-Girons, (Philippe Sers, 1990).

11 It is beyond the purpose of this study to trace the changing association of architectural elements like pediments or domes, from religious to secular uses.

12 P. Drew, "Poetic Paradox", in *Building a Masterpiece: the Sydney Opera House*, Anne Watson (ed.), (Powerhouse Publishing, 2006), pp. 68–83.

13 See: http://australia.gov.au/about-australia/australian-story/sydney-opera-house

14 "The Yale Centre for British Art", in *Burlington Magazine*, CXIX(890), (1977), p. 315.

15 V. Scully, "Yale Center for British Art", in *Architectural Record*, (1977).

16 For an architectural survey of the campus of Yale University, see P. Pinnell, *The Campus Guide, Yale University*, (Princeton Architectural Press, 1999).

17 Available at: http://web.archive.org/web/20080226003714/http://www.guggenheim.org/exhibitions/past_exhibitions/gehry/millenium_30.html

18 Casey C.M. Matthewson, *Frank O. Gehry, Selected Works: 1969 to Today*, (Firefly Books, 2007), pp. 574–7; G. Deleuze, *Le Pli: Leibniz et le baroque*, (Les éditions de Minuit, 1988).

19 See Chapter 5.

Conclusion
The Usefulness of Conflict for Judgment

> *If man lived an Arcadian shepherd's existence of harmony, modesty and mutuality, man, good-natured like the sheep he is herding, would not invest his existence with greater value than that his animals have. Man would not fill the vacuum of creation as regards his end, rational nature. Thanks are due to nature for this quarrelsomeness, this envious competitive vanity, and for this insatiable desire to possess or to rule, for without them all the excellent natural faculties of mankind would forever remain undeveloped. Man wants concord but nature knows better what is good for his kind; nature wants discord.*[1]
>
> Immanuel Kant

In the preceding chapters we considered five general themes: the first four exert a notable influence on external architectural judgment, and the fifth theme plays a vital role in internal architectural judgment.

1. We have seen that the retreat of grand historical narratives has given way to a multitude of smaller histories and how historicism collapsed into egalitarian relativism. Yet, to a limited degree, some integrative possibilities are also clearly evident. The categories of type, character, and style allow for an alternative writing of architectural history that avoids the sweeping claims of grand narratives and the fragmentary nature of particularized histories; while the cluster of differentiated forces vaguely assembled under the term modernity hold the hope for a possible cultural synthesis that may prove beneficial in the future.
2. We noted that even though modernity proves to be an elusive concept on account of its frequent shifts in meaning, architects still make definitive judgments based on modernity as if it had one single fixed and stable definition that enjoyed general approbation.
3. We emphasized the ways in which architecture and politics are called to serve the public realm, but observed that architecture suffers from

C.1   Looking toward the finials of Sant'Ignazio, Rome.
Source: Photo by Author.

two kinds of monism: the first inculcates external political content onto architectural form, the second claims legitimacy to one single way of practicing or teaching architecture. We differentiated political freedom from artistic freedom, and showed that the conflation between the two causes a blurring of the distinction between artistic genres, and weakens the clarity of their definitions.
4. We observed how imitation and desire for form play a formative role in the intellectual and emotional life of architects. But we also noted the paradox presented by imitation, notwithstanding its superlative qualities. Imitation was at once a basis for learning as well as a basis for the mimetic rivalry between architects – a phenomenon that contributes to destabilizing the architectural discipline.
5. Finally, we examined the concept of architectural character in relation to imitation and invention; to self-expression and civic expression; to the private and the civic realms. We also examined the limits (in the sense of boundaries) of architectural expression.

These considerations concerned the intersection between history and philosophy, cultural theory, politics, psychology, and architectural expression, forming a varied set of external and internal criteria that significantly condition architectural judgment. For several decades now, architects and historians have saturated the architectural discourse with polemics deriving from these five cultural areas. Architectural conflicts have brought the five themes into the arena of judgment, interpenetrating their tenets and augmenting their influence; yet not one single theme constitutes by itself *the* privileged battle-ground. As we noted in the introduction, in order to be comprehensive architectural judgment needs to include the external as well as internal criteria. But rare are the architects who examine these criteria comprehensively before pronouncing their judgment. Instead, individual architects deploy their judgments, at times in a definitive manner, while considering only a few of these criteria, and sometimes only superficially. For an inclusive examination of these criteria we need the wisdom assured by a certain historical distance. We need to consider how opposing architectural groups elaborate the intellectual discourse (theory) and how they structure the formal material (creativity and practice) available to them over the span of generations in relation to the larger cultural currents in which they are situated. Understanding the larger intellectual ecology in which architectural judgment arises makes it evident to us why it is exceedingly rare for an architect today to stand facing a building without any previous preconception, without any previous mediation. And this mediation, which includes the external as well as the internal criteria for architectural judgment, is to a considerable degree formed by the cultural commonplaces of contemporary pluralistic democracies.

THE PLURALIST CONTEXT

Perhaps the most prevailing commonplace today is the declared commitment to cultural pluralism. Architects may disagree on what is an architectural paradigm, or whether architectural paradigms still play a vital role today, but many of them have come to uphold one single overarching cultural paradigm. This shared paradigm can be described as a pluralistic outlook, one that allows a multiplicity of architectural forms to thrive unfettered by the annoying impositions of competing architectural judgments, one that avoids unyielding categorizations, single-minded orthodoxies, and determining grand narratives. Some have characterized this outlook as a laissez-faire attitude deriving from a certain fatigue, a certain weariness caused by intense conflicts between short-lived theories. Others, such as Jurgen Habermas, feeling the same weariness, recommended a certain "letting things be", a backing-away from decades of relentless bickering. The pluralist outlook now forms the larger cultural milieu in which the themes we discussed in this book move and have their being. But this broad cultural tolerance was not always the case. If cultural pluralism is widely accepted today, it was to a large extent due to the compelling forces of political pluralism. Modern society developed political pluralism much earlier (and this is one of the greatest achievements of modernity) than artistic pluralism, for this is an indispensable condition for its internal stability. The pluralist outlook brought some noted benefits as well as some unintended detrimental results.

Although conflicts and antagonisms are quite acute amongst architects this condition is not altogether different in other disciplines. Adherents to different disciplines are concerned about the effects of their conflicts on themselves, and they rarely calculate the effects on the whole of society. They take it for granted that pluralistic democracy provides a cultural space so vast in its reach as to contain a multitude of smaller conflicts, yet without loosing stability in the whole. They take it as a given that this cultural space embraces all positions, including those that claim exclusive validity. Graver concerns are usually expressed about political conflicts than cultural conflicts that have their internal political relationships, their own periods of stability or turmoil. Contrary to Le Corbusier's categorical admonition that if architecture was not reformed then social revolution will inevitably result, few believe today that cultural conflicts such as the ones that proliferate amongst architects will lead to political unrest.

Quite significantly, whereas it wishes to contain political conflicts, pluralistic democracy does not seek to contain conflicts over cultural forms such as architecture or the arts, for that would be contrary to its encouragement of intellectual or artistic freedom. Crises and conflicts in these cultural forms are phenomena that plumb the psychological depths of architects and artists, but they are, unfortunately, considered to be surface phenomena when it comes to the stability of political life. Intellectual or artistic crises that shake the theoretical foundations of architecture do not destabilize political life. And yet, as we outlined in Chapter 5, politics and architecture are both called to serve the public and private realms (the *res publica* and *res privata*) in a reciprocal way; and when architecture fails, for instance, to serve the public realm symbolically (e.g. architectural character) and practically (e.g. by providing commodious shelter), the damage to the architectural-symbolic dimension of political life is noteworthy. One example of such a failure concerns the contemporary understanding of the monument. So divisive have theoretical conflicts been about what constitutes a monument that architects frequently produce buildings of such reductive architectural characters that the nature of monumentality, of commemorativeness, is altogether ignored or avoided. Because there is such widespread disagreement on the architectural character(s) that befits each purpose that needs to be monumentalized (peace memorials, war memorials, Olympic gymnasia) the monument's symbolic nature has been in retreat for several decades.

Pluralistic democracy, then, assumes the substantial responsibility of containing, rather than resolving, political conflicts, and it allows cultural conflicts to develop according to their own dynamics. But here, pluralistic democracy also cultivates an apparently contradictory practice that exerts a strong influence over cultural conflicts – a practice that is usually overlooked. The apparent contradiction revolves around the simultaneous practice of containment and expansion. Conflicts and rivalries are acceptable as long as they do not destabilize the social order (political containment), while freedom of expression is broadly encouraged (expansion of cultural forms). This apparent contradiction stems from the understanding of war and peace as irreconcilable Manichaean opposites. Qualities such as belligerence, hostility, and confrontation, are set in opposition to qualities such as concord, serenity, and harmony. These qualities are then transposed, *mutatis mutandis*, from political conflicts onto cultural ones. Cultural conflicts are classified within the "war camp", while the permissive acceptance of cultural differences is classified within the "peace camp". It has become commonplace today to speak of "cultural wars" or "architectural wars", when in reality these are conflicts between cultural groups who are encouraged by pluralistic democracy to express their full volition and who are left to vie for primacy within the same cultural space alongside other cultural groups. The result of this "war versus peace" understanding is that the useful side of conflicts is overlooked. In order to avoid the "war versus peace" impasse, we might also avoid the confusion between war and conflict. More precisely, we might avoid a *strictly narrow theory of war*, on the one hand, and an *overly general theory of conflict*, on the other. Some social elements in a given culture are capable of provoking war, whereas others produce only conflicts.[2]

This leads us to consider the dual role that conflict plays in constructing culture in general, and the ways in which it affects architectural culture in particular. As we shall see, one aspect of this role can be considered detrimental – especially in the short term – while the other is constructive – especially in the long term. As we noted previously, when conflicts become excessive they turn into antagonisms threatening to destabilize the discipline by undermining the very sociability between architects and the legitimization of their judgments. *This is a narrow theory of "cultural war"*. Although architects accept their discord as a given, they necessarily expect that society on the whole be stable, if only for their selfish interest in exercising their will-to-make unfettered by obstacles. As differentiated groups and differentiated individuals, architects accept the idea of stability in the whole but discord in the groups that compose that whole. They expect the pluralist political context to assure the stability in the whole. It is easy to ask that architects turn away from their conflicts and even their antagonisms. But this is a naïve and largely insufficient question. Those who wish to end conflicts and those who enjoy them (for even those who seek conflicts eventually desire their end) un-enviably share the same disappointment that conflict will simply not cease. *This is an overly general theory of cultural conflicts*. There will be conflicts and antagonisms as long as there is mimetic rivalry between individuals who desire the same cultural forms. There will be conflicts and antagonisms as long as architects conflate their mode of being with the buildings they make. But conflict has another role, one that is useful and even necessary for the improvement of culture in general and architecture in particular. We examine this useful role to conflict and inquire if the cure for the problem might not reside in the problem itself. Indeed, we may ask, with only a modest degree of exaggeration, if concord between opinions is even possible today without some kind of preceding conflict?

CONFLICT THREATENS AND PROTECTS CULTURE

The aspiration to achieve a just civic constitution compels us to believe that democratic society is moving toward pacified human relations, toward the cessation of violence, destruction, conflicts and antagonisms, or at least their gradual diminution. We believe that conflicts, in society, in international politics, or in artistic culture, can be surpassed and eventually eliminated, and we content ourselves with pluralism as a beneficial intermediate answer. However, the persistence and proliferation of conflicts in all socio-cultural levels runs contrary to such wishes causing concerns, anguish, disappointments, and pessimism. We worry that the increase in cultural conflicts will be accompanied with an increase in "cultural barbarism" because we identify barbarism with chaotic cultural conditions, violent oppositions, ignoble sentiments, or decadent comportments. We tend to forget that by identifying barbarians as those who threaten a city or a civilization from outside its borders, we implicitly mean that barbarians play a role in the way in which a city or civilization defines itself. Yet, by belonging inside one culture and standing outside another, "barbarians" visit many cultural ramparts, many cities, many cultures, and the cultures of smaller groups within society, thus helping to transmit many ideas, artistic forms, and techniques. So, appreciation must be expressed to the "cultural barbarians" among us for their role in the spreading of culture. Moreover, amongst the cultural groups and their closely entwined conflictual relations, cultural borders are as much inside as they are outside, and so are the "cultural barbarians". In an age of differentiation accompanied by widespread mistrust, each of us is at once a citizen in one context and a "barbarian" in another. It is therefore beneficial to accept the role of cultural conflicts in building civilization, in building the city, because if conflicts are unrecognized or repressed, if they are relegated to the shadow area of the personality, or the personality of a group, they can become barbarisms in the worst sense of this word. Analogically, it is important not to assume that architectural conflicts stand separate from the building of architectural culture even though judgmental comportments, mordant criticism, and deceptive sophistry have the capacity to exasperate conflicts in a most infuriating way.

In his *Idea for a Universal History with Cosmopolitan Intent*, Kant praises the value of conflict on three interconnected scales: that of individuals, that of society, and that of nature as it contains society.³ He gives particular importance to what he calls quarrelsomeness – that "unsociable sociability" among citizens who come together in society while resisting this togetherness. Without mutual resistance and raucous quarrelsomeness they may not have been compelled to realize their intellectual and moral potentials, and to eventually combine their talents. The greater the freedom of expression in society, the greater the possible conflicts among its members. Freedom and conflict combine to develop the full capacities of citizens. But freedom, conflict, and even antagonisms, are only useful if they eventually become the cause of lawful order within society. Freedom of expression is not indefinite as it needs to coexist with other freedoms, hence the need for law in politics and for principles and rules in art and architecture. From the perspective of an individual who is directly involved in cultural conflicts, these conflicts may appear very divisive and traumatic; but for an external observer who is considering the cumulative individual endeavors in a society, it will appear that society is continually advancing. Quarrelsomeness, conflicts and antagonisms, according to Kant, are the means used by nature to bring about the advancement of society. They are at the basis of culture and of the arts. Ultimately, Kant suggests that war is nature's way to teach humans to reach the goals that reason had already made available to them without the need for such an unfortunate experience. The Kantian point is worthy of reiteration in the words of psychologist James Hillman: "the martial spirit constructs civilization by promoting internal dissension between parties".⁴

It takes little to awaken Mars inside the architect-polemicist, the architect as a mimetic rival within the arena of public debates, or the courtroom of competitions where the desire to challenge a rival is passionately animated by the thrill of the risk. The risk makes the play. Architectural judgment turns into a performance of agonistic play (Greek *agon*: competition as a play or ludic function), of competitive impulse, and polemical play (Greek *polemos*: war).⁵ These qualities are part and parcel of the formation of architects' personae as they amalgamate their identities with their forms. Nothing confirms or exasperates identities or beliefs like the mimetic rivalry that plays out in public as a competition of minds and forms, as a martial exchange of opposing stances. Competition is usually heralded for its supposed useful effects on cultural and architectural innovation; and this belief predisposes us to overlook the *excesses* of competitiveness especially when incited, ritualized, and institutionalized by the architectural academy and the profession. Conflicts and competitions sustain architects by sustaining their group identities as well as their individual identities. Winning a competition helps to cohere a group who now feels culturally vindicated, whereas the loosing group begins to mimetically study their rivals' methods while waiting for a better day. Conflicts and competitions have the tremendous potency of converging into one point in time all the qualities of the architect as a maker of form and a slayer of form. There, in the midst of conflict, architects display their multiple facets. They are more than *homo sapiens* in the sense of knowing and knowing that they know; or *homo faber*, the maker; or *homo oeconomicus* in the sense of calculating their personal interests in relation to the interests of their patrons; or *homo aestheticus* who values beauty; or *homo militis*, the fighter, and sometimes the revolutionary who violently upsets the status quo. They are also *homo ludens*, the game-player who exalts in the prowess of devising rules for composition and rules for judging composition, as well as the consumption of all of the previously listed qualities. Conflict and play threaten and protect architectural culture.

TWO ARCHITECTURAL CONFLICTS AND THEIR SUBSEQUENT VALUE

How could Kant's "envious competitive vanity", "quarrelsomness", and the qualities of contesting, of dissenting, competing, modifying, or severing, take part in building and protecting architectural culture? What constructive outcome can derive from such qualities? We examine a few elements belonging to two architectural conflicts that have had considerable importance for architectural thought. The first, which includes a small cluster of architects represented by François Blondel and Claude Perrault, occurred in the late seventeenth century and presaged developments whose resonance continues to animate architectural and aesthetic judgments. The second, which includes a larger cluster of architects represented by Peter Eisenman and Léon Krier, summarizes the polar opposites within contemporary architectural thought over the past three decades or so. It is important to note that whereas the first was termed a conflict between ancients and moderns, the second can be termed as conflict between moderns and moderns. It is not our purpose to describe these architectural conflicts by drawing attention to their protagonists as personae or clusters of personae, or to the contrarianism that accompanies their critical minds. Nor is it our purpose to expand on the intellectual lineages and contexts that led to the formulation of their positions. Their intellectual histories are well known. Instead, we will examine some of the results of these conflicts from the standpoint of their usefulness to architectural culture at large.

Within the larger context of rationalism (e.g. René Descartes) and sense based theory (e.g. John Locke), it is significant that the conflict between the two principal architectural figures of the *Querelle des anciens et des modernes*, both steeped in Cartesian rationalism, both erudite savants of the principles of classical architecture, was to take place initially around the concept of beauty in architecture. For François Blondel, as well as many members of the Académie Royale d'architecture, artistic and architectural rules imitated the laws of Nature. Natural beauty was the basis for the beauty found in the arts and in architecture. Beauty, affirmed Blondel in his *Cours*, was a concept that connected all the arts and architecture (including music and dance).[6] Beauty was an objective property of beautiful things (buildings, sculptures) and the proper arrangements of their parts. But beauty depended above all else on proportions. It pleases the mind and the senses universally; and although different individuals have different appreciations of beautiful objects, beauty was not relative, nor was it subject to time or varying historical conditions. Custom, or habit, according to Blondel, do not affect our judgment regarding beauty and proportions. In order to judge an object beautiful, it was not necessary for the observer to be accustomed to such an object. Conversely, being accustomed to ugly objects does not necessarily predispose an observer to judge them beautiful.

Claude Perrault's dissent from the concept of objective beauty assured by proportions initially emerged in his translation and commentary of Vitruvius,[7] and took resolute shape in his *Ordonnance* following the strong opposition to his views. For Perrault, proportions were not by their very nature beautiful or ugly, nor is one proportion inherently better than another. Proportions are not "positive", "necessary", or "convincing" in themselves. Perrault did not deny natural beauty, nor did he deny that some proportions appear beautiful and others ugly. He asserted, however, that preference for one set of proportions over another was due to custom, *accoutumance*, and the psychological associations made by individual observers as well as those conventionally accepted by society. He distinguished between a positive or objective beauty, and between an arbitrary or subjective beauty.[8] Positive beauty was founded on "convincing reasons" which are rationally understood by all, for example: grandeur in buildings, symmetry, fine materials, and skilled execution. He termed the second kind of beauty arbitrary because the proportions, shape, and outline of a building have been willed by the architect. Perrault then proceeded to make his most provoking assertion regarding beauty in architecture: if properties of buildings, such as proportions, can be modified without necessarily making the building appear ugly, then this proves that proportions do not ensure architectural beauty. Architectural properties are considered agreeable not because of universal reasons accessible to everyone, but because of custom, and because of a "link made by the mind between two things of a different nature. Through such a link, it so happens that the esteem the mind invests in one set of things, whose value is known, is then transposed onto another set of things whose value is unknown, leading the mind to imperceptibly esteem both sets equally".[9] Thus, evaluating and judging proportions in architecture as pleasing or disagreeable, according to Perrault, depended on custom and associative psychology.

Sir Christopher Wren took a middle position. He agreed with Blondel in seeing proportion as an aspect of natural beauty, and he also agreed with Perrault that customary beauty derived from familiarity with objects which in themselves might not be intrinsically beautiful.[10] Subsequent authors of architectural treatises such as Charles Etienne Briseux, the abbot Jean-Louis de Cordemoy, and Jacques-François Blondel, upheld the concept of objective beauty knowable through proportion and measure, whereas many philosophers, especially in the eighteenth century, adhered more to the concept of subjective beauty experienced through an array of emotions and associations based on custom. Philosophers such as Francis Hutcheson, Edmund Burke, David Hume, and others, went so far as to recognize only a minimal role to objective beauty. And although objective beauty found a strong resurgence in the late eighteenth and early nineteenth centuries in the work of Johann Joachim Winckelmann, Antoine Chrysostôme Quatremère de Quincy, Victor Cousin, and others, subjective beauty has been prevailing ever since. As the work of Polish historian of aesthetics Wladyslaw Tatarkiewicz aptly demonstrated, objective and subjective views on beauty have always accompanied aesthetic experience, but objective beauty tended to dominate from antiquity until the eighteenth century when subjective beauty began to take the upper hand.[11] The *Querelle* presaged much of the later debates about the objective properties of buildings and the observer's subjective experiences. Indeed, architects continuously debate the primacy of one position over the other in determining architectural judgment. But in considering the value of this conflict for architectural culture at large, and without any undue neutrality, one of the important lessons that the *Querelle* sharply delineated was that neither the objective properties of buildings nor the subjective experiences of these properties can be discounted. *That individual observers judge architectural beauty differently does not invalidate the fact that buildings have objective properties that have been willed by architects.* Furthermore, that observers have undeniable subjective experiences of beauty does not mean that there are as many kinds of beauty as there are observers.

Blondel and Perrault's conflict also covered other areas such the authority of tradition, and it is worthy of note that their opinions were sometimes complementary. Although Blondel was among those who acclaimed the great exemplariness and even the superiority of the ancients, and although Perrault was among those who believed that the experience of the moderns cannot be discounted simply because it was not yet justified by tradition, both men rejected the blind acceptance of the authority of the ancients.[12] The authority of the ancients did not prevail over the authority of reason. Both men did not question the principles and practice of classical architecture, nor did they question the validity of rules in architecture; but their conflict – whether about proportions, the analogy between musical harmonies and architecture, or the superiority of either the ancients or the moderns – pertained more to the elaboration of a set of criteria by which architectural preferences come to be justified or judged.

The second conflict might well be termed: *La querelle des modernes et des modernes*. It has been developing over the past three decades between Peter Eisenman and Léon Krier and has been rendered public in three documented debates in 1983, 1989, and 2006, as well as an academic conference that considered their work and debates in 2002. This conflict differs quite prominently from the first one. Blondel and Perrault's quarrel was about the justifications of classical architecture, not about classical architecture itself. The protagonists of the second conflict, Eisenman and Krier, hold a radical disagreement about architectural form. But the second conflict shares a common notion with the first in that architectural form needs to be justified on the basis of a broad framework of ideas. This significant framework for architectural conflicts is now much broader than the first *Querelle*, and as we shall see, its reasons are at once external and internal to architecture.[13] Since the late seventeenth century architectural characters and styles have increased considerably, leading, in the nineteenth century, to eclecticism and frequently to the confusion of architectural genres. Later on, modernist ideology sought to realize a definitive rupture with previous traditions and subjected the city, architecture, and art, to the dictates of technological determinism. Later still, the various architectures grouped under the rubric of post-modernism repealed some of the tenets and forms of modernism. Architectural forms and the theories that justified them proliferated, while their unrelenting divergences served to exasperate the increasingly tense psychologies of architects.

Eisenman emphasized that the previous theocentric and then anthropocentric views of the world have now been replaced by the forces of objective technocentrism "which are outside of man's control".[14] Moreover, collective anxiety and the threat of nuclear annihilation, operating well into the 1980s, instilled the uneasy feeling that an individual's natural life span may never be completed. These existential forces changed the relationship between humanity and nature, and between the individual and society making it such that it is no longer possible to use classical means of representation. The idea of universal wholes that justify and inform architectural form no longer applied and has instead been replaced by multiple fragmentary approaches. All great periods, the Renaissance, the Enlightenment, or Modernism, operated as ruptures from previous cultural conditions, and they themselves experienced ruptures by subsequent cultural periods. Ruptures produce irreversible historical conditions that justify the emergence of new architectural forms, which, in turn, respond to these conditions. Eisenman considered these facts to be undeniable, and reproached Krier for not having acknowledged them, and for being too certain about the solutions offered by traditional architecture.[15] For Eisenman, the nature of architectural form is dictated by the times, by the external ideas that make up the individual's understanding of the times. Architecture must change in order to maintain relevance, and this relevance is assured by presentness. Whether it is the Parthenon (fifth century BC), or the church of Notre Dame du Haut at Ronchamp (completed in 1955), the architecture of the past no longer has relevance today.

What could replace architecture?

Krier asserts that philosophy and theology are not ends in themselves; rather they are instruments that allow us to distinguish between phenomena that apply to universal as well as particular scales, to the public and the private realms. The city and architecture are such universals, and their elements can be combined and recombined to produce an infinite variety of forms. It is things that can be broken or fragmented, but not ideas. The fact that the city and architecture are in a desperate fragmented state does not mean that this is an irreversible historical condition, as long as there is the will and the moral courage to put the city and architecture back together. History unfolds on multiple lines, not one single direction, and these lines can be modified given the right will. Historical ruptures and personal anxieties resided in the individual's mind, but the practice of architecture "is not about expressing anxieties".[16] Personal anxieties do not inform the architect about how to build cities or shape the countryside. "To forbid a good architecture because we live in terrible times is absurd".[17] Krier sees his work and that of Eisenman as a conflict between architecture and anti-architecture. Hence Krier's question: "Is architecture still relevant or is anti-architecture a better expression of the mess we are in"?[18]

Central to Krier is the distinction between modernity and modernism. Tradition is modern; but there are two fundamental sets of differences between modern traditional architecture, on the one hand, and modernist architecture, on the other. First, in traditional culture and architecture, invention, innovation and discovery are means used to improve inherited knowledge, and the technology used to realize them is subordinate to larger ends. In modernist culture and architecture, invention, innovation and discovery are ends in themselves, while technology dominates all aspects of cultural production. Second, traditional culture and architecture produce objects for long-term use whereas modernist culture and architecture produce objects for short-term consumption. Architecture must not only have presentness; it must serve for a long time. It must be enduring. The teaching of architecture must operate based on some certainties assured by the intellectual and material enduringness of buildings, otherwise how could professors teach if they are full of doubts?

The cluster of themes around which Eisenman and Krier's intellectual conflict centered, include the nature of architectural character (e.g. the nature of the monument); universals and particulars; the uses of historical knowledge; the role of will in history; and certainty and doubt. These are some of the themes belonging to the conflict that emerged from architectural modernism and the culture of modern traditional architecture (also known as the Other Modern). Where Eisenman underscored irreversible historical conditions, adverse though they may be, Krier wished to reform architecture in spite of these adverse conditions; where Eisenman emphasized presentness, Krier emphasized enduringness; where Eisenman denied the cumulative aspects of architectural tradition and searched within "tradition for what tradition in its very real sense always obscures",[19] Krier founded his architecture on the cumulative aspects of tradition in the sense of a rationally proven body of forms and technologies; where Eisenman rejected universals and accentuated the fragment, Krier affirmed universals and accentuated wholeness; where Eisenman wished to transgress the limits of architectural syntax, Krier posited the notion of limits with respect to the uses of intelligence, means, and materials; where Eisenman's form-making put the lineaments of architecture into crisis, Krier's form-making aimed to elaborate a reconstructive system that includes ecology, the city, and architecture. Krier elaborated a broad-ranged architectural system that aims at establishing enduring cities rooted in a place, each region being distinguished by the continuity of its own architectural character(s). Eisenman elaborated a set of polemics aimed precisely at negating and deconstructing the idea of system itself, emphasizing uncertainty, estrangement from place, and discontinuity in architectural composition.

Both protagonists occupy the diametrically opposed limits of contemporary discourse on architecture. Both confirm the other's *esprit de contradiction*. They have little in common architecturally, and it is doubtful if their relationship is that of mimetic rivals. But it is significant that both accept the notion that socio-economic conditions, or a philosophy external to architecture, can justify or reject architectural forms. In varying degrees, both accept the influence of external criteria on the making of architectural form. They also share some common oppositions. Although both occupy two of the summits within the landscape of architectural fame, both wish to detach their architectures from media empires, from fashion, from pop culture, from the empire of kitsch. Both formed their architectural identities first by practicing modernism, and later by their opposition to modernism. Eisenman considered the modernist social program to be a failed utopian experiment, and he dedicated his work initially to transforming modernist forms and subsequently to shredding and decomposing these very forms. Krier unmasked the ecological, urban and architectural failures of modernism, elaborating a counter-project on the scale of the city and the territory, and dedicating his work to re-establishing traditional architecture, not as a revival but as the use of urban and architectural forms that have rationally been proven successful.

But one of the greatest lessons that one can extract from their conflict concerns their treatment of the architectural image, or rather the *limits of the architectural image*. Eisenman deployed considerable efforts to carry the fragmentation of the architectural image to its limits, to transgress the compositional limits of lines, planes, and volumes as such. Contrary to the experiments of *l'architecture parlante* that sought to associate architecture and social meaning, Eisenman did not wish to make a form that carried a social meaning. He aimed to dissociate architectural form from the social layering in which meaning emerges and worked on producing forms that answered this goal. Eisenman's architectural image is the fragment, the shard, the ultimate stage that began with differentiation, moved to dissociation, and then arrived at dissolution. It is in this sense that his fullest opposition to classicism occurs. Krier's architectural image is deeply rooted in the continuity of regional architectural character, wherever that region may be. His architectural image includes urban types (streets, squares, blocks), architectural types (courtyard, rotonda, gable roof) and tectonic types (trabeation, arcuation). Comprehensively, Krier's architectural image is type, character and style – an image that can differentiate, but where the architect exerts the artistic will to prevent this image from falling into dissolution.

One of the main values of this conflict, or quarrel between moderns and moderns, for architectural culture at large, resides in the difference between the differentiations of the architectural image and its dissolution. Put differently, one of the values of the Eisenman versus Krier conflict concerns the limits of differentiation – one of the principal phenomena unleashed by modernist thought, as we saw in Chapter 4. If the architectural image (type, character, and style), undergoes differentiations like other cultural forms, then to what extent can it continue to dissociate? If it reaches a state of dissolution, what next then? But more importantly, how has this experiment served the larger civic constitution? It is significant to note that the urban dimension is almost completely lacking in the work of the protagonists of what we have termed the dissolution of architectural form (the deconstruction project); while the urban dimension is the most fundamental basis for the work of the protagonists of traditional architecture (the reconstruction project).

We discussed these two *querelles* because they are linked on several levels. Historically speaking, the first *querelle* occurred at the dawn of the modern differentiations that were later fully launched by the Enlightenment, while the second occurred at the most pervasive stage reached by differentiation since modernism became the dominant cultural ideology. Both *querelles* stood on either side of differentiation. The first one showed:

1. that neither the objective properties of buildings nor their subjective properties can be denied, even if judging architects may decide to prefer one over the other;
2. that aesthetic judgment depended at once on objective properties as well as custom;
3. that tradition is highly influential in evaluating architecture, but tradition by itself was insufficient a reason to justify architectural preference; and
4. that the authority of reason was more important than then simple authority of tradition.

The second *querelle* showed that:

1. the choice now unmistakably lies between the use of architecture in order to build a just civic association using that broad rational collectivity called tradition, or the practice of architecture as self-expression;
2. it showed the polarization between the protagonists of the architectural sense-in-common, the essential and enduring aspects of architectural culture, on the one hand, versus the protagonists of architectural self-referentiality, the circumstantial and ephemeral, on the other;
3. it showed that the conflict around the architectural image, or more precisely architectural character, is also a conflict around the limits of architectural expression, e.g. a painting may well represent a painter's existential anxieties, but in essence cities or individual buildings are about building communities even if some architects intend on using architecture as a vehicle for their private anxieties.

ARCHITECTURAL JUDGMENT AND CONFLICT: HONORING THE PHENOMENON

We asked, a few pages ago, if the cure for the problem did not reside in the problem itself, that is, if the cure for conflict did not reside in conflict itself; and we suggested accepting and respecting the useful results deriving from conflict if we wish to arrive at reasoned judgment. Architects need some historical distance in order to more fully understand the possible beneficial, as well as detrimental, results of conflict. But two reasons usually combine to prevent architects from reaping the full benefits brought by judgment and by conflict. First, architects tend to associate reasoned judgment with intellectual serenity and concord between minds; and second, they tend to associate conflict with opposing architectural theories or with opposing personalities. Rather than thinking that good judgment occurs only when conflicts are suspended, architects might honor these two phenomena by remembering that architectural form, discourse, and practice, are inherently results of various conflicts; that reasoned judgment, discriminative choice, or rational accord between free minds emerge from a will to synthesize conflicting claims. Conflict not only accompanies change in form, e.g. stylistic change, it is present in the early adumbrations of form and its subsequent transformation. There is conflict when architects mentally select, eliminate, and combine forms, or when they analyze forms for the purpose of selecting preferred elements for a new combination. It is an often-overlooked truth that before a building eventually harmonizes with its context (if such was indeed the intention of the architect), it passes through various conflicts, whether it is between architects and builders, or between various materials brought together by the will of the architect, or between the building itself and the law of gravity. Before reaching its maturation, refinement, and full articulation, architectural composition passes through multiple conflicts, and so does the architect's mind. Architectural form and architectural judgment evolve through conflicts.

But the intent to honor the phenomenon also involves an acknowledgement of its possible disorders. Conflict and judgment have their disorders, and architects stand to benefit from the lessons of psychologists and physicians who have rightly observed that some of their methods, their scholarship, resulted in adverse effects on their patients and their discipline – effects that they have called iatrogenic disorders. Accordingly, architects may benefit by not equating rationality and judgment, with criticism. Whereas criticism requires reasoned judgment, reasoned judgment itself operates quite well without criticism. Architects may profit from K. Marx's wise maxim that the weapon of criticism should not replace criticizing the weapon itself. They may admit that many of the uses of architectural criticism are essentially displays of power, including an extensive amalgamation of reputation, ambition, exhibitionism, authority, and the expectation that architects should produce buildings that conform to the critic's demands. Criticism can then become a disorder of judgment, a pursuit of what Jacques Ellul called the "effectiveness of impact".[20] Architects may also acknowledge that some of the justificatory prose of architectural theory occasionally masks the delusion that architecture is the expression of the personality cult of the separate individual who makes new buildings out of no-thing; and the equally deluded expectation that the city's form is somehow the resulting agglomeration of buildings made by unique individualities who create unique expressions intended for unique patrons within a unique context at a unique point in time. Architects who proudly display their pluralistic banner may concede, even if temporarily, that pluralism and relativism are not the same. Far from being pluralistic, the indiscriminate acceptance of all competing architectural forms, all of them received as having equal value, is a corrupt understanding of pluralism and might itself develop into a disorder of judgment. Indiscriminate acceptance and its repetition may even cause a certain aesthetic non-response. The faculty of judgment is either sedated in the face of objects that simply rise and fall in the architect's consciousness without eliciting an aesthetic response; or to the contrary, aesthetic responses do indeed arise, except they are repressed and prevented from expression. Non-response may cause a disorder of judgment that inhibits in-depth architectural engagements. "Those who do not accuse you seek to excuse you, and that is even sadder", said Marguerite Yourcenar, placing these fictive words in the mouth of her aging Michelangelo.[21] In the final analysis, the contemporary condition of constantly shifting cultural priorities and constantly shifting personal preferences combine to weaken the intellectual frames of reference necessary for reasoned architectural judgment. And to explain-away these conditions as results of pluralism, is either inaccurate or disingenuous. For as we have seen, it is one thing to see pluralism as a desirable milieu that contains many frames of reference, and another to use pluralism to exclude *any* frame of reference in order to justify the architect's personal choices, or whims, as they are being made.

Because architects and architecture are always in a state of becoming, conflict remains their constant companion. No matter how talented and fortunate architects may be, they remain imperfect and incomplete as artists. No matter how well wrought and skillfully composed an edifice may be, it contains imperfect and incomplete parts.[22] The Socratic idea of artistic perfection, which was re-formulated by L-B. Alberti in the notion of a perfect building where nothing can be added or subtracted but for the detriment of the whole, is an exceedingly rare occurrence.[23] But the most refined work of architecture, on the one hand, and the most humble of buildings, on the other, share the overarching intention to resolve many smaller conflicts within a composition that transcends them all. The becoming of the maker and the becoming of the made are closely linked. Intellectual becoming is closely linked to architects' apprehension and judgment of artistic phenomena, to their very consciousness of history, to their sense of responsibility vis-à-vis architectural form as history in the making, and to their discerning perception that they are part of the becoming that historians wish to trace.

Images have the power to provoke thoughts, release feelings, and claim our attention imaginatively. They elicit associations, motivate admiration, encourage imitation, and arouse disapproval. They even provoke violence, recalling the old iconoclastic struggle. From type, to character, to style, the architectural image animates the psyche of architects. By its very multiplicity their imagistic life forms a living totality through which they become conscious of their selves, sculpt their selves, while giving meaning to their reality as artists-intellectuals. The real, for architects, is almost always thought of in terms of images – those of the self, considered as a center of perception, and those of the world. Their intimate relation to the image is rarely a passive perception because they are constantly analyzing, judging, and reconstituting the world they see. The architectural image is at once the *subject* of architects' accords and conflicts, the *material* with which accords are made and conflicts disputed, and the *ground* upon which accords are built and conflicts waged. Because the architectural image is at once subject, material and ground, it also contains the possible cures for the conflicts that beset it.

NOTES

1. I. Kant, "Idea for a Universal History with Cosmopolitan Intent" in *The Philosophy of Kant, Moral and Political Writings*, Carl Friedrich (Tr.), (Modern Library, 1977), p. 121.

2. Gaston Bouthoul, the founder of the study of polemology, suggests the differentiation between the "belligenous" from the "polemogenous": the elements of culture that engender wars from the elements that involve conflicts. See his *La paix*, (Presses Universitaires de France, 1974), p. 77

3. *Op. cit.*, pp. 116–31.

4. *A Terrible Love of War*, (Penguin, 2004), p. 204.

5. Having initially applied to games with spectators, the word agon came to be applied to judicial debate and also to oratorical competition. This ensemble of connotations regarding competition in front of a public following an arbitration or judgment based on rules, closely resembles philosophical dialogue. On the agon and the play function see the classic texts of J. Huizinga, *Homo Ludens*, (Beacon Press, 1950); and R. Caillois, *Les jeux et les hommes*, (Gallimard, 1958).

6. The *Cours d'architecture* comprised Blondel's teaching at L'Académie Royale d'Architecture (founded in 1671) between 1675 and 1683. Book VI contains Blondel's perspective on the debates held between him and Perrault on the nature and origin of beauty.

7. See *Les dix livres d'architecture de Vitruve*, 1673, (Mardaga, 1988), notes 8, 9, 13, 14 to Chapter II, pp. 11–12.

8. *Ordonnance des cinq espèces de colonnes ...* 1683, Préface, pp. 6–7. This same distinction will be reiterated by his brother Charles in the *Parallèle des anciens et des modernes*, 1692, Vol. I, p. 138.

9. *Ibid*, p. 7, my translation.

10. In his memoirs, the *Parentalia*, Wren opined on beauty stating: "There are two causes of beauty – natural and customary. Natural is from geometry, consisting in uniformity, that is equality and proportion. Customary beauty is begotten by the use, as familiarity breeds a love for things not in themselves lovely. Here lies the great occasion of errors, but always the true test is natural or geometric beauty. Geometrical figures are naturally more beautiful than irregular ones: the square, the circle are the most beautiful, next the parallelogram and the oval. There are only two beautiful positions of straight lines, perpendicular and horizontal; this is from Nature and consequently necessity, no other than upright being firm". Quoted by Colin Rowe in *The Mathematics of the Ideal Villa*, (MIT Press, 1976), p. 2.

11. See his "Objectivity and Subjectivity in the History of Aesthetics", in *Philosophy and Phenomenological Research*, XXIV(2), (1963); and his *History of Aesthetics*, (1970-74), Vol. 3, (Thoemmes Press, 1999), pp. 415–58.

12. See the discussion by Wolfgang Hermann in *La théorie de Claude Perrault*, (Mardaga, 1974), pp. 38–44.

13. For a comprehensive view of the ideas defended by Eisenman and Krier, see: P. Eisenman and L. Krier, "A Conversation", in *Skyline*, (February 1983), Rizzoli; *Reconstruction/Deconstruction, P. Eisenman vs. L. Krier*, "My Ideology is better than yours". *Architectural Design*, 59(9–10), (1989); Léon Krier, *Architecture, Choice of Fate*, (Papadakis, 1998); *Blurred Zones: Investigations of the Interstitial: Eisenman Architects, 1988–1998*, (Monacelli, 2003); *Eisenman/Krier: Two Ideologies*, (Monacelli, 2004);

Eisenman/Krier, Il colloquio romano, (held at E.U.R) Aion Edizioni, (Firenze, 2007); *Eisenman Inside Out: Selected Writings, 1963–1988*, (Yale, 2004); José Rafael Moneo, *Theoretical Anxiety and Design Strategies in the Work of Eight Contemporary Architects*, (MIT Press, 2004); Léon Krier, *The Architecture of Community*, (Island Press, 2009).

14 *Op. cit., Skyline*, p. 31.

15 The ideas inherent to this debate have been expanded and comprehensively examined by historians Robert van Pelt and Carroll William Westfall in their *Architectural Principles in the Age of Historicism*, (Yale, 1989).

16 *Op. cit.*, p. 33.

17 *Ibid*, p. 37.

18 *Op. cit., Reconstruction Deconstruction*, p. 7.

19 *Ibid*.

20 J. Ellul, *L'Empire du non-sens*, (Presses Universitaires de France, 1980), p. 276.

21 M. Yourcenar, *That Mighty Sculptor, Time*, Walter Kaiser (Tr.), (Noonday, 1993), p. 20.

22 The fact that some of the most preferred buildings contain several flaws does not diminish their paradigmatic role. The Pantheon's interior, for example, has always elicited criticism for the lack of alignment between the columns, the attic pilasters and the coffers in the dome, compelling many architects to propose projects that corrected this apparent compositional deficiency. These corrections were either theoretical projects such as those of Francesco di Giorgio and Antonio da Sangallo the younger, or actual buildings such as the church of San Francesco di Paola (1817–1846) in Naples which attempts to remedy the internal alignment problem, or the Tempio canoviano (1819–1830) in Possagno which avoids the problem altogether by eliminating the columns and the attic altogether, leaving simply a drum and a coffered dome.

23 "Beauty is that reasoned harmony of all the parts within a body, so that nothing may be added or taken away, or altered but for the worse …", L. Battista Alberti, *De re aedificatoria On the Art of Building in Ten Books*, J. Rykwert, N. Leach, and R. Tavernor (Tr.), (MIT Press, 1988), VI, 2, p. 156.

Bibliography

Alberti, L-B. *On Painting*, J. Spencer (Tr.), Yale University Press, New Haven, CT, 1956.

Alberti, L-B. *De re aedificatoria, On the art of building in ten books*, J. Rykwert, N. Leach, and R. Tavernor (Tr.), MIT Press, Cambridge, MA, 1988.

Alperson, Philip. *The Philosophy of the Visual Arts*, Oxford University Press, Oxford, 1992.

Althusser, Louis and Balibar, Etienne. *Lire le capital*, 2 vols., Maspero, Paris, 1968.

Arendt, Hannah. *Juger: Sur la philosophie de Kant*, M. Revault d'Allonnes (Tr.), Seuil, Paris, 1991.

Arendt, Hannah. *Vies politiques*, Gallimard, Paris, 1974.

Arnheim, Rudolf. *New Essays in the Psychology of Art*, University of California Press, Berkeley, CA, 1986.

Arnold, Dana, Elvan Altan Erqut, and Belin Turan Ozkaya (eds). *Rethinking Architectural Historiography*, Routledge, 2006.

Archives d'architecture moderne, Prix européen pour la reconstruction de la ville, Nº35/36, Brussels, 1987.

Aron, Raymond. *Introduction à la philosophie de l'histoire*, Gallimard (1938), Paris, 1986.

Aschenbrenner, Karl and Isenberg, Arnold, (eds). *Aesthetic Theories: Studies in the Philosophy of Art*, Prentice Hall, Englewood Cliffs, NJ, 1965.

Aubenque, Pierre. *La prudence chez Aristote*, Presses Universitaires de France, Paris, 1963.

Azoulay, Vincent and Boucheron, Patrick. *Le mot qui tue: Une histoire des violences intellectuelles de l'antiquité à nos jours*, Champ Vallon, Seyssel, 2009.

Banham, Allan. *The Architecture of the French Enlightenment: From Soufflot to Ledoux*, University of California Press, Berkeley, CA, 1989.

Barasch, Moshe. *Theories of Art*, Vol.III, Routledge, New York, 1998.

Barey, André. *La déclaration de Bruxelles*, Archives d'Architecture Moderne, Brussels, 1980.

Barthes, Roland. *Eléments de sémiologie*, Seuil, Paris, 1968.

Bateson, Gregory. *Steps to an Ecology of the Mind*, Ballantine, New York, 1969–72.

Baudrillard, Jean. *Le système des objets*, Gallimard, Paris, 1968.

Baudrillard, Jean. *Simulacres et simulations*, Galilée, Paris, 1981.

Baxandall, Michael. *Patterns of Intention: On the Historical Explanation of Pictures*, Yale University Press, New Haven, CT, 1985.

Beardsley, Monroe. *Aesthetics from Classical Greece to the Present*, University of Alabama Press, Tuscaloosa, AL, 1966.

Belting, Hans. *L'histoire de l'art est-elle finie?*, Folio, Paris, 1989.

Benevolo, Leonardo. *The Origins of Modern Town Planning*, Routledge & Kegan Paul, 1967.

Benevolo, Leonardo. *Storia dell'architettura del rinascimento*, 1968.

Benevolo, Leonardo. *History of Modern Architecture*, Routledge & Kegan Paul, 1971.

Benevolo, Leonardo. *The History of the City*, MIT Press, Cambridge, MA, 1980.

Bernier, Georges. *A. Carême (1783–1833). La sensibilité gourmande en Europe*, Grasset, Paris, 1989.

Bivier, Marie-Louise. *Le Panthéon à l'époque révolutionnaire*, Presses universitaires de France, Paris, 1982.

Blondel, Jacques-François. *Cours d'architecture, ou traité de la décoration, distribution & construction des bâtiments; Contenant les leçons données en 1750, & les années suivantes*, 8 vols., Paris, 1771–77.

Bly, Robert. *A Little Book on the Human Shadow*, Harper & Row, New York, 1988.

Boffrand, Germain. *Book of Architecture* (1745), Caroline van Eck (ed.), David Britt (Tr.), Ashgate, Aldershot, 2002.

Bordes, Philippe and Michel, Régis. *Aux armes & aux arts!*, Biro, Paris, 1988.

Bouillon, Jean-Paul, Mosser, Monique and Rabreau, Daniel. *Les fêtes de la Révolution*, Musée Bargoin, Clermont-Ferrand, 1974.

Boullée, Etienne-Louis. *Essai sur l'art*: *Boullée's Treatise on Architecture*, H. Rosenau (Tr.), Tiranti, London, 1953.

Broadbent, Geoffrey, Bunt, Richard, and Jencks, Charles (eds). *Signs, Symbols and Architecture*, Wiley, New York, 1980.

Burckhardt, Jakob. *Force and Freedom, Reflections on History* (1929), Pantheon Books, New York, 1943.

Caillois, Roger. *Les jeux et les hommes*, Gallimard, Paris, 1958.

Le Camus de Mézières, Nicolas. *The Genius of Architecture; or the Analogy of that Art with our Sensations*, (1780) Introduction by Robin Middleton, David Britt (Tr.), The Getty Center for the History of Art and the Humanities, 1992.

Carême, Antonin. *Le Pâtissier pittoresque, précédé d'un traité des cinq ordres d'architecture* (1828), *L'art de la cuisine française au XIXème siècle*, 5 Vols. (1833–44), Payot-Rivages, Paris, 1994.

Carroll, Noël. *Philosophy of Art: A Contemporary Introduction*, Routledge, London, 1999.

Cazeaux, Clive (ed.). *The Continental Aesthetics Reader*, Routledge, London, 2000.

The Charlottesville Tapes, Rizzoli, 1985.

The Chicago Tapes, Rizzoli, 1986.

Chipp, Herschel B., *Theories of Modern Art: A Source Book by Artists and Critics*, University of California Press, Berkeley, CA, 1968.

Collingwood, Robin G. *The Idea of History*, Clarendon Press, Oxford, 1946.

Colquhoun, Alan. *Modernity and the Classical Tradition*, MIT Press, Cambridge, MA, 1989.

Colquhoun, Alan. *Modern Architecture*, Oxford University Press, New York, 2002.

Le Corbusier. *Towards an Architecture* (Org. 1923), Frederick Etchells (Tr.), Praeger, New York, 1927.

Le Corbusier. *Croisade, ou le crépuscule des académies*, Editions G. Crès, 1933.

Le Corbusier. *Oeuvre complète*, 1910–1929, Septième Edition, Gisberger, Zurich, 1960.

Corneille, Pierre. *Le Cid* (1636), L. Lejealle and J. Dubois (eds), Larousse, Paris, 1970.

Coulton, John James. *Ancient Greek Architects at Work*, Cornell University Press, Ithaca, NY, 1977.

Croce, Benedetto. *Logica come scienza del concetto puro*, Laterza, Bari, 1947.

Croce, Benedetto. *Estetica*, (1902), Adelphi, 2005.

Crowe, Norman, Economakis Richard, and Lykoudis, Michael (eds). *Building Cities: Towards a Civil Society and Sustainable Environment*, Artmedia Press, London, 1999.

Danto, Arthur C. *The Transfiguration of the Commonplace*, Harvard University Press, Cambridge, MA, 1981.

Derrida, Jacques. *Speech and Phenomena and Other Essays on Husserl's Theory of Signs*, D. Allison (Tr.), Northwestern University Press, Evanston, IL, 1973.

Diderot, Denis. *Paradoxe sur le comédien*, Sautelet, Paris, (1777) 1830.

Drachline, Pierre (ed.). *Le grand livre de la méchanceté*, J'ai lu, Paris, 2009.

Dray, William. *Perspectives on History*, Routledge & Kegan Paul, London, 1980.

Dripps, Robin. *The First House*, MIT Press, Cambridge, MA, 1997.

Eco, Umberto. *La struttura assente*, Bompiani, Milan, 1968.

Economakis, Richard (ed.). *Building Classical: A Vision of Europe and America*, Academy Editions, London, 1993.

Eisenman, Peter. *Eisenman, Inside Out: Selected Writings 1963–1988*, Yale University Press, New Haven, CT, 2004.

Ellul, Jacques. *La technique ou l'enjeu du siècle*, A.Colin, Paris, 1954.

Ellul, Jacques. *Propagandes*, A.Colin, Paris, 1962.

Ellul, Jacques. *Le système technicien*, Calmann-Lévy, Paris, 1977.

Ellul, Jacques. *L'empire du non sens*, Presses Universitaires de France, Paris, 1980.

Ellul, Jacques. *Le bluff technologique*, Hachette, Paris, 1988.

Feurbach, Ludwig. *Manifestes philosophiques, 1839–1845*, Gallimard, Paris, 2001.

Fichet, Françoise. *La Théorie architecturale à l'âge classique*, Mardaga, Brussels, 1979.

Finke, Ronald A. *Principles of Mental Imagery*, MIT Press, Cambridge, MA, 1989.

Folkierski, Wladyslaw. *Entre le classicisme et le romantisme* (Org. 1925), Champion, Paris, 1969.

Foucault, Michel. *L'archéologie du savoir*, Gallimard, Paris, 1969.

Foucault, Michel. *Power/Knowledge: Selected Interviews and Other Writings, 1972–1977*, C. Gordon (Tr.), Pantheon Books, New York, 1980.

Fox-Genovese, Elizabeth and Lasch-Quinn, Elizabeth (eds). *Reconstructing History*, Routledge, London, 1999.

Fox Weber, Nicholas. *Le Corbusier: A Life*, Random House, London, 2008.

Frampton, Kenneth. *Modern Architecture: A Critical History* (Org. 1980), Thames & Hudson, London, 2007.

Freud, Sigmund. *Moïse et le monothéisme*, (1939), Gallimard, Paris, 1967.

de Fusco, Renato. *Archittetura Come Mass Medium*, Dedalo, Rome, 1967.

Gazda, Elaine (ed.). *The Ancient Art of Emulation, Studies in Artistic Originality*, University of Michigan Press, Ann Arbor, MI, 2002.

Giedion, Sigfried. *Mechanization Takes Command*, Oxford University Press, Oxford, 1948.

Giedion, Sigfried. *Space, Time, and Architecture*, (1941), Harvard University Press, Cambridge, MA, 1967.

Giedion, Sigfried. *The Eternal Present: A Contribution on Constancy and Change*, (1962), Princeton University Press, Princeton, NJ, 1981.

Girard, René. *La violence et le sacré*, (1972), Pluriel, 1990.

Girard, René. *Des choses cachées depuis la fondation du monde*, Grasset, Paris, 1978.

Girard, René. *To Double Business Bound*, Johns Hopkins University Press, Baltimore, MA, 1978.

Girard, René. *Celui par qui le scandale arrive*, Desclée de Brouwer, 2001.

Girard, René. *La voix méconnue du réel*, Grasset, Paris, 2002.

Girard, René. *The Girard Reader*, James Williams (ed.), Crossroads Herder, 2003.

Girard, René. *Les origines de la culture*, Pluriel, 2004.

Girard, René. *Politiques de Cain*, Domenica Mazzù (ed.), Desclée de Brouwer, 2004.

Gisel Pierre (ed.). *Histoire et théologie chez E. Troeltsch*, Labor et Fides, Geneva, 1990.

Goldthwaite, Richard. *The Building of Renaissance Florence*, Johns Hopkins University Press, Baltimore, MA, 1980.

Goodman, Nelson. *Languages of Art*, Hackett, Indianapolis, IN, (1969), 1976.

Gombrich, Ernst. *Art and Illusion*, Princeton University Press, Princeton, NJ, 1960.

Gombrich, Ernst. *Art, Perception and Reality*, J. Hochberg and M. Black (eds), Johns Hopkins University Press, Baltimore, MA, 1972.

Gombrich, Ernst. *The Sense of Order: A Study in the Psychology of Decorative Art*, Cornell University Press, Ithaca, NY, 1979.

Gros, Pierre. *L' architecture romaine*, 2 Vols., Picard, Paris, 1996.

Habermas, Jurgen. *Habermas: Critical Debates*, J.B. Thompson and D. Held (eds), MIT Press, Cambridge, MA, 1983.

Habermas, Jurgen. *The Habermas Reader*, William Outhwaite (ed.), Polity Press, Cambridge, 1996.

Hart, Vaughan and Hicks, Peter (eds). *Paper Palaces*, Yale University Press, New Haven, CT, 1998.

Hayes, Michael (ed.). *Architectural Theory since 1968*, MIT Press, Cambridge, MA, 1998.

Howard, Deborah. *The Architectural History of Venice*, Yale University Press, New Haven, CT, 2002.

Hegel, Georg W.F. *Phenomenology of Spirit*, A.W. Miller (Tr.), Oxford, 1977.

Hegel, Georg W.F. *Principle of Right*, S.W. Dyde (Tr.), Batoche, Ontario, 2001.

Heidegger, Martin. *Poetry, Language, Thought*, A. Hofstadter (Tr.), Harper & Row, New York, 1971.

Herrmann, Wolfgang. *The Theory of Claude Perrault*, Zwemmer, London, 1973.

Hillman, James. *The Dream and the Underworld*, Harper & Row, New York, 1979.

Hillman, James. *A Terrible Love of War*, Penguin, New York, 2004.

Hitchcock, Henry-Russell. *Architecture: Ninenteenth and Twentieth Centuries*, Penguin, New York, 1958.

Hitchcock, Henry-Russell and Johnson, Philip. *The International Style*, Norton, New York, 1932.

Hochman, Elaine. *Architects of Fortune, Mies van der Rohe and the Third Reich*, Fromm International Publishing, New York, 1990.

Huizinga, Johan. *Homo Ludens*, Beacon Press, Boston, MA, 1950.

Husserl, Edmund. *Phenomenological Psychology*, John Scanlon (Tr.), Martinus Nijhoff, The Hague, (1925), 1977.

Jacques, Annie. *Les Architectes de la Liberté*, Gallimard, Collection Découvertes, Paris, 1988.

Jameson, Frederic. *Postmodernism, or, the Cultural Logic of Late Capitalism*, Duke University Press, Durham, NC, 1991.

Jencks, Charles. *The Language of Post-Modern Architecture*, Rizzoli, New York, 1977.

Jenkins, Keith. *Re-thinking History*, Routledge, 1991.

Jenkins, Keith. *The Postmodern History Reader*, Routledge, 1997.

Jenkins, Keith, Morgan, Sue, and Munslow, Alun (eds). *Manifestos for History*, Routledge, London, 2007.

Jung, Carl. *The Essential Jung*, Anthony Storr (ed.), Princeton University Press, Princeton, NJ, 1983.

Junod, Philippe. *Transparence et opacité*, (1976), Jacqueline Chambon, Paris, 2004.

Kagis McEwen, Indra. *Vitruvius: Writing the Body of Architecture*, MIT Press, Cambridge, MA, 2003.

Kant, Immanuel. *Idea for a Universal History* (Org. 1784), Modern Library, New York, 1977.

Kant, Immanuel. *Critique of Judgement* (Org. 1790), James Meredith (Tr.), Oxford, 2007.

Kaufmann, Emil. *Three Revolutionary Architects: Boullée, Ledoux, and Lequeu*, American Philosophical Society, Philadelphia, PA, 1952.

Kivy, Paul (ed.). *Essays on the History of Aesthetics*, Library of the History of Ideas, University of Rochester Press, Rochester, NY, 1992.

Krauss, Rosalind. *The Originality of the Avant-garde and other Modernist Myths*, MIT Press, Cambridge, MA, 1985.

Krier, Léon. *Albert Speer Architecture, 1932–1942*, L. Krier (ed.), Archives d'architecture moderne, Brussels, 1982.

Krier, Léon. *The Architecture of Community*, Island Press, Washington, DC, 2009.

Krier, Rob. *Architectural Composition*, Rizzoli, New York, 1988.

Kristeva, Julia. *Etrangers à nous mêmes*, Gallimard, Paris, 1991.

Kruft, Hanno-Walter. *A History of Architectural Theory from Vitruvius to the Present*, Princeton Architectural Press, New York, 1994.

Koenig, Giovanni Klaus. *Analisi del linguaggio archittetonico*, Fiorentina, Florence, 1964.

Lasch, Christopher. *Culture of Narcissism*, W.W. Norton, New York, 1991.

Laugier, Marc-Antoine. *Essai sur l'architecture*, 1752.

Laugier, Marc-Antoine. *Observations sur l'architecture*, Avertissement, Desaint, Paris, 1765.

Leach, Andrew. *What is Architectural History?*, Polity Press, Cambridge, 2010.

Ledoux, C-N-L. *L'architecture considérée sous le rapport des mœurs et de la legislation*, Paris, 1804.

Linazasoro, José Ignacio. *Le Projet Classique en Architecture*, Archives d'architecture moderne, Brussels, 1984.

Lemagny, Jean-Claude. *Visionary Architects: Boullée, Ledoux, Lequeu*, Gulf Print Co., Houston, TX, 1968.

Leith, James. *Space and Revolution*, McGill-Queen, Montréal, 1991.

Lovejoy, Arthur O. *The Great Chain of Being*, Cambridge, MA, 1936.

Maalouf, Amin. *Les identités meurtrières*, Grasset, Paris, 1998.

Mallgrave, Harry Francis (ed.). *Architectural Theory, An Anthology, From Vitruvius to 1870 and 1871–2005*, 2 Vols., Blackwell, Hoboken, NJ, 2006.

Manuel, Frank and Manuel, Fritzie. *Utopian Thought in the Western World*, Harvard University Press, Cambridge, MA, 1979.

Matthewson, Casey C.M. *Frank O. Gehry, Selected Works: 1969 to Today*, Firefly Books, Buffalo, NY, 2007.

Meinecke, Friedrich. *Historism*, J.E. Anderson (Tr.), Routledge and Kegan Paul, London, 1972.

Merleau-Ponty, Maurice. *Phénoménologie de la perception*, (1945), Gallimard, Paris, 2002.

Mileti, Nick. *Beyond Michelangelo*, Xlibris, NJ, 2005.

Moneo, José Rafael. *Theoretical Anxiety and Design Strategies in the Work of Eight Contemporary Architects*, MIT Press, Cambridge, MA, 2004.

Morrissey, Jake. *The Genius in the Design*, Duckworth, London, 2005.

Mortier, Roland. *L'originalité, une nouvelle catégorie esthétique du siècle des lumières*, Droz, Paris, 1982.

Mosser, Monique and Teyssot, Georges (eds). *The Architecture of Western Gardens*, MIT Press, Cambridge, MA, 1991.

Mumford, Lewis. *The Transformations of Man*, Collier Books, New York, 1962.

Mumford, Lewis. *The Future of Technics Civilization*, Freedom Press, London, 1986.

Munslow, Alan. *The Routledge Companion for Historical Studies*, Routledge, London, 2000.

Nebel, Cécile. *The Dark Side of Creativity*, Whitston Publishing, New York, 1988.

Ockman, Joan, Berke, Debora, McLeod, Mary (eds). *Architecture, Criticism, Ideology*, Princeton Architectural Press, New York, 1985.

Olin, Margaret. *Forms of Representation in Alois Riegl's Theory of Art*, Pennsylvania State University Press, University Park, PA, 1992.

Onians, John. *Bearers of Meaning*, Princeton University Press, Princeton, NJ, 1988.

Payne, Alina. *The Architectural Treatise of the Italian Renaissance*, Cambridge University Press, New York, 1999.

Pérez-Gómez, Alberto. *Architecture and the Crisis of Modern Science*, MIT Press, Cambridge, MA, 1983.

Pearlman, J. "Joseph Hudnut's other modernism at the Harvard Bauhaus", *Journal of the Society of Architectural Historians*, 56(4), December 1997.

Pérouse de Montclos, Jean-Marie. *Étienne-Louis Boullée, Theoretician of Revolutionary Architecture*, Brazilier, New York, 1974.

Pérouse de Montclos, Jean-Marie. *Jacques-Germain Soufflot*, Monum, Paris, 2004.

Perrault, Claude. *Les dix livres d'architecture de Vitruve*, 1673, Mardaga, Liège, 1988.

Perrault, Claude. *Ordonnance des cinq espèces de colonnes* … Paris, 1683.

Pevsner, Nikolaus. *An Outline of European Architecture*, (1948), Penguin Books, London, 1968.

Pevsner, Nikolaus. *Pioneers of Modern Design: From William Morris to Walter Gropius*, (1949), Yale University Press, 2005.

Pevsner, Nikolaus. *The Sources of Modern Architecture and Design*, Oxford University Press, Oxford, 1968.

Pevsner, Nikolaus. *Studies in Art, Architecture and Design*, Vol. II, Walker & Co, New York, 1968.

Pevsner, Nikolaus, *History of Building Types*, Bollingen, Princeton, NJ, 1970.

Picon, Antoine. *Claude Perrault, La curiosité d'un classique*, Picard, Paris, 1988.

Podro, Michael. *The Critical Historians of Art*, Yale University Press, New Haven, CT, 1982.

Popper, Karl. *The Poverty of Historicism*, (1944), Routledge, London, 2002.

Popper, Karl. *Objective Knowledge: An Evolutionary Approach*, Clarendon Press, Oxford, 1972.

Porphyrios, Demetri (ed.). *On the Methodology of Architectural History*, Architectural Design Profile, London, 1981.

Porphyrios, Demetri (ed.). *Classicism is Not a Style*, Architectural Design, London, 1982.

Porphyrios, Demetri. *Classical Architecture: The Living Tradition*, McGraw-Hill, New York, 1992.

Prinz, Jesse. *Furnishing the Mind: Concepts and their Perceptual Basis*, MIT Press, Cambridge, MA, 2002.

Quatremère de Quincy, Antoine-Chrysostome. *Dictionnaire d'architecture*, 3 vols., *Encyclopédie Méthodique*, C.J. Panckoucke, Paris, 1788–1825.

Quatremère de Quincy, Antoine-Chrysostome. *Essai sur la nature, le but et les moyens de l'imitation dans les beaux-arts*, Paris, (1823); Introductions by L. Krier and D. Porphyrios. Archives d'Architecture Moderne, Brussels, 1980.

Quint, David (ed.). *Creative Imitation: New Essays on Renaissance Literature in Honor of Thomas Greene*, Mediaeval and Renaissance Texts & Studies, Binghamton, NY, 1992.

Reill, Peter. *German Enlightenment and the Rise of Historicism*, University of California Press, Berkeley, CA, 1975.

Ricoeur, Paul. *Histoire et vérité*, Seuil, Paris, 1955.

Rorty, Richard. *Objectivity, Relativism and Truth*, Cambridge University Press, New York, 1991.

Riegl, Alois. *Grammaire historique des arts plastiques*, É. Kaufholz-Messmer (Tr.), Klincksieck, Paris, 1978.

Rigault, Hippolyte. *Histoire de la querelle des anciens et des modernes*, Hachette, Paris, 1856.

Rosenblum, Robert. *Transformations in Late Eighteenth Century Art*, Princeton University Press, Princeton, NJ, 1967.

Rousseau, Jean-Jacques, *Discours sur l'origine et les fondements de l'inégalité parmi les hommes*, (1755), Paris, Editions Sociales, 1983.

Rowe, Colin. *The Mathematics of the Ideal Villa*, MIT Press, Cambridge, MA, 1976.

Rowe, Colin. *The Architecture of Good Intentions*, Academy Editions, London, 1994.

Ruskin, John. *The Seven Lamps of Architecture*, (1880), Dover reprint, New York, 1989.

Rykwert, Joseph. *On Adam's House in Paradise*, Museum of Modern Art, 1972.

Rykwert, Joseph. *The First Moderns*, MIT Press, Cambridge, MA, 1980.

Rykwert, Joseph. *The Dancing Column*, MIT Press, Cambridge, MA, 1996.

Saint-Girons, Baldine. *Esthétique du XVIIème siècle. Le modèle français*, Philippe Sers, Paris, 1990.

Saisselin, Rémi. *The Rule of Reason and the Rules of the Heart*, Press of Case Western Reserve University, Cleveland, OH, 1970.

Salvini, Roberto. *La critique de la pure visibilité et du formalisme*, E. Dickenherr, C. Jatosti, A. Pernet, A. Real-Charrière (Tr.), Klincksieck, Paris, 2000.

Sanford, Kwinter. *Architectures of Time*, MIT Press, Cambridge, MA, 2001.

Scalvini, Maria Luisa. *L'architettura come semiotica connotativa*, Bompiani, Milan, 1975.

Scamozzi, Vincenzo. *Dell'idea dell'architettura universale*, Centro Internazionale di Studi di Architettura Andra Palladio, Edizioni Colpo di fulmine, Verona, 1997.

di Schino, June and Luccichenti, Furio, *Il cuoco segreto dei Papi*, Gangemi, Rome, 2007.

Schopenhauer, Arthur. *The World as Will and as Idea* (1883), R.B. Haldane and J. Kemp (Tr.), Routledge and Kegan Paul, New York, 1950.

Scruton, Roger. *The Aesthetics of Architecture*, Princeton University Press, Princeton, NJ, 1980.

Scruton, Roger. *The Classical Vernacular*, St. Martin's Press, London, 1995.

Semper, Gottfied. *Style in the Technical and Tectonic Arts*, (1860–1863), H. Mallgrave and M. Robinson (Tr.), Getty, Los Angeles, CA, 2004.

Sennett, Richard. *The Fall of Public Man*, Norton, 1992.

Simmel, Georg. *Sociologie, études sur les formes de la socialisation*, Presses Universitaires de France, Paris, 1999.

Snow, Charles. *The Two Cultures*, New American Library, New York, 1959.

Soufflot et l'architecture des lumières, Actes du colloque à Lyon, Mosser, Monique, Rabrean Daniel, Eds., Ecole Nationale Supérieure de Beaux-Arts, 1986.

Southgate, Beverly. *What is History For?* Routledge, New York, 2005.

Spencer, Herbert. *First Principles*, (1880), De Witt Revolving Fund, New York, 1958.

Starobinski, Jean. *1789, Les emblèmes de la raison*, Flammarion, Paris, 1973.

Szambien, Werner. *Symétrie, goût, caractère*, Picard, Paris, 1986.

Tafuri, Manfredo. *Teorie e storia dell' architettura*, Laterza, 1986.

Tafuri, Manfredo and Francesco Dal Co. *Modern Architecture*, (1976), Harry Abrams, New York, 1979.

Tassin, Etienne, "Sens-commun et communauté: La lecture arendtienne de Kant", in *Les cahiers de philosophie*, 4, Presses Universitaires de France, 1987.

Tatarkiewicz, Wladyslaw. *History of Aesthetics*, Vol. 3, (1970–74), Thoemmes Press reprint, Bristol, 1999.

Tatarkiewicz, Wladyslaw. *A History of Six Ideas,* Martinus Nijhoff, PWN, Polish scientific publishers, 1980.

Taylor, Charles. *Sources of the Self*, Harvard University Press, Cambridge, MA, 1989.

Todorov, Tzvetan. *L'esprit des lumières*, Robert Laffont, Paris, 2006.

Tournikiotis, Panayotis. *The Historiography of Modern Architecture*, MIT Press, Cambridge, MA, 1999.

Tzonis, Alex and Lefaivre, Liane. *Classical Architecture: The Poetics of Order*, MIT Press, Cambridge, MA, 1986.

Tschumi, Bernard and Cheng, Irene (eds). *The State of Architecture at the Beginning of the 21st Century*, Monacelli Press, New York, 2003.

Valéry, Paul. *Oeuvres*, Pléiade, Gallimard, Paris, 1957.

van Eck, Caroline. *Organicism in Nineteenth Century Architecture*, Architectura & Natura Press, Amsterdam, 1994.

van Eck, Caroline. *Classical Rhetoric and the Visual Arts in Modern Europe*, Cambridge, New York, 2007.

Van-Pelt, Robert and Westfall, Carroll William. *Architectural Principles in the Age of Historicism*, Yale University Press, New Haven, CT, 1991.

Vattimo, Gianni. *La fine della modernità*, Garzanti, Milano, 1985.

Veeser, H. Aram (ed.). *The New Historicism*, Routledge, New York, 1989.

Venturi, Robert. *Complexity and Contradiction in Architecture*, Museum of Modern Art, New York, 1966.

Venturi, Robert, Scott-Brown, Denise, and Izenour, Steven. *Learning from Las Vegas*, MIT Press, Cambridge, MA, 1972.

Vidler, Anthony. *The Writing of the Walls*, Princeton Architectural Press, New York, 1986.

von Ranke, Leopold. *The Theory and Practice of History*, Georg Iggers and K. von Moltke (eds), Irvington Publishers, New York, 1983.

Walton, Kendal. *Mimesis as Make-believe: On the Foundation of the Representational Arts*, Harvard University Press, Cambridge, MA, 1990.

Watkin, David. *Architecture and Morality*, Clarendon Press, Oxford, 1977.

Watson, Anne (ed.). *Building a Masterpiece: The Sydney Opera House*, Powerhouse Publishing, Sydney, 2006.

Weber, Max. *Selections from his work*, with an Introduction by S.M. Miller, Crowell, New York, 1963.

White, Hayden. *Tropics of Discourse*, Johns Hopkins University Press, Baltimore, MA, 1978.

Wilber, Ken. *Sex, Ecology and Spirituality*, Shambhalla Publications, Boston, MA, 1996.

Wilber, Ken. *A Brief History of Everything*, Shambhalla Publications, Boston, MA, 1996.

Wilber, Ken. *The Marriage of Sense and Soul, Integrating Science and Religion*, Random House, New York, 1998.

Wilber, Ken. *Boomeritis*, Shambhalla Publications, Boston, MA, 2002.

Wilson, Edward. *Consilience*, Vintage, New York, 1998.

Wittkower, Rudolf and Wittkower, Margot. *Born Under Saturn*, Norton, New York, 1963.

Wolfe, Tom. *From Bauhaus to our House*, Farrar Straus Giroux, New York, 1981.

Wollheim, Richard. *Art and its Objects*, Harper and Row, New York, 1968.

Wollheim, Richard. *On the Emotions*, Yale, 1999.

Younés, Samir. *The True, the Fictive and the The Real: The Historical Dictionary of Architecture of Quatremère de Quincy*, Papadakis, Newbury, 1999.

Yourcenar, Marguerite. *That Mighty Sculptor, Time*, Walter Kaiser (Tr.), Noonday, New York, 1993.

Zöllner, Frank, Popper, Thomas, and Thoenes, Christof. *Michelangelo: Complete Works*, Taschen, Cologne, 2007.

Zweig, Connie and Abrams, Jeremiah (eds). *Meeting the Shadow*, Tarcher/Putnam, New York, 1991.

Index

Aesthetics, 105, 157
Agon and *polemos*, 13, 229, 239
Alberti, Leon Battista, 146, 147, 162, 163, 191, 192, 238, 240
American Revolution, 104
Antagonism, 5, 11, 13, 15, 109, 123, 124, 125, 126, 130, 131, 134, 226, 227, 228, 229
Ara Pacis, 121, 123, 157, 189
Architecture parlante, 57, 103, 166, 199, 204, 219, 235
Arendt, Hannah, 79, 105
Aristotle, 28, 72, 83, 112, 113, 127, 135, 162
   Aristotelian "ought", 153, 154, 155, 156, 186, 220
   Quartet of causes, 72
Aron, Raymond, 27, 29, 37, 42, 46
   Perspectivism, 42
Architectural Image, 7, 154, 214, 235, 236
   Type, Character, and Style, 12, 51, 52, 65, 73, 149, 154, 199, 223, 235, 238
Artistic Freedom, 6, 7, 10, 77, 78, 86, 91, 93–7, 103, 106, 225
Avant-garde, 67, 77, 100, 101, 124, 197

Bachelard, Gaston, 42
Barbarians (Cultural), 228
Baroque, 34, 99, 203, 212, 221, 218
Barthes, Roland, 27, 74, 196
Bateson, Gregory, 129, 138
Batteux, Charles, 45, 66, 166
Baudrillard, Jean, 43, 47, 49, 135, 185
Beauty, the beautiful, 28, 32, 70, 71, 73, 75, 83, 85, 87, 105, 119, 134, 153, 156, 157, 163, 166, 168, 169, 177, 196, 212, 230, 231, 232, 239, 240
Being and making, 78, 127
Bellori, Gian Pietro, 164
Beginning and origin, (Distinction), 37, 38, 39, 47, 59, 165, 173, 190, 192

Bienséance, 55, 159, 167
Blondel, François, 15, 44, 124, 129, 148, 193, 230, 213, 232, 239
Blondel, Jacques-François, 55, 66, 168, 169
Boffrand, Germain, 143, 166, 168, 193
Boullée, Etienne-Louis, 47, 66, 107, 170, 194
Boule, boulesis, bouleterion, 15, 112, 135
Briseux, Etienne, 45, 231
Le Brun, Charles, 160–70
Building purpose, 11, 51, 52, 55, 83, 88, 134, 143, 144, 150, 151, 152, 165, 171, 175, 190, 202, 219, 227
   Civic, 11, 12, 52, 55, 88, 147, 149, 154, 155, 175, 182, 187, 188, 189, 190, 191, 200, 201, 202, 206, 209, 212, 214, 219, 220, 216, 218, 225
   Private, (vernacular) 12, 147, 149, 155, 175, 188, 189, 190, 191, 219
Burckhardt, Jakob, 13, 15, 43
Burke, Edmund, 28, 231

Le Camus de Mézières, Nicolas, 55, 66, 169, 170
Capriccio, 96, 128
Cataneo, Pietro, 162
Causality, cause, 9, 11, 18, 25, 26, 27, 36, 37, 41, 53, 71, 72, 74, 80, 82, 111, 112, 113, 130, 148, 165, 166, 169, 219, 229, 239
Character, 1, 6, 7, 11, 12, 13, 25–7, 32, 51–9, 62, 65, 72, 79, 83, 86, 96, 97, 102–5, 117, 141, 143–59, 161, 164, 165, 166–75, 180–83, 186–91, 199, 200, 201, 202, 203, 207, 208, 211–20, 223, 225, 227, 232–6
Charter of Venice, 12
Church
   Santa Maria della Salute, 205, 206, 221,
   Sainte Geneviève (Panthéon), 104, 208, 221

City, 1, 7, 15, 17, 55, 69, 70, 73–6, 80, 88, 94, 119, 124, 127, 146, 148, 150, 177, 199, 214, 233,
  The Good City, 86–90
City Beautiful Movement, 212
Classicism, 9, 18, 31, 32, 34, 185, 186, 196, 210, 211, 235
Clérisseau, Charles-Louis, 156
Cogito, 73, 85, 212
Composition, 1, 4, 7, 12, 17, 21, 24, 27, 34, 51, 53, 59, 62, 70, 72, 81, 83, 97, 103, 104, 121, 136, 143, 144, 150, 151, 153, 154, 155, 156, 157, 164, 165, 166, 172, 175, 180, 181, 185, 186, 187, 188, 191, 199, 201, 202, 203, 204, 205, 207, 210, 216, 219, 230, 234, 235, 237, 240
Conflict (Cultural, Architectural) 5, 11, 13, 15, 25, 120, 121, 124, 128, 129, 130, 132, 134, 219, 225, 226, 227, 228, 232, 229, 230, 236, 234, 235, 237, 238
Continuity, 22, 39, 44, 74, 80, 101, 176, 181, 217, 234, 235
Convenance, 55, 159, 169, 190
Convenienza, 55
Convention, 21, 22, 31, 34, 35, 37, 78, 88, 91, 105, 175, 182, 200, 149, 152, 156, 171, 173, 190, 184, 191, 199, 209, 214, 231
Copy, 73, 97, 128, 154, 155, 156, 163, 186, 172, 173, 174, 182, 201, 205, 220
Cordemoy, Jean-Louis, de, 193, 231
Covering law theory, 36
Cousin, Victor, 232
Creatio ex nihilo, 22, 131, 181, 183
Creativity, 43, 45, 77, 133, 154, 225
Crisis, 5, 9, 13, 14, 75, 103, 130, 183, 184, 234
Critic, Criticism, 1, 4, 8, 11, 13, 14, 18, 22, 25, 27, 35, 36, 40, 41, 42, 43, 45, 48, 89, 120, 124, 125, 126, 130, 132, 137, 147, 154, 156, 186, 189, 229, 230, 237
Le Corbusier, 29, 42, 100, 121, 129, 138, 156, 176–80, 214, 226
Corneille, Pierre, 95, 106
Croce, Benedetto, 21, 27, 28, 29, 37, 45, 46, 134

Danti, Vincenzo, 164
Deconstruction, 41, 65, 69, 75, 235
Desire (Mimetic), 4, 11, 109, 121, 127, 128, 129, 130, 225, 228, 229
Decorum, 55, 190, 217, 220
Determinism, 18, 34, 75, 102, 134, 183, 233
Diderot, Denis, 28, 66, 70, 87, 157, 146

Doxa, 94
Durand, J-N-L., 45, 52, 53, 55, 136, 210

Ecclecticism, 62
Eisenman, Peter, 184, 185, 230–40
Ellul, Jacques, 15, 75, 81, 82, 176, 182, 237, 240
Encyclopédie, 53, 65, 70, 75, 81, 173
Enduringness, 32, 44, 51, 52, 65, 69, 74, 81, 85, 94, 155, 161, 163, 185, 186, 200, 212, 234, 236
L'Enfant, Pierre-Charles, 104
Enlightenment, 10, 12, 13, 24, 32, 40, 41, 71, 74, 75, 77, 78, 80, 82, 144, 153, 159, 161, 164, 165, 174, 176, 177, 190, 233, 236
Ethics, 17, 28, 70, 71, 73, 74, 78, 79, 80, 87
Ethos and *locus*, 83
Eurythmia, 133
Expression, 6, 7, 8, 12, 14, 23, 34, 37, 81, 86, 90–99, 103, 105, 106, 121, 127, 129, 137, 143–59, 164, 168, 170, 172, 181, 186, 188–91, 199, 200–202, 214–18, 219, 220, 225, 236, 237

Face and architectural character, 11, 99, 147, 149, 170, 195
  Face and mask, 99, 107
Fictive, 65, 95, 128, 154, 155, 173, 174, 201, 202, 209, 238
Filarete, 163
Form, 1, 7, 11, 12, 18, 21, 25, 27, 34–8, 43, 55, 57, 59, 65, 69, 72, 74, 80, 83, 88, 94, 103, 109, 111, 114–20, 121, 128, 147, 148, 151–3, 169, 171–9, 182–6, 225, 229–33, 235, 237
  Form, quality, and purpose, 143–50
Foucault, Michel, 42, 49, 81
French Revolution, 14, 38, 74, 87, 93, 103, 104, 106, 209

Gehry, Frank,
  Pritzker Music Pavilion, 149, 214, 217, 218
Genera (Columns), 52
Giedion, Sigfried, 29, 46, 47, 176
Di Giorgio, Francesco, 162, 163, 240
Girard, René, 1, 4, 15, 114, 124, 128, 129, 137, 138
Gothic, 26, 27, 34, 42, 39, 62, 85, 102, 168, 181, 184, 193, 195, 202, 208, 209, 211, 212, 216, 217
Grand narratives
  Classicism and Historicism, 9, 18, 21, 22, 28, 31, 32, 35, 36, 43, 44, 51, 65, 226

Great Chain of Being, 10, 69, 70, 72, 74, 76, 78, 80, 81
Gropius, Walter, 47, 99, 102, 176, 196

Habermas, Jurgen, 79, 81, 226
Hansen, Theophil Edvard,
  Academy of Athens, 210
Hegel, G.W.F., 25, 28, 34, 39, 40, 44, 76, 113, 124, 135, 137
Heidegger, Martin, 28, 35, 46, 79, 83, 114, 134
Hillman, James, 120, 121, 132, 136, 138, 229
Hitchcock, Henry-Russell, and Johnson, Philip, 29, 47, 176, 180, 181
Historians, 5–9, 15–18, 19, 22–44, 48, 51–9, 64, 65, 83, 86, 91, 100, 101, 107, 121, 191, 219, 225, 238
Historicism, 9, 18, 21, 26, 28, 32, 31, 34, 35, 36, 41, 45, 46, 90, 137, 223
History, 13, 17, 31, 43, 44, 65, 67, 102
  Philosophy of, 5, 6, 8, 10, 18, 21, 24–9, 36–48, 51, 52, 74, 104, 219, 223, 233, 238
  Sanctioning by, 9, 19, 22, 23, 64, 65
Historiography, 21, 29
Hudnut, Joseph, 102, 107
Huizinga, Johan, 239
Humanism, 14, 45, 49, 94, 125
Hume, David, 26, 231
Hut, 38, 47, 117, 165, 166, 173
Hypostyle type, 55, 179
  Temple of Amon, 39
  Palace of one hundred columns in Persepolis, 39
  Porticus Margaritaria in the Roman Forum, 39
  Mosque of Cordoba, 63
  Market in Siena, 64

Idea, Ideal, 5, 14, 17, 18, 19, 22–4, 28, 32, 34, 38, 40, 48, 53, 55, 69–71, 77, 78, 81, 82, 93, 103, 113, 114, 120, 132, 146, 148, 151, 164, 172–4, 182–5, 202, 204, 210, 218, 219, 228, 233
Identity, 43, 55, 62, 72, 75, 78, 80, 109, 119, 120, 121, 123, 124, 126, 129, 130, 131, 133, 137, 143, 144, 148, 149, 174, 211, 214, 215
Infinity, 40, 71, 75–9, 182
Imitation, Mimesis, 7, 11, 12, 28, 31, 43, 69, 73, 77, 78, 109, 127, 128, 130, 138, 148, 154, 155, 156, 159, 161, 162, 164, 165, 166, 167, 173–6, 180–95, 199, 220, 225, 238
Image-maker, 6, 120, 121, 124, 149, 154
Imaginal, 51, 62, 87, 123
Invention, 7, 12, 22, 25, 77, 78, 109, 127, 133, 149, 154, 156, 159, 161, 162, 164–7, 170, 183, 188–92, 220, 225, 234

Jefferson, Thomas, 104, 155, 156, 202
Jones, Inigo, 128
Judgment, Architectural, 4, 6, 7, 8, 18, 22, 23, 25, 28, 49, 85, 87–91, 99, 103, 109, 119, 126, 133, 143, 153, 154, 156, 162, 191, 223, 225, 232, 237
  Definition, three kinds of, 1–5
Justification, 5, 6, 7, 9, 17, 21, 22, 23, 24, 26, 36, 38, 40, 47, 90, 91, 93, 95, 100, 104, 112, 131, 134, 162, 189, 200, 218, 232

Kahn, Louis,
  Yale Centre for British Art, 215, 216
Kant, Immanuel, 28, 85, 88, 105, 113, 119, 135, 223, 229, 230, 239
  Disinterestedness, 119
  Unsociable sociability, 229
Kent, William, 128
Kostof, Spiro, 31
Krier, Léon, 45, 66, 88, 105–7, 187–9, 230, 232–40

Lacan, Jacques, 116, 135, 137
Language-architecture analogy, 121, 126, 149, 152, 155, 182, 184–7, 189, 196
Laugier, Marc-Antoine, 15, 38, 45, 65, 165–6, 167, 172, 193
Ledoux, C.-N.L., 47, 55, 57, 66, 83, 107, 136, 171, 202
License, 154, 164, 166
Limits, bounds, 10, 12, 43, 55, 57, 75–8, 94–7, 103, 124, 156, 159, 171, 199–202, 218, 219, 225, 234–6
Links and boundaries, 72, 77–80, 95–7, 186, 200
Lovejoy, Arthur, 81

Maalouf, Amin, 137
Maniera, 59, 121, 164
Mars, 131, 204–5
Marx, Karl, 14, 25, 34, 48, 74, 87, 237
Mass culture, 79

Meinecke, Friedrich, 45, 46, 74
Michelangelo, 48, 49, 121, 130, 136, 137, 138, 148, 192
Mimetic rivalry, 4, 5, 11, 15, 124, 127, 129, 130, 131, 132, 137, 225, 228, 229
Mimesis, see Imitation
Model, 7, 11, 19, 38, 42, 44, 46, 53, 73, 102, 104, 118, 127, 128, 129, 130, 131, 155, 163, 164, 166, 172, 173, 174, 182, 190, 201, 212
Modernity, 6, 8, 9, 10, 11, 34, 67, 69, 70–82, 100, 101, 102, 223, 226, 234
   Differentiation, 10, 51, 52, 71–81, 86, 93, 117, 132, 154, 165, 184–5, 192, 228, 235–6
   Dissociation, 10, 44, 71–4, 78–80, 81, 105, 154, 235
   Dissolution, 40, 72, 74, 78, 81, 86, 186, 235
Modernism, 6, 9, 10, 12, 25, 28–9, 35–40, 46, 69, 74, 78, 100–102, 107, 130, 138, 159–61, 171, 175–7, 181–3, 186–9, 195, 199, 233–6
Monism, 10, 75–6, 89–91, 99, 101, 103, 106, 225

Nature, 7, 19, 32, 34, 52, 73, 77, 79, 80–82, 87, 97, 127, 138, 148, 155, 159, 162–70, 171, 173–5, 188, 190–93, 199, 214, 219, 223, 229, 233–4
   Natura naturans, 31, 73, 127, 148
   Natura naturata, 31, 73, 127
   Natural law, 31, 37, 127, 230

Originality, 133, 171–2, 191, 197
Ornament, 11, 59, 69, 117, 130, 148, 152, 164, 169, 177, 180, 181, 186–7, 189, 193, 202, 219
Other Modern, 69, 111, 197

Paradigm, 9, 21, 27–8, 31, 34, 36, 38, 41, 43, 69, 80, 103, 127, 155–6, 161–2, 165, 168, 173–6, 189–90, 199, 200, 226, 240
Perrault, Claude, 15, 44, 124, 129–30, 138, 193, 230–32, 239
Periodization, 5, 19, 26, 48, 59, 38
Pevsner, Nikolaus, 46, 47, 65, 195
Phantasia, 87
Philosophy, 8, 15, 17–18, 21, 23, 24–5, 26–9, 41, 46, 66, 70, 71–2, 74, 125, 134–5, 157, 225, 233–4, 239
Philosophers, 5, 9, 17–18, 24–8, 35, 37, 78, 184, 231

Plato, 28, 53, 85, 87, 113, 119, 127, 155, 162, 174
Pluralism, 6, 9–10, 73–4, 89–91, 93–4, 102–3, 105–6, 219–20, 226, 237–8
Poein, poietic, 6, 69, 111, 154, 190
Polemos, 13, 229
Politics, 6, 10, 17, 28, 46, 70–73, 78–80, 83, 85–9, 91, 99, 102, 106, 133, 223, 225–6, 228–9
Political Freedom, 6–7, 10, 13–15, 73, 85–97, 103, 106, 225–7
Popper, Karl, 45–6, 106, 137
Porphyrios, Demetri, 186–7, 197
   Magdalen College, Oxford, 216
Post-modernism, 35, 36, 40, 41, 42, 43, 49, 69, 74, 75, 86, 196, 233
Presentness, 5–6, 24, 74, 233–4
Progress, 21, 25, 34, 36–40, 43, 67, 74, 76–7, 101, 163, 182, 212
Propriety, 4, 6, 11, 28, 32, 55, 57, 73, 77, 83, 85, 88, 143, 147, 150, 154–5, 159, 166–9, 171–3, 175, 189–90, 201–2
Psychology of Architect, 4–5, 7–8, 11–12, 29, 37, 42–3, 72, 107, 109, 111, 119–21, 126–8, 130–32, 134, 137, 147–8, 164, 178, 225–6, 229, 231, 233, 237

Quatremère de Quincy, Antoine-Chrysostôme, 15, 45, 53, 55, 65–6, 97, 106, 114, 135, 171–4, 191, 194–5, 208, 232
Querelle des anciens et des modernes, 129, 138, 163, 230, 232, 236
Querelle des modernes et des modernes, 232–6

Relativism, 9–10, 18, 28, 43–5, 49, 73–4, 89–91, 93, 103, 105, 153, 223, 237, 248
Renaissance (Italian), 12, 24–5, 29, 34, 42, 45–6, 48, 49, 71, 80, 87, 122, 159, 161–5, 176, 190, 192, 210, 233
Representation, 7, 11, 21, 41, 43, 49, 76–7, 86, 99, 102–6, 112–13, 127, 134–5, 137, 150, 154, 156, 157, 174, 178, 182, 185, 187, 196, 199, 200, 214, 151–2, 157, 233
Res publica, res privata, 11, 154, 187, 226
Ribart de Chamoust, 65, 167, 193
Ribera, Juan de, 133
de La Rochefoucauld, François, 126
Rousseau, Jean-Jacques, 73, 81, 209
   Contrat social, 71

Sansovino, Jacobo, 136
   Zecca and Biblioteca Marciana, 206–7
Sartre, Jean-Paul, 74, 124, 134
Scamozzi, Vincenzo, 164
Schinkel, Karl Friedrich, 202, 210
Seeing as and seeing in, 6
Semantics, 86, 89, 184–5
Semiology, 184
Semiotics, 41, 190
Subjectivism, subjectivity, 7, 10, 14, 26, 42–3, 85, 91, 105, 111, 116, 119, 128, 153, 156–7, 239
Syntax, 151, 184, 189, 234
Sense-in-common, 88–9, 93–4, 105
Soufflot, Jacques-Germain, 107, 193, 208–9, 221
Soviet Union, 100–101, 212
Spinoza, Baruch, 113, 135
Spirit of age, *zeitgeist*, 33–34, 46, 67, 77, 102, 148, 176, 182, 190, 219
Style, 11–12, 25–7, 34–5, 51–3, 59, 62, 64–6, 69, 73, 86, 103, 121, 149, 151, 154, 176–7, 179, 180–81, 186, 196–9, 223, 232, 235, 238
Symmetria, symmetry, 32, 70, 174, 180–81, 185, 187–8, 190, 231
Synthesis, 10, 21, 46, 69, 79, 80–81, 176 223

Tabularium, 203, 207
Tafuri, Manfredo, 27, 29, 47, 195
Tatarkiewicz, Wladyslaw, 48, 66, 81, 134, 157, 192, 232
Technique, 10, 15, 69, 75–9, 80, 82, 103, 161, 175–6, 182–3, 189–90, 195, 199, 219
Telos, Teleology, 18, 34–40, 111, 118
Temple of,
   Antonino and Faustina, 165
   Concord, 203–4, 221
   Hercules, 204–5
   Mars Ultor, 204–5
   Venus Genetrix, 38
Theatre of Marcellus, 165
   Vaudoyer, Léon, 121–2
Thematismos, 173
Theory, 1, 4, 6, 8, 11, 15, 18, 21–2, 24–5, 28, 31–2, 35–6, 41, 45–7, 66, 67, 70, 89, 104, 116, 124–5, 127, 133–4, 137, 151, 155, 157, 161–3, 165, 174, 177, 185, 190–91, 195, 219, 220, 225, 227, 228, 237
Third Reich, 99–100, 106, 107
Tradition, 5, 10, 12, 21, 22, 32, 34, 42, 44–5, 64–5, 67, 69–70, 73–5, 76–7, 80, 88–9, 91, 93–5, 99–101, 102, 104, 107, 121, 127, 130, 134, 137, 138, 149, 156, 161–2, 164–5, 175–7, 179–84, 186, 188–91, 196, 199, 202, 206, 211, 218–19, 232–5, 236
Trompe-l'œil, 151
True, the Beautiful and the Good, 70, 87, 91, 174
   The true and the factual, 70, 73, 96, 174, 182
Type, 12, 24, 38, 51–3, 55, 62, 64, 65, 73, 149, 154–5, 162, 165–7, 172–3, 174, 179, 181–3, 190, 192, 199, 223, 235, 238

Universal communicability, 85, 105
ut pictura poesis, 97
Utopia, 28, 67, 87–8, 105, 235
Utzon, Jorn,
   Sydney Opera House, 213–14

Valéry, Paul, 83, 111, 135,
Vasari, Giorgio, 42, 44, 48, 136, 163–4, 192
Venturi, Robert, 117, 182–4, 196
Viollet-le-duc, Eugène-Emmanuel, 29, 85, 191, 220
Virginia State Capitol, 155–6, 202
Vitruvius, 15, 29, 47, 52, 109, 132, 161, 162, 174, 191, 204, 221, 231
   Triads, 32
Von Klenze, Leo,
   Munich Glyptothek, 209

Weber, Max, 79, 81, 107
Weltanschauung, 35, 82
Westfall, Carroll William, 45, 46, 53, 65, 240
White, Hayden, 29,
   Emplotment, 42
Wilber, Ken, 81, 132, 138, 139
Will-to-make, 22, 111, 113, 227
Winckelmann, Johann Joachim, 15, 136, 232
Wolfflin, Heinrich, 66
Wollheim, Richard, 15, 59, 66, 157
World Fairs, Universal Expositions, World's Columbian Exhibition in Chicago, 203, 211, 212, 213
Wren, Christopher, 231, 239
Yourcenar, Marguerite, 238, 240, 250

Zecca, 206–7

Made in the USA
Las Vegas, NV
28 December 2020